Battles
and Battlescenes of World War Two

Other works by the Author

A Traveller's Guide to the Battlefields of Europe (2 vols.), (1965)
The Campaigns of Napoleon, (1966)
Two Soldiers of Marlborough's Wars: Parker & Mérode-Westerloo, (1968)
Marlborough as Military Commander, (1973)
The Art of War on Land, (1974)
Napoleon, (1974)
The Art of Warfare in the Age of Marlborough, (1975)
A Dictionary of the Napoleonic Wars, (1979)
Waterloo – the Hundred Days, (1980)
Atlas of Military Strategy, 1618–1878, (1980)
A Journal of Marlborough's Wars: J. M. Deane, (1984)
Sedgemoor 1685 – an Account and an Anthology, (1985)
Napoleon's Marshals, (1987)
A Dictionary of Battles, (1987)
The Military Maxims of Napoleon, (1987)

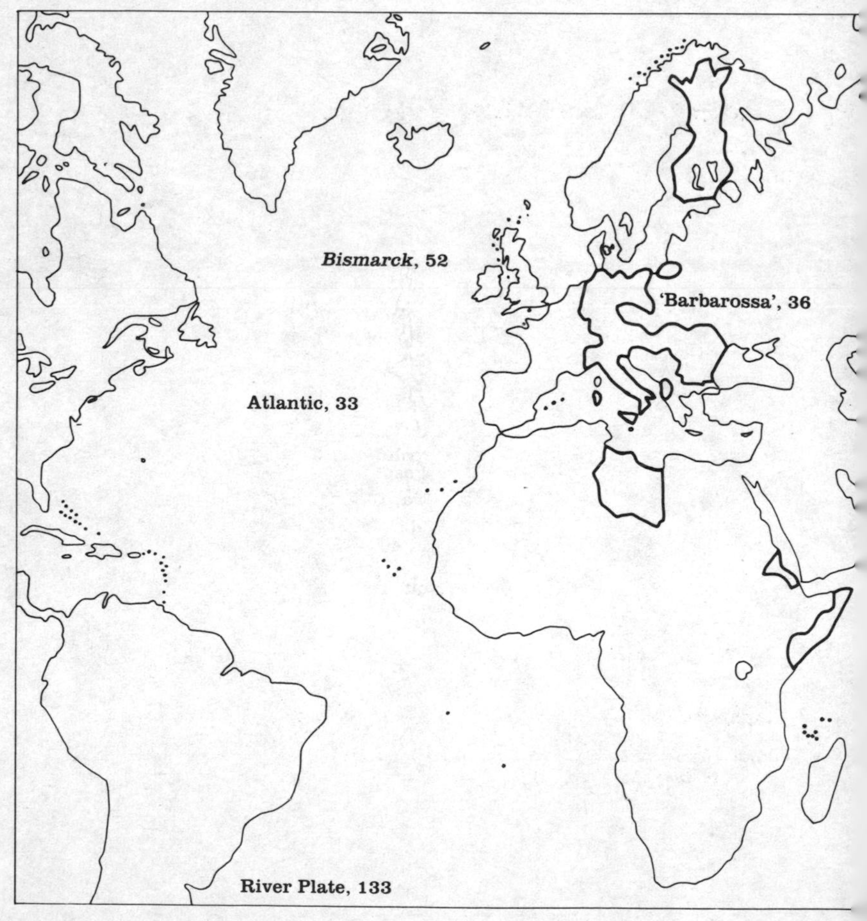

Battles and Battlescenes of World War Two

DAVID G. CHANDLER

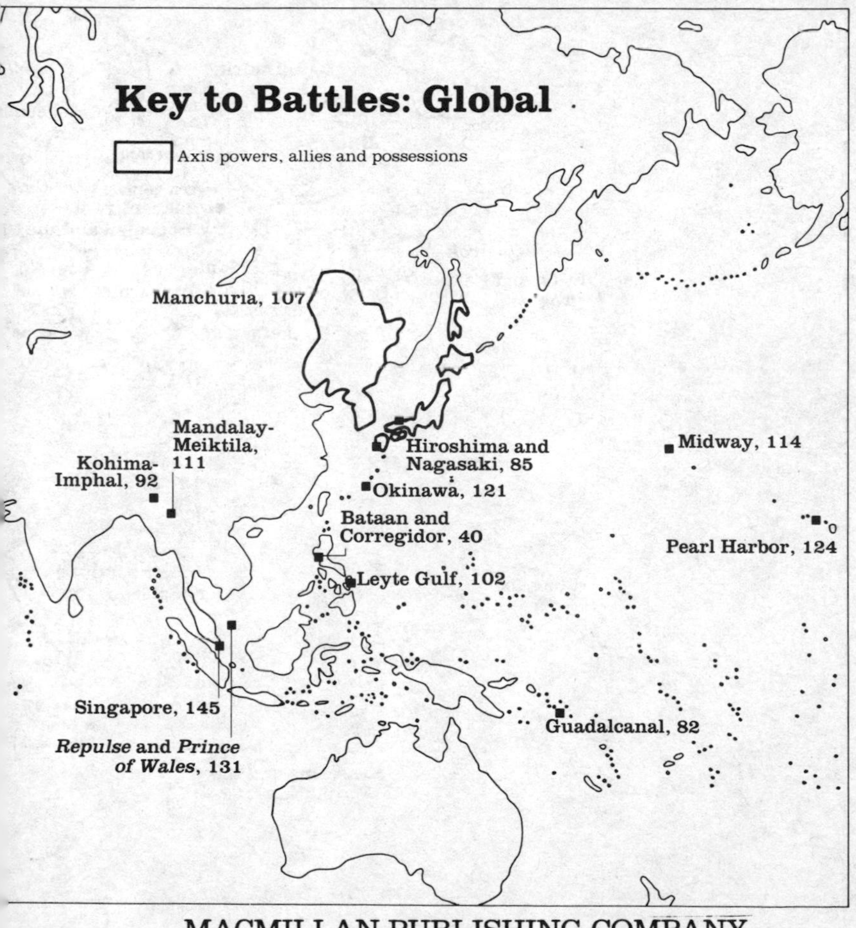

MACMILLAN PUBLISHING COMPANY
NEW YORK

Oslo
Dunkirk, 71
Eben Emael, 75
Battle of Britain, 42
Blitz, 54
London
Amsterdam
Berlin
Arnhem, 26
Aachen, 14
D-Day, 68
Brussels
Ardennes, 22
Prague
St-Lô and Falaise, 135
Caen, 58
Paris
Sedan, 139
Arras, 30
Belfort, 48
Vienna
Rome
Anzio, 20
Cassino, 60
Salerno, 137
Gibraltar
Algiers
Tunis
Kasserine and the Mareth Line, 87

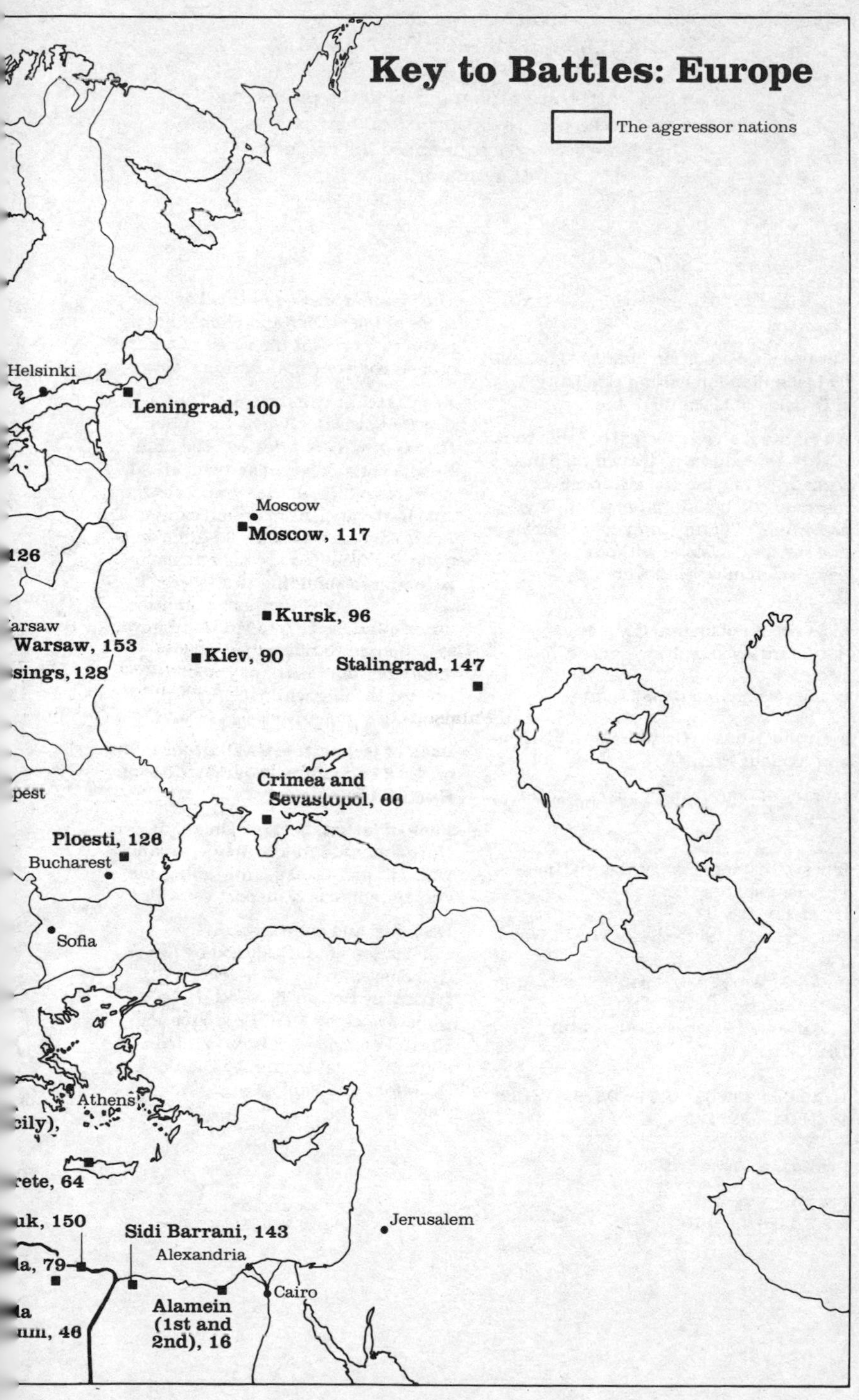

Key to Battles: Europe
The aggressor nations
Helsinki
Leningrad, 100
Moscow
Moscow, 117
Kursk, 96
Warsaw, 153
Kiev, 90
Stalingrad, 147
Crimea and Sevastopol, 66
Ploesti, 126
Bucharest
Sofia
Athens
Jerusalem
Sidi Barrani, 143
Alexandria
Cairo
Alamein (1st and 2nd), 16

This book is respectfully dedicated to my Uncle,
CHARLES FREDERICK (BOB) DEANS
of Beverley,
who first introduced his nephew to the pleasures
of overseas travel, and thus opened up new perspectives
that have strongly influenced his life as a
military historian.

First American edition published in 1989 by Macmillan Publishing Company
A Division of Macmillan, Inc.

Macmillan Publishing Company
866 Third Avenue, New York, NY 10022
Collier Macmillan Canada, Inc.

First published in Great Britain by Arms and Armour Press

Library of Congress Catalog Card No: 89-12122

Library of Congress Cataloging-in-Publication Data
Chandler, David G.
Battles and battlescenes of World War Two.
1. World War, 1939–1945 – Campaigns – Dictionaries.
2. Battles – History – 20th century – Dictionaries.
I. Title
D740.C45 1989 940.54'1'03 89-12122
ISBN 0-02-897175-2

Printed in Great Britain

printing number
1 2 3 4 5 6 7 8 9 10

The views expressed in this book are those of the author and should not be taken to represent the views of an official body or organization.

Front Jacket illustration: The Soviet flag flies over the Reichstag in Berlin; Nazi Germany is defeated. The final Russian attack began at dawn on 30 April targeting all the symbols of Nazi rule in the ancient Prussian capital. The Red Army massed some 90 guns on a 200-yard front to take the Reichstag, reducing the building to a façade. By dawn of 1 May Hitler had committed suicide and Sergeants Mikhail Egorov and Meliton Kantaria had earned enduring fame as they symbolically hoisted the flag while the fighting continued in many streets below.

Back of jacket, top: RAF fighter pilots of No. 87 Squadron 'scramble' to their Hurricanes.

Back of jacket, bottom: Omaha Beach, Normandy. US follow-up forces land with M3 half-tracks, anti-tank guns and amphibious transport vehicles.

Designed and edited by DAG Publications Ltd. Designed by David Gibbons; edited by Michael Boxall; typeset by Ronset Typesetters Ltd; camerawork by M&E Reproductions, North Fambridge, Essex; printed and bound in Great Britain by Biddles Ltd, Guildford and Kings Lynn.

Contents

Author's Note

1. For the convenience of readers seeking rapid information, the battle-studies have been placed in *alphabetical* order. The inclusion of a *chronological chart* (*see* p. 156) will show inter-relationships and assist a reader to follow-through a particular theatre of war. Similarly, use of the index will aid the study of a particular commander through his various battles.

2. For purposes of easy quick reference, each entry is headed by a data table giving in tabulated form the minimum of vital information, namely: Date, Location (see also end-paper maps), Object, Opposing sides, Forces engaged, Casualties, Result and Suggested reading (*see* para 4. below). Please note that strengths of forces and totals of casualties are often estimates and approximations – it being very difficult to obtain precise information on these subjects. Calculations of 'wounded', for example, vary from country to country: the Japanese regarded no soldier as wounded if he were capable of crawling and handling a weapon.

3. Each battle is illustrated with at least one map or diagram, and the vast majority with a contemporary photograph too. In some cases, entries treat two battles together: for example, Alamein I and II; Sevastopol and the Crimea; Mount Etna and Sicily; Kohima-Imphal, etc.

4. *Suggested Reading*. Only a selection of books that have been of particular use to the author are included. Because a book may have been published in the late 1940s or 1950s – and the subject has been re-written more recently – does not necessarily invalidate the earlier title. Many older books, for example Chester Wilmot's *Struggle for Europe* (1948), have attained the status of at least minor classics and well repay reading even if much newly available information has come to light subsequently. Often the older books are better than their supposed successors, *pace* the claims of later authors and publishers. Similarly, every entry will contain a reference to the *Purnell History of the Second World War* a part-work edited by Barrie Pitt and published from 1966. This source (also available in bound volume format) is of particular value in that it contains many articles by participants in the events described as well as by informed by-standers (who proverbially '. . . see more of the game') and scholars. It serves, therefore, as a form of 'control' on the whole book, although the views expressed here are very much those of the present author and do not necessarily accord with those in the *Purnell* chapters and parts. Those desiring to read an overall history of the Second World War are directed to Winston S. Churchill's masterpiece, *The World War*, 12 volumes (London, 1949 and numerous subsequent editions and reprintings); for a shorter, but authoritative treatment, attention is directed to Brigadier Peter Young's one-volume work, *World War Two: 1939-1945* (London, 1964). There are of course many others, including John Pimlott's *World War II in Photographs* (London, 1984), which is also recommended.

Introduction

During the 1940s a famous radio comedian invariably prefaced his act with the phrase: "The day war broke out, I said to the wife. . . ." Almost 50 years on from that September day in 1939, I remember my uncle telling the assembled family that he very much doubted that all present would live to see the end of it. But our family proved more fortunate than many another, and all of us lived to celebrate VE- and then VJ-Day in 1945. Even better, a fair number of us have lived on to see the approach of the 50th anniversary of the outbreak of the Second World War on 3 September 1939 – truly an important date in the annals of history.

As a small, five-year-old boy living in a Yorkshire seaside town, my recollections are vivid but necessarily limited. I remember the Black Watch on Church Parade soon after Dunkirk, bringing both rifles and ammunition to the service at my father's church. I remember being fitted with my gas-mask, air raid precaution drills at my first school, the black-out, and the concrete pillboxes, anti-tank obstacles, barbed wire entanglements, anti-aircraft guns on Waxholme Road the searchlight batteries on England's Hill that suddenly sprouted along our peaceful piece of coast during that 'invasion summer'. I recall the sentries checking identity cards on the Hull Road barricade at Stevenson's Farm, and my own particular adopted soldier, Frank, for whom my mother knitted scarves and 'caps-comforter'. Did he survive the war I wonder? I recall the arrival of busloads of evacuees from Hull and elsewhere – our share of the influx was a school-master – Mr Harvey – who helped dig our air-raid shelter while awaiting his call-up papers. Did he survive the next five years?

I vividly remember the blitz of Hull and, after one 'All Clear', leaving our eventual shelter beneath the back-stairs at Owthorne Vicarage (where I spent many long nights scrawling disrespectful graffiti about Nazi leaders on the whitewashed walls – they were still there eight years ago), and going outside to see the whole western horizon glowing an angry red (and it was not a sunset), and hearing the drone of German bombers. Did, as we believed, their engine-notes really vary between 'full' and 'empty'? I remember the excitement of being taken to see the remains of a shot-down Heinkel 111 at Holmpton, and the pride of owning small pieces of the raider that always had a special smell. I remember finding a large piece of shrapnel – still warm if I do not fool myself – on our front-door step, and of seeing an unexploded incendiary bomb sticking out of St Matthew's

Church roof. I recall the unexploded bomb at Rimswell corner, and the cheery Army Bomb Demolition squads driving to work up Hull Road in their red-mudguarded vehicles, singing as they returned to peril. I can see the bomb craters on Withernsea bowling-green and the wreck of Mr Turner's house on Queen Street (he had a truly miraculous escape) after a sneak raid.

Above all we feared the parachute land-mines, one of which, far from any military target, totally destroyed Halsham Church, but left untouched the farm next door (did the farmer and his wife, as we heard, sleep on undisturbed to wake and draw back the curtains the next morning and make the immortal remark, 'Eee lass, t'church is gorrn'?). And there were the parades, the military exercises through our gardens, the weekly 'Build a Spitfire', 'Salute the Soldier' or 'Buy War Bonds' drives, the eagerly awaited Nine O'clock News ('. . . and this is Frank Hibberd reading it') not to forget the occasional addresses by the Prime Minister. How we liked the broadcasts by the Radio Doctor and Mr Woolton, Minister of Food, extolling the virtues of the potato-pie that bore his name. I remember my uncle donning his black 'tin-hat', proudly inscribed 'Senior Warden', at the sandbagged telephone-post built into his house in Beverley, and the building of prototype prefabricated fighter hangars at his works. My future (never-to-be) father-in-law died of pneumonia resulting from long, cold winter nights of fire-watching at Withernsea – reminding me that not all of war's casualties are caused by shell, bullet or bomb.

I *think* I can recall seeing a V-1 'doodle-bug' (presumably Heinkel-launched) off the Humber streaking up Hull Road past our camouflaged lighthouse, a well-known landmark for would-be daylight raiders who would often dump their bombs on our small seaside town and, honour at least partly satisfied, head for home rather than tackle the growing air defences protecting Hull fifteen miles away. I recall rationing and ration books, clothes coupons (but not bread-units – they only came in *after* the war) and 'points' for almost everything. I well remember receiving my banana – 'one for every child in Britain' – and the excitement of receiving our first food-parcel from an unknown Chandler family in North America . . . and so I could go on.

Very different was the war of millions of soldiers, sailors and airmen of many nations who fought the battles of the Second World War on land, sea and in the air, from that of a small boy on the 'Home Front', who never received a scratch but lost his second teeth a few years later through calcium deficiency resulting from war-time milk shortages. But to all of us who survived it 'the War' will always remain in our memories and, it is to be hoped, in those of later generations. War was terrible, as it always is, but, in the words of William Wordsworth relating to the French Revolution of 1789 as it appeared to enthusiasts:

> 'Bliss was it in that dawn to be alive,
> But to be young was very heaven!'

And now Europe and the Super-Powers can claim to have enjoyed almost 45 years of freedom from direct exposure to large-scale shooting wars. This is unique in Europe's history. But we need remember that since 1945 there have been well over 200 separate wars in the Second and Third Worlds. It would therefore seem, alas, that mankind as a whole has still not learnt the folly of indulging in warfare for all the horrendous loss of life and maiming, physical and mental, that was the inevitable price of the Second World War.

We commonly speak and read of 'the Second *World* War, 1939-1945', but it is not strictly accurate to speak of the struggle in such terms until late 1941, and even then large parts of the earth's surface (much of South America for instance) were only minimally or indirectly affected. The war began as essentially a European struggle, with Middle Eastern and North African theatres eventually tacked on from mid-1940, although from the outset the lands of the British Commonwealth and Empire rallied to the Motherland's call – as did the colonial possessions of France. But the war only developed truly global proportions by stages. Winston Churchill once remarked that he recalled two absolutely crucial dates in the War's history: 22 June 1941 (the German invasion of Russia) – 'On that date I knew we would not *lose* the War'; – and 7 December 1941 (Japan's pre-emptive strike on Pearl Harbor that brought the USA somewhat belatedly into the struggle) – 'On that date I knew that we would undoubtedly *win* it.' Small wonder he sub-titled the relevant fifth and sixth volumes of his great work *The Second World War* 'The Grand Alliance – Germany Drives East' and 'The Grand Alliance – War Comes to America' respectively. No doubt he was referring to the vast man-power and economic resources the Allies could call upon from 1941 onwards that were bound in long-term attritional terms to wear down the Axis to eventual defeat. But was it really so inevitable? Had German scientists perfected the atomic bomb ahead of the Allies, who can say what the outcome would have been – a grave thought that bears some pondering. The race of the scientific war was neck-and-neck, and the German 'Victory Weapons' – the V-1 flying-bombs and above all the supersonic V-2 rockets – wrought grievous damage on Great Britain (especially London) from mid-1944 to early 1945, and the V-3 was not too far away.

As it was, the Second World War cost the world at least 54 million dead, all of 20 million of them Russians. And of course posterity may adopt a different viewpoint. Already there are historians who prefer to regard the two great world struggles of the first half of the twentieth century as one massive war – with a 19-year interval in the middle. True, apart from Italy (which changed sides twice – in 1940 and again in 1943 if the wider perspective is applied), the main antagonists were the same, and both wars, 1914-18 and 1939-45, were mainly Eurocentric and focused upon Germany's wrongs and ambitions, although there are those who would challenge even those assumptions. 'History is indeed an argument without end,' as Professor Geyl sagely remarked, and that is particularly true of military history in its many forms.

In 1979 it was decreed by authority that the commemoration of the Second World War would be concentrated on its fortieth anniversaries as it was realized that by 1989-95 the surviving combatants would have become rather fewer or certainly ten years older. As a result, there was a flurry of commemorative activities (good and bad), both on the ground and on paper, with perhaps the D-Day Anniversary ceremonies receiving pride of place, certainly in Great Britain and France. However, the proximity of the Fiftieth Anniversaries seems to be unleashing in many countries a second flood of books containing commentary, analysis and recollection that will at least rival that of a decade ago, although in 1989 it is likely that in France, at least, the prior claims of the bicentennial of the onset of the French Revolution will be regarded as paramount (as the young William Wordsworth would doubtless have approved as well). But the French are setting their hand to a long haul that will continue all the way to AD 2015 as all the great Napoleonic bicentennary anniversaries will inevitably follow – and there should be room for more than a little commemoration of the Second World War's fiftieth anniversaries amid all the French rejoicing.

In any case, this little book has been written in that belief, indeed certainty. Its particular purpose it not to add a great deal that is new to the official record – there have after all been tens of thousands of titles already devoted to one aspect or another of the great theme. Rather it is to reassess certain judgements and beliefs in the light of experience – and above all to provide the reader (there have been at least two whole new generations of mankind born over the past 50 years, and one of those has reached reading-age since 1979) with a source of quick reference material to a selection of battles whose names will be freely bandied to and fro in the media and the conversation of veterans, which may conjure up only a dim echo in his or her mind.

It is not our intention to bring back recollections of '. . . old, unhappy, far-off things, And battles long ago' except insofar as these are a vital part of our common heritage which certainly set the scene for the turbulent times we are called upon to live in – and therefore deserve to the recognized and understood. As the poet Fitzgerald wrote in the *Rubaiyat of Omar Khyam* (admittedly in another context), 'Oh, the brave Music of a *distant* drum!' and it is in the hope that this will continue to be the case for ourselves and generations yet unborn that this book has been written.

Inevitably, any selection of just 52 subjects from the several hundreds available – for it was a war almost incomprehensible in extent and complexity – leaves huge gaps unfilled. It is hoped, however, that a reasonable balance has been achieved between Europe, the Atlantic and the African and Far Eastern theatres of war. I am aware that one vast war area receives no attention whatsoever – that of Nationalist China, which was at war with Japan from 1933 to 1945. Strange to say, however, even now, well over 55 years after the onset of a great war that became subsumed into an even larger struggle from December 1941, there is no truly definitive English-language history available. So there is still a field of virgin exploration and research to be undertaken by some gifted British or American historian endowed with a knowledge of both the Chinese and Japanese languages. It may be felt that I have given undue preference to subjects of an Anglo-Saxon significance. I would justify this through two observations. A large part of the old Aryan-Saxon race comprises what we would today call the German peoples – and they were in the Second World War from 3 September 1939 (some purists would prefer no doubt from 1 September – the date of Hitler's invasion of Poland from which all else followed) until 9 May 1945. The second part – the Anglo-Saxons *per se* – comprise a vital part of the racial make-up of the British people, who were, after all, the ONLY participants in the Second World War (together with the loyal members of the British Empire and Commonwealth) to see it through from the first day to the very last. It is felt, therefore, that such a slight bias in representational terms is perfectly justified.

It was equally difficult to decide in many instances which subjects should receive fuller treatment at 1,000 words apiece, and which should be allocated only 500. All I can say is that I have followed my own personal estimation based upon almost 29 years of teaching military history to successive generations of officer-cadets and young officers at the Royal Military Academy, Sandhurst, and of attending at least thirty international conferences on related subjects under the auspices of the *Commission Internationale d'Histoire Militaire*, of which I have been an active member since 1964 and an officer since 1975. On that, my case must rest. However, each of the 52 subjects has at its head an identically designed data-table, which provides the irreducible minimum of factual information. It is hoped, therefore, that the result will be both interesting and useful as a source of ready-reference for those who were born long after 1945, but whose interest is attracted to the subject, and will equally help veteran participants, some of whose memories may not be quite so good as they once were, to answer the inevitable question, 'And what did *you* do in the War, Granddaddy?'

DAVID G. CHANDLER
Sandhurst and Yateley

Acknowledgements

The author would like to thank his many friends and colleagues who consciously or unbeknowingly contributed to the writing of this book. He would like to thank Mr Orgill and the staff of the Central Library, Royal Military Academy, Sandhurst for their professional assistance and advice. He also owes a debt of gratitude to Roderick Dymott of Arms & Armour Press whose original brain-child this volume represents. Both publisher and author wish to acknowledge the Robert Hunt Library for permission to reproduce photographs in whole or in part. Every effort has been made to trace the holders of original copyrights, but the passage of up to half a century has not always made this feasible.

Aachen

Date: 4 October – 1 December 1944.

Location: Just within West Germany in the Aachen–Huertgen Forest area.

Object: The Americans were trying to break through the German defences to take Cologne on the River Rhine and also the Roer valley.

Opposing sides: (a) General Omar Bradley commanding the US 12th Army Group; (b) Field Marshal Walther Model commanding German Army Group B.

Forces engaged: (a) Four US and one British armoured, and thirteen US and one British Infantry divisions. Total: approx. 300,000 men (750 tanks); (b) Five Panzer and eleven infantry divisions. Total: 250,000 men (500 tanks).

Casualties: (a) approx. 85,000 Allies; (b) approx. 70,000 Germans.

Result: Although the Allies successfully breached the vaunted 'West Wall', they called off the attempt to reach Cologne after the US First Army's failure to capture the Roer dams at Schmidt.

Suggested reading: O. Bradley. *A Soldier's Story* (London, 1952); D. Eisenhower. *Crusade in Europe* (London, 1948); A. Kemp. *The Story of a Battle – Metz* (London, 1975); H. Essame. *43rd Wessex Division at War* (London, 1952); B. Pitt (ed.). *The Purnell History of the Second World War* vol. 6, No. 1 (London, 1968).

The rapid Allied advance through France and the Low Countries in August and September 1944 brought them to the Siegfried Line or 'West Wall'. It was soon clear that the German forces would make a determined stand to protect the Fatherland. For the Allies, the hope of finishing the war by Christmas began to fade with the failure of Operation 'Market Garden' at Arnhem. Their problem was in large part logistical as the supply lines still stretched back to Normandy; Antwerp's port, although captured intact on 3 September, was not operational for unloading until 26 November because of mines in the Scheldt and stiff resistance at Walcheren.

Patton's US Third Army had played a malign part in 21st Army Group's failure at Arnhem by, against SACEUR's orders, attacking Metz and also purloining fuel intended for Montgomery's armies. Soon, in conformity with Eisenhower's 'Broad Front' policy, 21st Army Group, 12th Army Group and 6th Army Group were all advancing on the Rhine. Three months of fierce fighting ensued as von Rundstedt, Supreme Commander West, deployed Model's and Balck's army groups to defend Germany's frontiers.

On the Allied central front, Bradley had reached the defences around Aachen as early as 12 September. The US First Army fought its way, house by house, into the city from 13 October, and by the 21st the Americans could claim to be masters of the first large German city to be taken. Next, in November, General Henry Simpson's US Ninth Army (which had moved up on General Courtney Hodge's left), joined with US First Army in a major assault against the German defences east of Aachen on a 24-mile front.

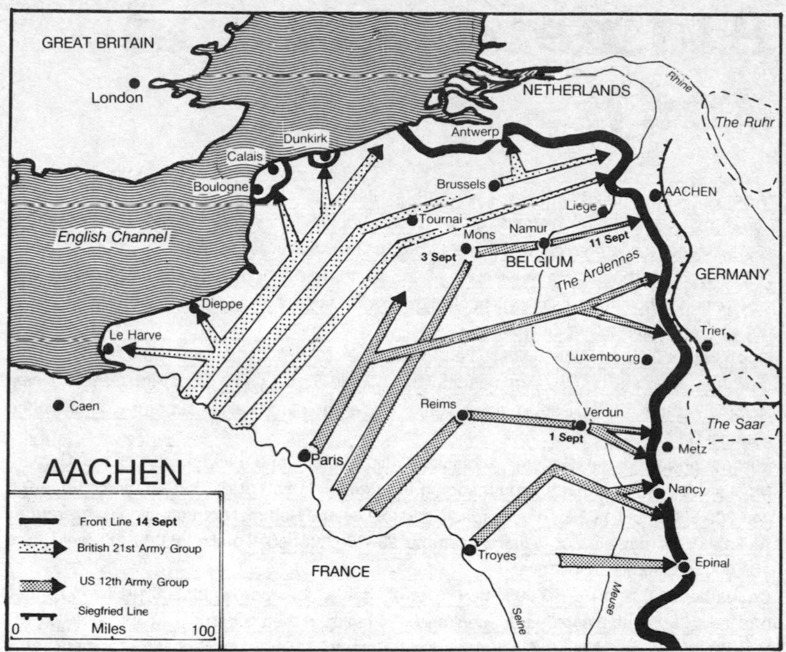

Preceded by heavy RAF and USAAF bombing, ten divisions attacked on 16 November, while British XXX Corps under Lieutenant-General Horrocks co-operated on the northern flank by taking Geilenkirchen. The US V Corps fought one of the hardest battles of the European Campaign in the defiles of the Huertgen Forest. By 1 December the Americans had reached the River Roer, some 25 miles west of Cologne on the Rhine, but all of seventeen American divisions were now engaged in the fighting, the weather was appalling and German resistance relentless. Model threw in five Panzer and eleven infantry divisions, while Sixth Panzer Armee shielded Cologne.

On 1 December Bradley took the hard decision to call off the battle on the grounds that further advance was impossible as Hodge had failed to capture the Roer dams, and problems associated with flooding were immense. Patton's US Third Army, meanwhile, continued to batter itself against Metz in three separate battles. A major German counter-attack by Fifth Panzer and First Armies had been repulsed in early October, but by mid-December grave news from the Ardennes sector took all attention.

Alamein (1st and 2nd)

Date: 1–27 July and 23 October–4 November 1942.

Location: Egypt. The town stands on the coast about 65 miles west of Alexandria. The battle areas extended southwards for 40 miles from the Mediterranean to the Qattara Depression.

Object: In both battles Rommel was striving to break-through to Cairo; Eighth Army was determined to hold the Axis troops back in the first battle (and also in that of Alam Halfa); and to defeat them decisively in the second.

Opposing sides: (a) General Sir Claude Auchinleck (first battle) and General Sir Harold Alexander (second battle), commanding the Middle East Land Forces; (b) General Erwin Rommel commanding Panzerarmee Afrika under nominal Italian supreme commander, Marshal Cavallero.

Forces engaged: (a) General Auchinleck (first battle) and Lieutenant-General Bernard Montgomery (second battle) commanding the Eighth Army. Totals: 35,000 men (160 tanks) and 200,000 men (1,029 tanks) respectively; (b) General Rommel commanding Panzerarmee Afrika in both battles (but General Stumme 23–26 October). Totals: 20,000 (90 tanks) and 104,000 (489 tanks) respectively.

Casualties: (a) approx. 13,000 men in each battle; (b) approx. 22,800, including 7,000 prisoners (first battle) and 59,000 men (and 454 tanks) in the second.

Result: In the first battle, Auchinleck held Rommel to a draw; then Montgomery, after achieving a similar result at Alam Halfa, launched an ultimately successful attack which led to a decisive defeat for Rommel.

Suggested reading: M. Carver. *Alamein* (London 1962); C. Barnett. *The Desert Generals* (London, 1960); R. Lewin. *Rommel as Military Commander* (London, 1968); B.Pitt (ed.). *The Purnell History of the Second World War* vol. 3, Nos. 7 and 10 (London, 1967).

The loss of Tobruk and the setback at Mersa Matruh left Auchinleck with one last position before Alexandria and Cairo – stretching from El Alamein to the cliffs edging the impassable salt marshes of the Qattara Depression – where it was possible to hold a reasonably continuous line. Both armies were almost exhausted, but much was at stake.

Auchinleck placed the two infantry divisions of General Norrie's XXX Corps on the coastal sector and General Gott's regrouping pair of armoured divisions with the New Zealand Division in XIII Corps on the desert flank, and prepared to fight a fluid defensive battle.

Rommel attacked the right-centre of the British position near Miteiriya and Ruweisat Ridges with 6,500 infantry and 90 tanks (almost half of them damaged) on 1 July – but was checked twice by 4th and 22nd Armoured Brigades' artillery fire over the next three days. The Italians were also repulsed on the coastal sector, and again on the desert flank. Auchinleck, realizing that the way to contain Rommel was to launch counter-strokes against his weaker Italian allies, launched the fresh 9th Australian Division against the Sabratha Division in the north, and took the ridge of

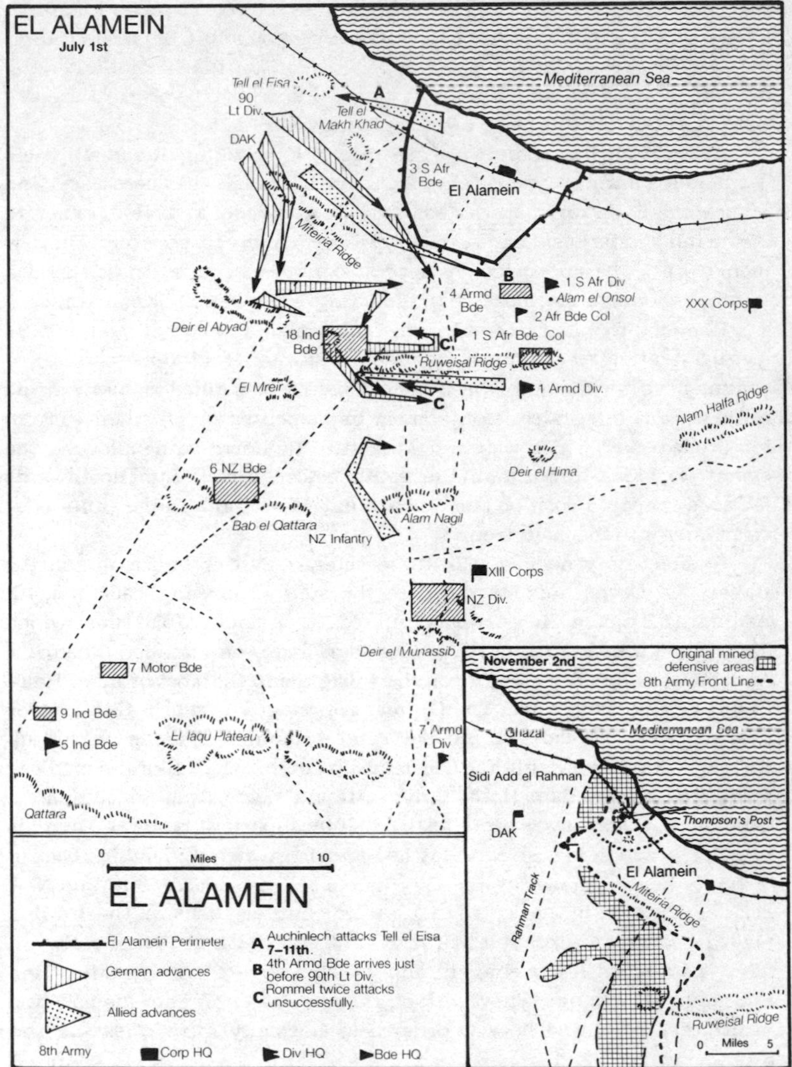

Tell el Eisa on the 11th. This forced Rommel to bring his German armour north, only to be repelled after two days' hard fighting on 13 and 14 July. Auchinleck then used XIII Corps in a northward drive on 21 and 22 July attempting to cut the Axis communications running west from Ruweisat Ridge. Only Point 63 eluded this attack, but Rommel was able to extricate his forces. The Germans were now down to only 26 serviceable tanks, while Auchinleck still had 119 running. Both sides were wholly exhausted, and over the next five days the battle gradually petered out into a stalemate.

Both sides began to lay minefields and protective barbed-wire entanglements, and dug in to await the arrival of reinforcements from the Delta and Benghazi respectively. The sinking of three out of four Axis tankers by forces operating out of Malta over this period was to be of great significance, but the failure of forward supply was more critical.

Auchinleck had achieved a great deal by checking Rommel in this battle, but Churchill decided that a change of leaders was necessary, and after a visit to Egypt he appointed Generals Alexander and Montgomery to command Middle East Land Forces and Eighth Army respectively. The new men were to be supported by several convoys bringing much-needed reinforcements to the Suez Canal, including American Sherman tanks.

Rommel, too, had received some tanks, men and supplies, and on 31 August he attacked again just over two weeks after Montgomery had taken command, determined to win a victory before the Allied reinforcements could be fully integrated. Montgomery implemented a plan inherited from his predecessor, which was to hold fast in the north while allowing the enemy to break-through in the south before luring him northwards towards prepared positions on and around Alam Halfa Ridge running at right angles to the main front.

Rommel duly obliged. His three veteran Panzer divisions and the Italian XX Corps broke-through in the south, pressing back the 4th Armoured Brigade. He next encountered 7th Armoured Division, which forced his tanks to turn north earlier than had been intended. The main Axis blow then fell on 22nd Armoured Brigade to the west of Alam Halfa Ridge around Point 102. The Germans managed to work 15th Panzer round the eastern flank to prevent 22nd Armoured Brigade linking up with 8th, but that brought the Germans up against the tanks and artillery positioned along Alam Halfa Ridge. After a fierce fight throughout 1 September, Rommel was brought to a halt by superior firepower – and his growing shortage of fuel. Next day he began to give ground, falling back to virtually his original start-line. Montgomery then sent forward 2nd New Zealand Division in the centre in a limited counter-attack on the 3rd, but made no attempt to exploit it. For a loss of 1,750 men and 68 tanks, Eighth Army had defied Rommel again and inflicted some 3,000 casualties and knocked out 51 tanks. Short of fuel, Rommel had now shot his bolt. His health was poor, and he was ordered to Germany to rest, leaving von Stumme in command.

Eighth Army used the next two months to prepare for a mighty attack. The initiative was now Montgomery's, but he made no move until he was ready. New divisions from the Commonwealth and the 75mm gunned Sherman tanks, together with large numbers of 6pdr anti-tank guns, were now arriving. In due course, Eighth Army comprised nine infantry divisions and three armoured – two of the latter placed in the new X Corps. By late October, facing them were four reinforced Axis armoured divisions, two German and two Italian, and eight infantry divisions, seven of them Italian. On the ground, Montgomery enjoyed a 2:1 advantage in manpower and a 3:1 advantage in tanks. Overhead, the Desert Air Force had gained the upper hand.

At 0940 hours on 23 October 600 British guns opened a devastating bombardment. Twenty minutes later the first troops advanced. Surprise was achieved in both the timing and direction of the attack, Montgomery striking in the north after creating the illusion of doing so in the south. Rommel was still in Germany, and von Stumme fell dead of a heart-attack. Despite these advantages, Eighth Army failed to punch the pair of intended corridors through the enemy minefields near Miteiriya Ridge, and much armour was destroyed by Axis fire as it became bottled up. By the 25th the advance had been halted, and from the third day Rommel was back in command. His counter-attacks on the 27th and 28th were beaten back, but Eighth Army had lost 10,000 men without a victory.

Montgomery realized he must regain the initiative. He reorganized his forces, and launched the 9th Australian Division in an attack along the coast road. This was a preliminary to a new main blow just north of Miteiriya Ridge, Operation 'Supercharge', which was flung against the Italian Trento Division on 2 November. This time the breach was made, and the superior British armour poured through to seek battle with Rommel's fewer, and petrol-starved, tanks. Two more days of heavy fighting and the issue was decided. With only 35 tanks left operational, Rommel disregarded Hitler's directive 'to stand and die', and began to retreat, leaving most of his Italian infantry to their fate. This action was inevitable, because on 8 November Allied armies began to come ashore in north-west Africa in Operation 'Torch'. Caught between two fires, Rommel had to look to the security of his base at Tripoli.

The great victory of Second Alamein proved the final turning-point of the Desert War, and after six months' more hard fighting in Tunisia the Axis would be driven from the shores of Africa.

Anzio

Date: 22 January – 22 May 1944

Location: On the west coast of Italy, 30 miles south of Rome

Object: The Allies were mounting an amphibious operation designed to outflank the Gustav Line and thus hasten the occupation of Cassino and the taking of Rome.

Opposing sides: (a) Under Lieutenant-General Mark Clark; Major-General John Lucas commanding the US VI Corps; (b) Under Field Marshal Albrecht Kesselring; General Eberhard von Mackensen commanding the German Fourteenth Army.

Forces engaged: (a) At first one US and one British division, with one armoured formation and supporting troops, later reinforced by more infantry divisions. Total: 50,000 men at first; (b) Initially four rising to a maximum of nine German divisions (by mid-February). Total: 90,000 men.

Casualties: (a) Approx. 40,000 Allies; (b). Approx. 35,000 Germans.

Result: Although the Germans contained the Allied bridgehead for four months, the final break-out from the perimeter did assist the ultimate breaching of the Gustav Line and the winning of the battle of Cassino.

Suggested reading: M. W. Clark. *Calculated Risk* (New York, 1950); G. A. Shepperd. *The Italian Campaign, 1943–1945* (London, 1968); A. Kesselring. *Memoirs* (London, 1954); B. Pitt (ed.). *The Purnell History of the Second World War* vol.4, No. 13 (London, 1967).

Once the first Allied attacks on Cassino had ended in failure, General Sir Harold Alexander, Allied Army Group commander, ordered US VI Corps to plan and undertake Operation 'Shingle', an amphibious landing at Anzio, 70 miles behind the Gustav Line and 30 miles south of Rome. On 22 January – after much trouble securing the necessary landing craft – the British 1st Infantry and the US 3rd Infantry Divisions landed to the west and east of Anzio respectively, while five American battalions attacked the port itself. At first little opposition was encountered, but Lucas was slow to exploit his advantage and press inland, being dominated by the wish to mass his forces ashore (including no less than 18,000 vehicles of all sorts) in the hope of avoiding the type of problems that had detrimentally affected the earlier Salerno landings. As a result, the key Highway 7 to Rome was not cut.

In fact this hesitation provided von Kesselring with time to react. The German Fourteenth Army was brought up to seal off the crowded Allied bridgehead. Lucas thereupon dug-in around his 15-mile by 7-mile perimeter and a bitter series of battles began. A major break-out attempt was frustrated on 31 January by the six available German divisions. The bridgehead was reinforced by elements of the US 1st Armoured Division and three more infantry divisions (two being British) in anticipation of a German counter-attack. Already Allied losses stood at almost 7,000 men, and when the German attack duly materialized it was only just beaten back. On 16 February it even seemed that the 29th Panzer Division might split the bridgehead in two, as four divisions supported by 450 guns mounted determined attacks. But by the 18th, the Germans were pulling back, and,

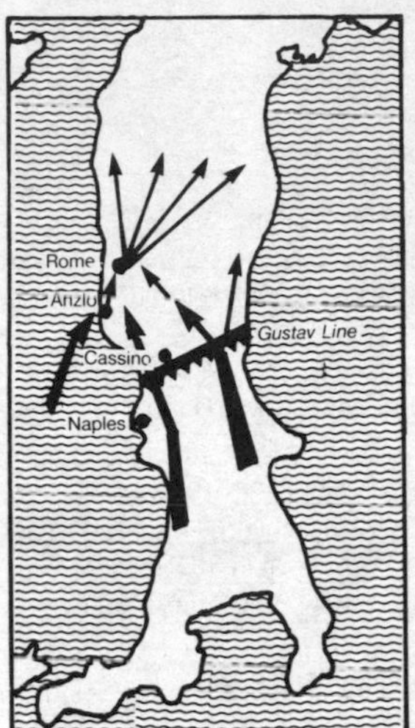

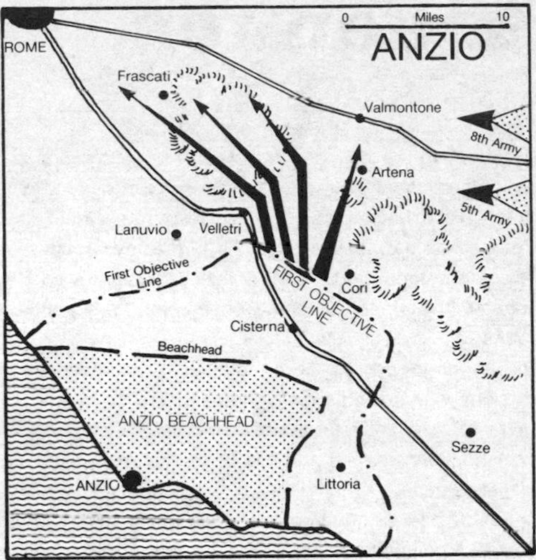

after surviving a second onslaught in late February, the bridgehead could be deemed secure.

A period of stalemate ensued. Rome remained uncaptured, and Cassino still held out. However, on 17 May – the day on which Cassino at last fell – Major-General Lucius Truscott (the new commander at Anzio in succession to the discredited Lucas) at last managed to break-out to link with US II Corps of Mark Clark's US Fifth Army. Four months' fighting had cost an estimated 9,200 British and 29,000 American casualties. As Winston Churchill said of the disappointing outcome, 'We had intended to fling ashore a screaming wild-cat; instead we found ourselves with a stranded whale.' In fairness to Lucas, he was forced to land prematurely owing to the higher priorities accorded to the shipping requirements for D-Day.

Ardennes

Date: 16 December 1944–1 February 1945.

Location: In the hilly and forested Ardennes region of eastern Belgium and Luxemburg, centring around the key communication centres of St. Vith and Bastogne.

Object: Hitler had ordered one last, desperate, all-out attempt to reach Antwerp, and thus split Montgomery's 21st from Bradley's 12th Army Group.

Opposing sides: (a) General Dwight D. Eisenhower, SACEUR; (b) Field Marshal Gerd von Rundstedt, German Supreme Commander, West (replaced by Model towards the end of the battle).

Forces engaged: (a) Seven armoured, eighteen infantry divisions and two parachute divisions, comprising the US First and Third Armies. Total: 400,000 men and 1,100 tanks; (b) Nine Panzer and fourteen infantry divisions, comprising the German Sixth SS Panzerarmee, the Fifth Panzerarmee and the Seventh Army. Total: 250,000 men, 1,000 tanks and self-propelled guns.

Casualties: (a) 77,000 troops and 733 tanks; (b) 90,000 troops and 600 tanks.

Result: A complete defeat for the German Army in the West following hard upon a considerable initial success. The American line was re-established by late January, but the Germans had held back the Allied arrival on the Rhine in the north-central sector by some six weeks.

Suggested reading: J. MacDonald. *The Battle of the Bulge* (London 1984) and *The Last Offensive* (Washington: 1973); H. Manteuffel. *The Fatal Decisions* Part 6 (London, 1956); O. Bradley. *A Soldier's Story* (London 1949); B. Pitt (ed). *The Purnell History of the Second World War* vol. 6, Nos. 3 and 4 (London 1967).

Aware that time was running short for the Third Reich, but still deluding himself that even at the eleventh hour he might save Germany from conquest, Adolf Hitler imposed on his higher command one last desperate all-out gamble on the Western Front. If he could drive a wedge between the Allies by capturing Antwerp, and thereafter eliminate the forces trapped in Holland to the north, he believed that Churchill and Roosevelt might be prepared to negotiate a cease-fire in the west which would permit Germany to employ all her remaining military resources against the remorseless advance of the Red Army from the east.

To produce sufficient men and *matériel* for the big effort every resource was exploited. Old men, hospital cases, and Hitler Youth were rushed into uniform and given rapid training. The brilliant Minister of Production, von Speer, made up the shortage in tanks by manufacturing pre-fabricated self-propelled guns throughout the smaller towns of Germany. One thousand aircraft were transferred for the time being to the Western Front. However, there was one critical shortage that could not be extemporised – fuel. Since the loss of the Roumanian oilfields, Germany had become increasingly short of this key commodity. Brushing aside Field Marshal von Rundstedt's plea for 'the little solution' – namely, an attack only as far as the Meuse – Hitler insisted on his own concept, stating that his forces would have to rely upon capturing Allied fuel dumps to supplement their meagre supplies. He similarly discounted anxieties that there were

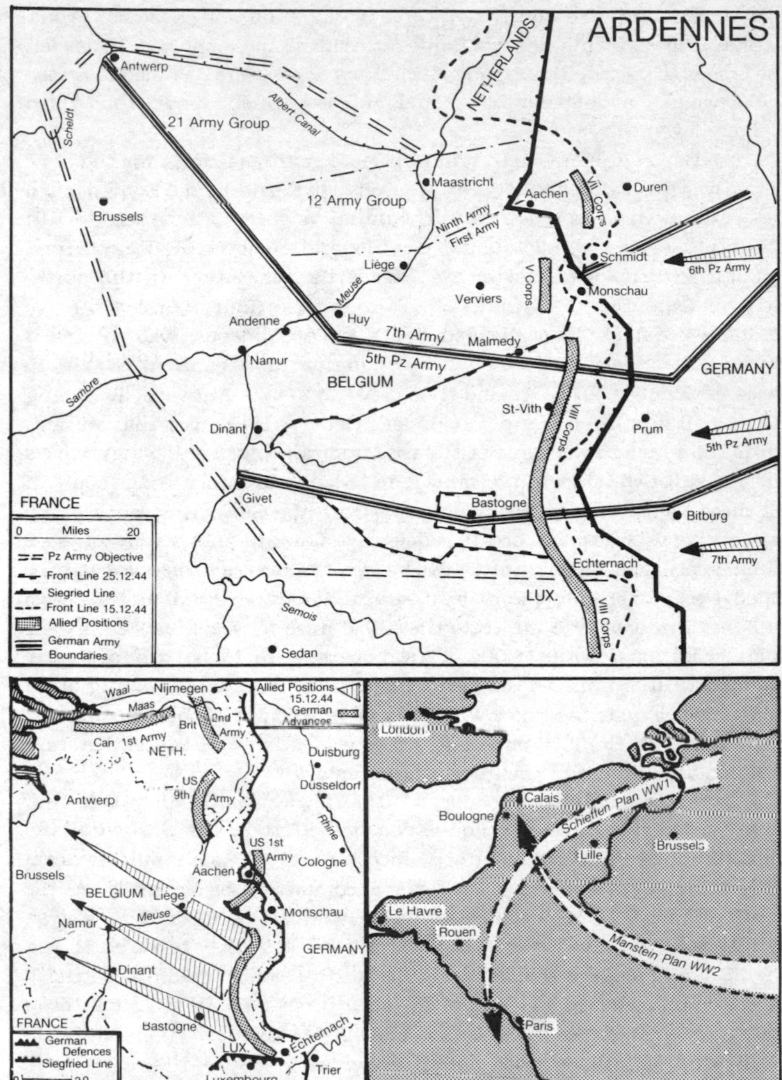

insufficient reserves to exploit an initial success, even if Allied air power could be negated.

Hitler dreamt of a repetition of the triumphs of May and June 1940 – and for his attack selected the very same sector of the front – namely the Ardennes Forest. Its hilly eastern approaches – the Eiffel – would conceal the German build-up; the frequent fogs and bad weather of December might well ground the Allied air forces, while the low temperatures would help demoralize the Allies whereas at least a proportion of their attackers had experience of earlier, far worse winters on the Eastern Front. Capitalizing on Montogmery's failure at Arnhem in September, Hitler felt the omens to be propitious. Indeed, circumstances were destined to afford the Germans a considerable initial success which shook the Allied command very severely.

The German plan was to build up secretly three armies for the blow which was to be launched between Monschau in the north and Echtenach in the south along a 70-mile front. The initial target was to be the US VIII Corps of General Middleton, part of General Hodge's US First Army, holding an extended front in the 'safe' Ardennes region. In the north, General Sepp Dietrich's Sixth SS Panzerarmee (four Panzer and five infantry divisions), spearheaded by Task Force Pieper, was to smash through the American front near the communications centre of St. Vith to force the Meuse near Liège and then drive on to take Antwerp, absorbing Allied fuel dumps en route. On its left, General Hasso von Manteuffel's Fifth Panzerarmee was to seize the road and rail centre of Bastogne, pass the Meuse between Liège and Namur, and occupy Brussels. To the south of all these, General Ernst Brandenberger with the German Seventh Army (mainly infantry) was to create a defensive flank to hold off Patton's US Third Army. This surprise offensive by twenty German divisions was to be aided by Colonel Otto Skorzeny's special forces, dressed in American uniforms, who were to infiltrate the Allied lines to wreak havoc on their communications, while 1,000 paratroopers were to be dropped near Malmédy. Hitler imposed the utmost security to conceal the coming blow, and very few generals knew what was to be expected of them until a few days before H-Hour. Camouflage, foggy weather and deceptive unit insignia were all used to heighten the deception.

The Allies ignored certain signs that a blow was impending, believing that Germany could never mount a major effort in the west after the appalling losses already sustained since June 1944. As a result, General Troy Middleton's command was taken complctely by surprise by the attacks on his VIII Corps which began early on 16 December. Soon a large salient had been driven into US First Army, but US V Corps to the north and the US 7th Armoured Division at St. Vith to the south, held up Dietrich's progress and pushed his line of advance further south than had been intended. On 27 December St. Vith at last fell. Meanwhile farther south von Manteuffel also made good initial progress – indeed he might have triumphed had Hitler been prepared to transfer armour from the Sixth SS Panzerarmee to reinforce Fifth Panzerarmee's success – but as the Fuehrer was determined that SS troops should have the glory of winning the campaign, just enough time was won for General Eisenhower to rush up 101st Airbourne Division by road to reinforce US 10th Armoured Division at Bastogne before the Germans surrounded the town. In a classic battle fought amidst deep winter conditions – including day after day of foggy weather which neutralized the Allied air forces – every German assault was repulsed by General Anthony McAuliffe from 20 to 26 December. Summoned to surrender, that commander returned the immortal reply: 'Nuts!' At length, on the 26th, a column of Patton's US Third Army managed to fight its way through to relieve the beleagured Bastogne garrison and the worst crisis had passed. The weather was now clearing, and Allied air strikes became increasingly effective from the 23rd. Two days later, the US 2nd Armoured Division checked the westernmost German formation (2nd Panzer) near Celle – the nearest the Germans came to reaching the Meuse. Colonel Pieper's Battlegroup had achieved much, but almost within sight of Huy was halted on the edge of a huge petrol dump which he was just not strong enough to capture.

Meanwhile, on 20 December, Eisenhower had taken the brave decision to entrust command of all troops north of 'the Bulge' to Montgomery – to the consternation of many of his American generals. This restored the balance at the cost of abandoning St. Vith. Then, striking south on 3 January, US VII Corps drove forward to cut the La Roche–Vielsalm road on the 7th. Next day Hitler at last authorized a fighting retreat, and on the 16th the Allies at last restored their solid front. Heavy fighting continued, but Hitler's last great gamble had failed. In late January his last troops left the Ardennes. The final German strategic reserve had been destroyed with little to show for it – except a gain in time of six weeks to prepare the defences of the Rhine.

Arnhem

Date: 17–25 September 1944.

Location: Holland, on the north bank of the Neder Rijn, nine miles north of Nijmegen.

Object: The 21st Army Group was attempting to pass the Rhine by a *coup de main* to attack the sources of German heavy industry in the Ruhr, thus turning the northern flank of the Siegfried Line.

Opposing sides: (a) Field Marshal Sir Bernard Montgomery in command of 21st Army Group; (b) Field Marshal Walther Model commanding German Army Group 'B'.

Forces engaged: (a) Three airborne divisions (two US, one British); 1st Polish Parachute Brigade and British XXX Corps. Total: approx. 100,000 troops; (b) Two Panzer divisions, parts of First Paratroop Army, various battle-groups and garrison battalions. Total: approx. 85,000 troops

Casualties: (a) British 1st Airborne Division lost 7,200 men; (b) German forces lost some 3,300 men killed and wounded.

Result: The failure of the final stage of Operation 'Market Garden' postponed the crossing of the Rhine until March 1945. The capture of Nijmegen, however, opened a new route on to German soil.

Suggested Reading: C. Wilmot. *The Struggle for Europe* (London, 1952); C. Ryan. *A Bridge too Far* (London, 1964); B. Horrocks. *A Full Life* (London, 1960); C. Hibbert. *The Battle for Arnhem* (London, 1962). B. Pitt (ed.). *The Purnell History of the Second World War* vol. 5, No. 12 (London, 1968).

Following the battle of Falaise, the Allies soon occupied Paris (25 August), swept on into Belgium to liberate Brussels (3 September) and Antwerp (but not the heavily-mined Scheldt Estuary), and Liège five days later. It seemed that final victory was in sight. Unfortunately, however, a strategic dissension was now dividing the Allied high command which was to have a bearing on the planning and outcome of the Arnhem operation. Since the secondary invasion of the south of France ('Anvil-Dragoon', 15 August) there were three Allied Army Groups in north-west Europe, two of them American (commanded by Bradley and Devers) and one British-Canadian (under Montgomery). The preponderance of American troops encouraged Eisenhower to insist upon a 'broad front' strategy, attacking the German frontiers all the way from Switzerland to the North Sea simultaneously, on the assumption that the German defences would crack somewhere. Montgomery championed a subtler, so-called 'narrow front' concept, whereby full priority of supplies and reinforcements was to be accorded to his 21st Army Group in Holland, including the Allied Air Army (the Supreme Commander's reserve), for a concentrated rapier-thrust, involving twenty divisions, through Holland to pass the Rhine by way of Arnhem, before swinging southwards to envelop the Ruhr – the loss of whose heavy industries would effectively end the war for Germany. All other operations would, by this scheme, be placed in abeyance.

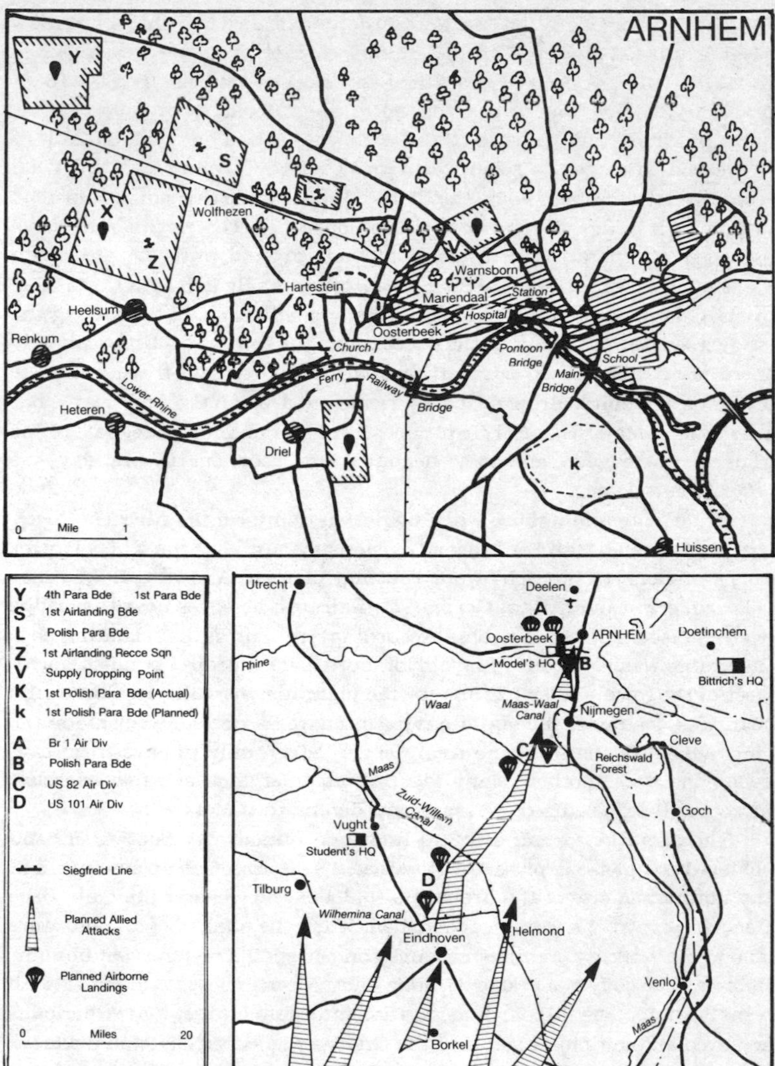

American objections to the British proposal were predictably strong, Patton (US Third Army) in particular having no wish to stand by as a virtual spectator while Montgomery won the war, Eisenhower felt he knew best, but under intense British pressure began to prevaricate, and on 12 September gave way – to the fury of his American commanders. Montgomery was awarded the use of the Air Army and full priority over supplies.

The plan for Operation 'Market Garden' envisaged two distinct phases. 'Market' was to be the creation of a 45-mile corridor from the Meuse-Escaut Canal (the current limit of the Allied advance) to Arnhem. The US 101st Airborne Division was to be dropped to secure bridges over two canals north of Eindhoven, while the 82nd Airborne carried out a similar role at Grave and Nijmegen to secure passages over the Rivers Maas and Waal respectively; simultaneously, the British 1st Airborne Division would drop to secure the bridge at Arnhem over the Neder Rijn. The 'river barrier' thus breached, the paratroops would hold their ground until, by Operation 'Garden', Lieutenant-General Sir Brian Horrocks's British XXX Corpıs (led by the Guards Armoured Division) linked up with them in turn along the single road before exploiting the success into the Ruhr area. Unfortunately there were insufficient aircraft available to drop all three complete divisions in a single drop; so it was decided to drop all the Americans, but only to land Major-General Urquhart's 1st Parachute Brigade, part of his glider-borne brigade, and some headquarters troops on the first day, the rest to follow later.

Inadequate intelligence work neglected to inform the Airborne Army that the 9th and 10th SS Panzer Divisions (comprising the XI SS Panzer Corps of General Bittrich) were refitting close to Arnhem. It was also believed, erroneously, that German anti-aircraft defences near the bridge over the Neder Rijn were strong. Accordingly, a *coup de main* landing near the bridge was ruled out in favour of more distant drops six miles north-west of the town. Other features of the planning were also less thorough than was desirable, the staffs having prepared a dozen schemes for the employment of the Airborne Army since D-Day, only to have them cancelled one after another. Many felt this was just another paper exercise. Moreover Patton refused to assume the defensive at Metz.

The operation began at 1300 hours on Sunday, 17 September, and achieved complete surprise at the outset. The Germans were astounded at the timing and size of the drops. Both Model and General Student of the German paratroops were near Arnhem when the attack began, and were able to start taking counter-measures on the spot, aided by a set of plans found on the body of a crashed glider-pilot. Nevertheless, to begin with all went well for the Allies. Except for Nijmegen bridge, the Americans achieved all their objectives, and the Guards Armoured Division made six miles up the road on the first day. Eindhoven was occupied on the 18th, and the Guards reached the 82nd 'Screaming Eagles' at Grave. The same afternoon a bold attack captured Nijmegen bridge.

Ill-fortune had dogged British 1st Airborne Division from the outset. The drops took place accurately enough, but the paratroops found their advance into Arnhem to seize the crucial bridge held by Krafft's battalion and a battle-group of the 9th SS Panzer. As a result it was not until 2000 hours that Lieutenant-Colonel John Frost's 2nd Parachute Battalion reached the northern end of the bridge – only to find a German force moving up to secure the southern end as Bittrich carried out countermoves based on the captured copy of the Allied plan. At the same time German paratroops aided by armour began to launch counter-attacks against the Allied corridor near Son and Veghel.

Then bad weather interposed, making it impossible to fly-in the second wave of Polish paratroops as per schedule. Many supply drops went straight into German hands, and many aircraft were shot down as the Flak defences were thickened up. Urquhart was trapped in a loft for a whole day in German-occupied Arnhem, so command slipped. The loss of large radio sets meant that XXX Corps had no news from Arnhem; nobody thought to use the railway telephone system which was open to Nijmegen.

The crisis came on the 21st. Frost's heroic resistance was quelled, and Urquhart (restored to command) began to withdraw his troops into a perimeter west of Arnhem at Oosterbeek on the banks of the Neder Rijn. In the afternoon the arrival of the delayed Polish Brigade near Driel to the south of the river made little difference. Further south, the Guards Armoured failed to force its way north from near Nijmegen, and German tanks and reinforcements had secured most of Arnhem itself.

German attacks on the corridor grew in intensity, and not until the 22nd was the 43rd Wessex Division able to approach the river at Driel. Three days later Montgomery ordered Urquhart to evacuate his shrinking perimeter. Some 2,000 crossed the river safely – but the Allied offensive had ended in failure, and both the Rhine barrier and the Ruhr beyond were safe until 1945.

Arras

Date: 21 May 1940

Location: On the River Scarpe, north-eastern France.

Object: Part of the British Expeditionary Force was attempting to slow the German post-Sedan advance towards the Channel coast.

Opposing sides: (a) Major-General Franklyn commanding 'Frank Force'; (b) Major-General Erwin Rommel commanding 7th Panzer Division and other German elements including the SS *Totenkopf* Division and 78th Artillery Regiment.

Forces engaged: (a) Two RTR regiments and two infantry battalions, twelve guns. Total: approx. 3,000 men; (b) 25th Panzer Regiment, two rifle regiments, SS *Totenkopf* Division, 45 guns. Total: approx. 16,000 men.

Casualties: (a) 57 British tanks and 220 men; (b) 20 German tanks and 378 men.

Result: A psychological check to the Germans although the British withdrew; Arras contributed to the Dunkirk evacuation by making the Germans cautious.

Suggested Reading: A. Horne. *To Lose a Battle* (London, 1969); B. J. Bond. *France and Belgium* (London, 1975); B. H. Liddell Hart (ed.). *The Rommel Papers* (London, 1953); K. Macksey. *The Shadow of Vimy Ridge* (London, 1965); B. Pitt (ed.). *The Purnell History of the Second World War* vol. 1, No. 9 (London, 1968).

Following their breakthrough near Sedan and Dijon, Army Group A's armoured elements raced westwards to drive a corridor between the Allied forces. On the inner flank of the thrust, Irwin Rommel's 7th Panzer Division (the 'Ghost Division') approached Arras on 20 May. The town was defended by 'Petre Force' of the BEF, with parts of British 5th and 50th Divisions ('Frank Force') behind Vimy Ridge to the north and west.

To carry out the French High Command's order to obstruct the German advance, General Franklyn extemporised two columns comprising (west) 7th RTR (Royal Tank Regiment), four companies of 8th Durham Light Infantry, 365 Field Battery RA, and some anti-tank guns, and (east) 4th RTR, four companies of 6th DLI, 368 Field Battery and more anti-tank detachments. As Rommel, on the 21st, began to advance around Arras towards Warlus and Wailly, these two columns – despite a confused and delayed approach march from Vimy Ridge – achieved a notable surprise attack. Crossing the Arras-Baumetz railway line at about 1400 hours the British struck the German 6th and 7th Rifle Regiments and the inexperienced SS *Totenkopf* Division as they prepared to advance through Wailly, Ficheux and Agny. The German light anti-tank guns proved useless against the British 'I' tanks, which brought chaos to the German transport and guns in the area.

Believing that he was under attack by five divisions and 'hundreds of tanks' (in fact only 83 were engaged in all), Rommel was at first taken off his guard and stupified. However, he was soon extemporising a gun-line to stop the British advance, and the arrival of the 25th Panzer Regiment late in the afternoon made it possible to counter-attack. Some of the British tanks had got ahead of their supporting infantry and guns, and heavy

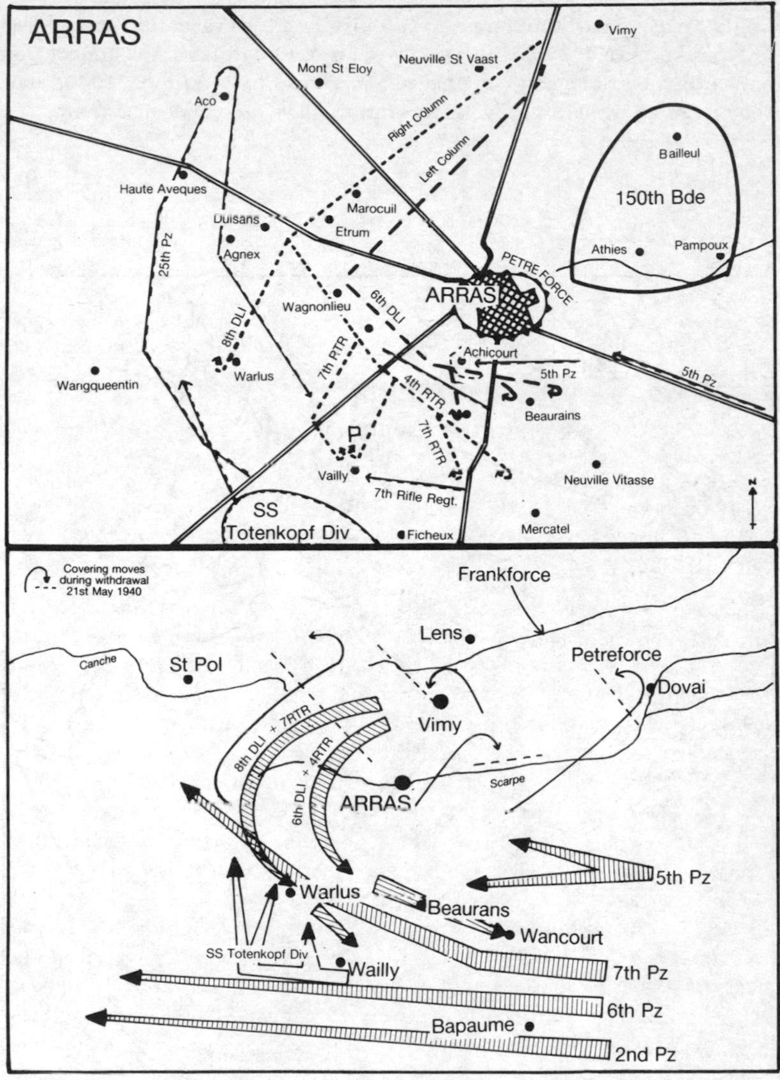

losses resulted. About dusk, the British survivors drew off in good order and retired towards Vimy. Arras was abandoned on the night of 23 May as the BEF drew back towards Dunkirk on the coast on the eve of the Belgian surrender.

This attack by a small British force against more powerful opponents who enjoyed almost complete control of the air, was an excellent example of a 'counter-stroke'. Its psychological impact on the enemy was out of all proportion to its physical size. The caution it engendered in the Germans would greatly assist the retreat to Dunkirk and the evacuation of the BEF to England over the following two weeks. Arras, in fact, was almost the only Allied battle success in the whole campaign of France, 1940, and demonstrated what might, with resolution, have been done elsewhere.

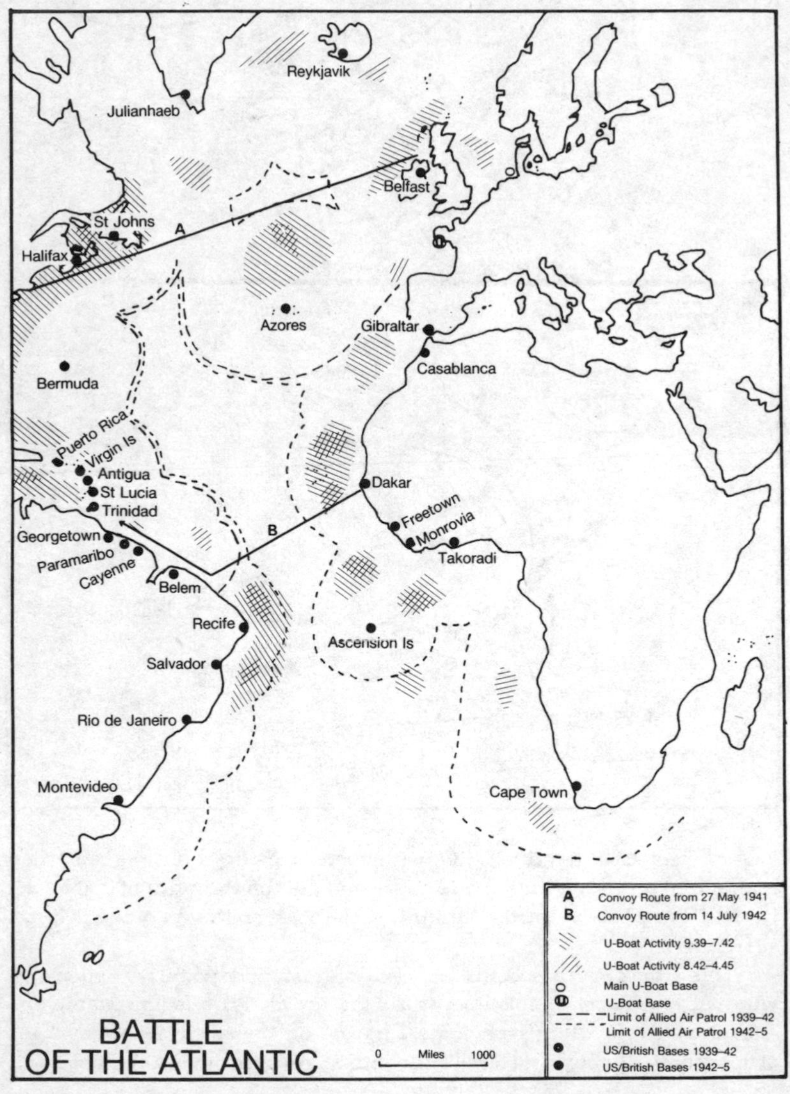

Atlantic

Date: 17 August 1940 – 12 November 1944.

Location: The North Cape to Greenland, the Cape of Good Hope to the Falklands.

Object: The German Kriegsmarine was attempting to blockade the British Isles by surface and submarine vessels (aided by the Luftwaffe when within range); the Royal Navy and the Allied fleets were determined to retain free use of the ocean, and impose a blockade on Germany.

Opposing sides: (a) The British First Lord of the Admiralty; (b) Grand-Admirals Raeder and Doenitz commanding the Kriegsmarine.

Forces engaged: (a) The Royal and Commonwealth Navies, and later the US Navy, with cover from the Fleet Air Arm (carrier and land-based); (b) U-boat arm of the Kriegsmarine.

Casualties: (a). Approx 2,828 vessels (14,500,000 tons) of British, American and Allied shipping; 82,000 British RN and Mercantile Marine sailors lost; (b). 781 U-boats and several heavy naval surface units sunk; 221 U-boats scuttled at the end of hostilities, 1945, and 156 more surrendered; more than 1,000 surface vessels sunk (1,800,000 tons).

Result: The frustration of the German blockade and the destruction of the power of the Kriegsmarine – but at very heavy cost.

Suggested Reading: S. W. Roskill. *The Navy at War* (London, 1960); P. K. Kemp. *The Battle of the Atlantic* (London, 1960); S. E. Morrison. *The Two Ocean War 1939-45* (Oxford, 1963); B. Pitt (ed.). *The Purnell History of the Second World War*, vols. 1 & 4, Nos. 14 & 4 respectively (London, 1966 and 1967).

Although the Battle of the Atlantic may be said to have commenced with the sinking by a U-boat of the SS *Athenia* on 3 September 1939, it was Hitler's declaration of a total blockade of Great Britain on 17 August 1940 that inaugurated the main struggle above, on and below the Atlantic Ocean. It was a war fought against surface-raiders, submarines, minefields and land-based German aircraft, and not least, during the long winters, against the cruel sea itself. Hitler was determined to cut Great Britain off from its sources of food supply, raw materials and military reinforcements, and neutral shipping was as much at risk as the vessels of Britain's allies. The struggle was relentlessly and bitterly fought by both sides.

The use of surface raiders palled after the loss of *Graf Spee* and above all of the mighty *Bismarck*, but by keeping its remaining capital ships in Norwegian fiords and French and German ports, the Kriegsmarine was able to tie down considerable elements of the far stronger Royal Navy in preventive roles. In December 1943 *Scharnhorst* put out to sea to raid convoys in the Arctic, but she was hunted down and sunk, while *Tirpitz* was put out of action by RAF bombing in Tromsö Fiord on 12 November 1944. So the main struggle was waged by the German U-boats, at first operating singly but later in wolf-packs, guided to their targets – the convoys – by high-flying, long-range Focke-Wulf *Condor* reconnaissance aircraft.

At first the shipping – especially American – tended to sail as single vessels, but it was soon found that the escorted convoy was the safest method to cross the Atlantic. Once British (and later American) forces had taken over Iceland, vital land-based air cover could be provided for more than two-thirds of the journey, but the gaps provided the main killing-grounds for the enemy. From June 1940 to July 1941 a total of 5,800,000 tons of shipping was lost (1,370 vessels of all types, including 899 British) – far exceeding the replacement capacity. Imports fell by a third, but there was less danger of national starvation than there had been under similar attack in 1917. By late 1940 the Germans had lost 31 U-boats to British air and naval action, but a year later German shipyards were building eighteen boats a month, and Raeder was able to keep 100 submarines at sea at a time. The American provision of 50 old destroyers under 'Lease-Lend' in September 1940 helped the Royal Navy find the myriad escorts required for convoys.

The menace of German surface raiders was considerable at the outset – but the sinking of *Bismarck* in May 1941 marked the end of that phase of the struggle to all intents and purposes. Then came the German invasion of Russia in June 1941, and the need to send war material to Murmansk and Archangel around the North Cape. The convoy routes, overlooked by a German-controlled Norwegian coast, added a huge new strain to the navy and merchant marine. The seasonal movement of the icefields restricted Allied freedom of action, and the winter convoys in particular were terribly exposed to bad weather and enemy air action. In all, 40 convoys carried 3,700,000 tons of supplies to the USSR, but in the process lost 91 ships. The worst losses were sustained by Convoy PQ. 17 in mid-1942, which lost 23 out of 34 merchant ships en route for Russia.

The main convoys were accompanied by squadrons of capital ships including fleet carriers whenever possible, and the building of a new class of escort carrier (converted merchant ships carrying six aircraft) helped ease the strain as more and more came into service; and the use of catapult-launched Hurricanes from selected ships helped destroy the menacing *Condors* which flew above the anti-aircraft gun range. Improved ASDIC detection methods, the introduction of surface radar (battery-driven U-boats had to surface regularly to recharge), and better hunting tactics and use of depth-charges, were progressively introduced, but the strain remained intense and losses mounted, although the American entry into the war in late 1941 shared the burden.

The worst year for shipping losses proved to be 1942. The Germans sank almost 8,000,000 tons, and the U-boats claimed 1,660 vessels. The escorts and aircraft had accounted for fourteen U-boats by June, and then fourteen in July capped by sixteen in October; but the Germans had managed to double their submarine fleet to 200 operational boats by December.

The replacement of Raeder by Doenitz early in 1943 assured an even greater emphasis on underwater attack. Half a million tons of shipping a month were being lost, but U-boat losses had also begun to mount (40 in May alone), and the graph-curve began to come down. Doenitz rested his crews and tried new tactics, but in the last quarter of 1943 all of 53 submarines were sunk and only 47 merchantmen lost. The main battle of the Atlantic was won, but, like Waterloo, it had been a 'near-run thing'.

The Atlantic struggle continued to the very end of the war but on a much reduced scale, and there was no question but that the Allies had gained, and retained, the upper hand. On 10 May 1945 Grand Admiral Doenitz ordered his submarine commanders to surrender to the Allies. Of 377 surviving U-boats only 156 complied – the rest preferring to scuttle themselves.

Over the duration of the struggle the Allies had lost more than 23,500,000 tons of shipping, well over half of this grim total to U-boat action. However, the combined US-British building capacity totalled more than 45,500,000 tons during the same period. Of the 781 U-boats sunk by the Allies, more than half were destroyed from the air. From first to last, as the loss of well over 82,000 British sailors alone demonstrates, it had been a grim struggle of heroic proportions.

'Barbarossa'

Date: 22 June – 21 August 1941.

Location: The western frontiers of the USSR, from the Baltic near Memel to the mouth of the River Pruth on the Black Sea.

Object: Three German Army Groups were to invade Russia, defeat the Red Army, capture Moscow, and ultimately penetrate to the Caspian Sea and the Ural Mountains.

Opposing sides: (a) Field Marshal von Brauchitsch commanding (under Hitler) the Wehrmacht; (b) Marshal Timoshenko commanding (under Stalin) the Soviet Red Army.

Forces engaged: (a) Army Groups North, Centre and South, altogether 145 divisions (including four Panzer Groups – 19 armoured and 12 motorized divisions) and three Luftwaffe Air Fleets. Total: approx. 3,000,000 German, Roumanian, Bulgarian and Hungarian troops; (b) Four Special Military Districts (Baltic, Western, Kiev and Odessa), altogether 132 divisions (including 34 armoured). Total: approx. 3,000,000 Russian troops.

Casualties: (to 21 August): (a) approx. 470,000 Germans and allies; (b) approx. 1,300,000 Russians.

Suggested Reading: Alan Clark. *Barbarossa* (London, 1965); J. Erickson. *The Road to Stalingrad* (London 1975); H. Guderian. *Panzer Leader* (London, 1952); V. I. Chuikov. *The Beginning of the Road* (New York, 1963); B. Pitt (ed.). *The Purnell History of the Second World War* vol. 2, Nos. 8 and 9 (London, 1967).

The German invasion of Russia in June 1941 unleashed the most devastating campaign – or series of campaigns –in military history. Even the disasters that befell Charles XII of Sweden in 1709–10 and Napoleon in 1812, pale into insignificance beside the fate of the German armed forces by 1945 on the Eastern Front, while the Russians lost twenty million soldiers and citizens in freeing their homeland from the invader and reaching Berlin. Yet the first campaigns – up to the winter of 1941/42 – were almost a continuous series of massive German victories.

Hitler had ordered the assembly of his vast army along the frontiers of the USSR early in 1941. It had been intended that his initial attack, code-named Operation 'Barbarossa', would begin in May, but the need to invade Greece and capture Crete caused a five-week postponement of the invasion – five vital weeks of good weather that probably made all the difference to the outcome of the campaign against Russia in 1941, although Hitler did not wish to strike in the east until the roads were well dried out.

The vast majority of his troops were Germans, but contingents of Hitler's Balkan allies were also included – perhaps some 210,000 men in the total. With the victories of Poland, Norway, the Low Countries, France and now Greece behind them, the morale of the German forces was extremely high. Von Brauschitsch set his Army Group commanders the following objectives. In the north, Field Marshal von Leeb (26 divisions including Hoepner's eight armoured formations and supported by the First *Luftflotte*) was to invade the Baltic States (recently seized by Russia) and head for Leningrad by way of Riga. In the centre, Field Marshal von Bock's

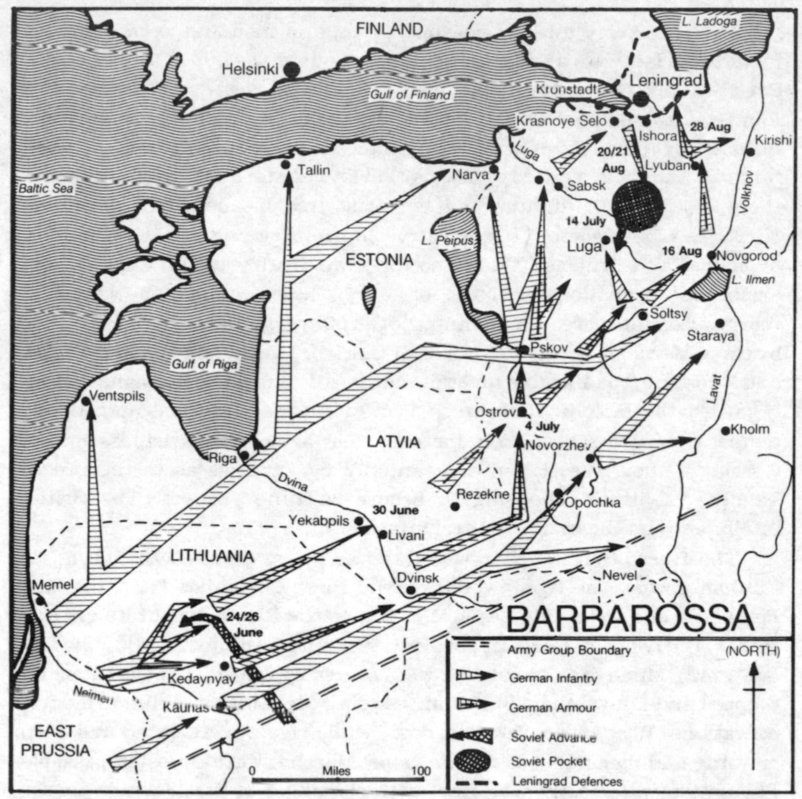

51 divisions (including one cavalry division and two Panzer Groups – all of 26 armoured and mechanized divisions under Guderian and Hoth, aided by the Second *Luftflotte*) were entrusted with the main blow – an all-out advance through Belorussia, skirting the northern side of the formidable Pripet Marshes, to capture Moscow. Further south Field Marshal von Rundstedt's Army Group (forty German and some eighteen allied divisions, including von Kleist's Panzergruppe of 14 armoured divisions supported by the 4th *Luftflotte*) was to cover a vast 500-mile front from Lublin to the Black Sea, with his main weight in the northern sector, and with it attack deep into the Ukraine and parts of Moldavia. A General Reserve of eighteen divisions (including two Panzers) stood behind Army Groups North and Centre, while the Finnish forces were preparing to strike into north-western Russia. Hitler expected a whirlwind victory against the huge but less well-equipped and supposedly ill-led Russian forces (Stalin's purges of officers had wrought havoc from 1935 onwards, and the Red Army's showing in the 1940–1 Winter War against Finland had not been impressive).

The Red Army totalled possibly 12 million men and women in all – including reservists and factory militias – but at the outset 75 per cent of Soviet trained forces were deployed to defend their western frontiers. Their four Special Military Districts (effectively Army Groups) were commanded initially by Generals Kuznetsov (Baltic sector – three armies, twenty infantry and six armoured divisions); Pavlov (Western sector – four armies, three cavalry, 23 infantry and ten armoured or motorized divisions); Kirponos (Kiev sector – two cavalry, 38 infantry and sixteen armoured divisions); and Tyulenev (Odessa sector – two cavalry, ten infantry and two armoured formations). From 11 July these commands would be reorganized into three – matching the German organization – commanded by three Marshals, namely Voroshilov (north), Timoshenko (White Russia) and Budenny (the Ukraine and the south). Although the Russians had not regarded the Molotov-Ribbentrop Pact of August 1939 as more than a temporary truce to be used to increase their armed preparedness against Germany, they were taken substantially by surprise as to the precise moment of attack, choosing to ignore warnings provided by British intelligence on the basis of 'Ultra' information.

The Russo-German War was to cover colossal areas. Including the Finnish sector, the front would extend for 2,000 miles from the Kola Peninsula and the White Sea all the way to the Black Sea. At its greatest extent, the depth of German penetration would be almost 1,700 miles (by late 1942). Much of this vast area was covered by forest, only the Ukranian Steppes and a few other limited areas being ideal for sweeping armoured operations. Roads were few and poor, while rivers were broad and deep, running mainly north–south. The Pripet Marshes were almost impassable. Population was mostly scattered, with a number of dense urban areas – around Minsk, Kiev, Smolensk, Leningrad and of course Moscow. The climate promised hot summers and very cold winters, with much rain and snow according to season.

The German attack began early on 22 June, and from the outset made tremendous gains. The Russians were ill-prepared to meet the German air-land *Blitzkreig* onslaughts, which were pressed with the greatest ruthlessness and skill. Vilna fell on the 24th, and six days later Lvov. The 1st July saw Guderian over the River Beresina, the same day that Hoepner entered Riga. As his forces reeled back Stalin called for an all-out, scorched-earth and partisan war; Hitler responded by ordering the razing of Moscow and Leningrad – once they were reached. On the 10th Finnish forces entered Russia. The crossing of the River Dniepr led to the capture of Minsk and Smolensk by 5 August, and brought the invaders 480,000 Russian prisoners, 4,500 tanks and more than 3,000 guns.

Timoshenko's Army Group was all but in dissolution, but in the north von Leeb was slowed by difficult terrain, and the same was true on von Rundstedt's sector in the south. German supply problems were rapidly mounting as the daunting effects of strategic consumption and the diminishing power of the offensive were encountered. But with von Bock's armoured spearhead at Beloj only 200 miles from Moscow, it seemed that nothing could save the fall of the Russian capital, and Leningrad was almost surrounded on 19 August. Voroshilov called for a last-ditch stand. Then Hitler made one of his disastrous interventions in the war – one that arguably cost him the outcome on the Eastern Front. In the first ten weeks of the campaign more than a million Russian casualties had been inflicted, but the *Wehrmacht* had lost more than 450,000 men. Hitler became concerned at the way his formations were being inexorably sucked into the depths of Russia, and against the advice of his Senior Staff Officers he decided to slow the advance on Moscow. Instead, he ordered Von Rundstedt and von Bock to trap Budenny's million troops at Kiev. Although this was to lead to another outstanding battle success, with the advantage of hindsight it is clear that this decision was a mistake: it robbed Hitler of the chance to take Moscow – an event which might have brought down Stalin, since 7 August supreme commander, and led to peace negotiations. But these possibilities were not to be.

Bataan and Corregidor

Date: 2 January – 6 May 1942.

Location: A peninsula and adjoining island on the west of Manila Bay, Luzon, the Philippines.

Object: The Japanese Imperial Army was determined to complete its conquest of the Philippines, and the Americans and Filipinos to delay this by making a determined last stand.

Opposing sides: (a) General Masahura Homma, commanding the Japanese Imperial Army; (b) General Douglas MacArthur commanding the US and Filipino forces.

Forces engaged: (a) The Imperial Japanese Fourteenth Army. Total: 50,000 troops; (b) US I and II Corps. Total: 35,000 Americans; 65,000 locals.

Casualties: (a) 12,000 Japanese killed and wounded; (b) 16,000 killed and wounded; 84,000 prisoners-of-war.

Result: The largest capitulation in United States' history completed the Japanese conquest of the Philippines with a major success.

Suggested reading: H. P. Willmott. *Empires in the Balance* (Annapolis, 1974); C. E. Morris. *Corregidor* (London, 1982); Clayton James. *MacArthur*, 3 vols. (New York, 1984); B. Pitt (ed.). *The Purnell History of the Second World War* vol. 3, No. 2 (London, 1967).

The Japanese invasion of the Philippines began on 10 December 1941, and by the end of the month the American and Filipino forces had been forced back on Manila, the capital, which was occupied on 2 January. General MacArthur had skilfully redeployed his troops to hold a 15-mile defence line protecting the Bataan Peninsula on the western side of Manila Bay, with headquarters and government established on the island of Corregidor. Major General Jonathan Wainwright held the western half of the line with US I Corps (or 'North Luzon Force') while Brigadier General George Parker's smaller US II Corps ('South Luzon Force') garrisoned the eastern sector. MacArthur hoped for substantial reinforcements – particularly aircraft – but Japanese naval and air supremacy was marked from the outset and very little aid got through.

On 10 January General Homma launched an all-out offensive against the eastern part of the line, but was repulsed with loss. New onslaughts forced the Americans back to the centre of the peninsula, but by 26 January the position had stabilized. Many of the American troops were sick with malaria, and medical resources were sparse, but the defence held firm. On 11 March President Roosevelt ordered MacArthur to leave with his staff for Australia, there to become Supreme Commander South West Pacific, leaving General Wainwright to command in the Philippines, with Major General Edward King commanding the Bataan forces. Rations – which had been cut to half from the outset – now had to be cut again to a quarter, and by late March some 24,000 men were sick.

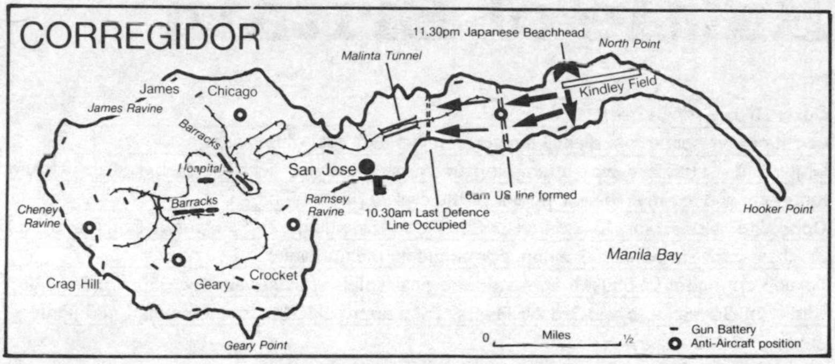

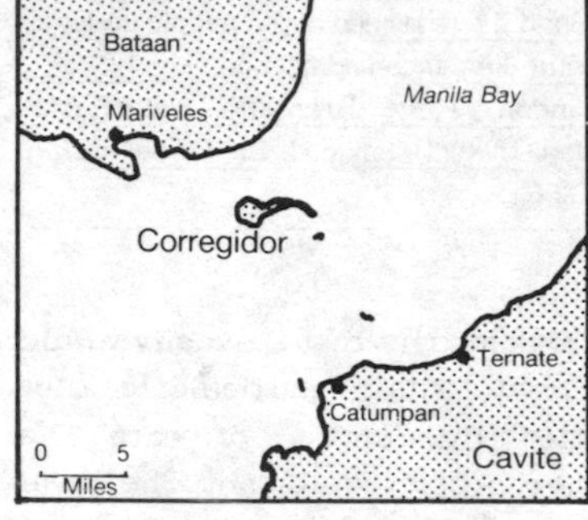

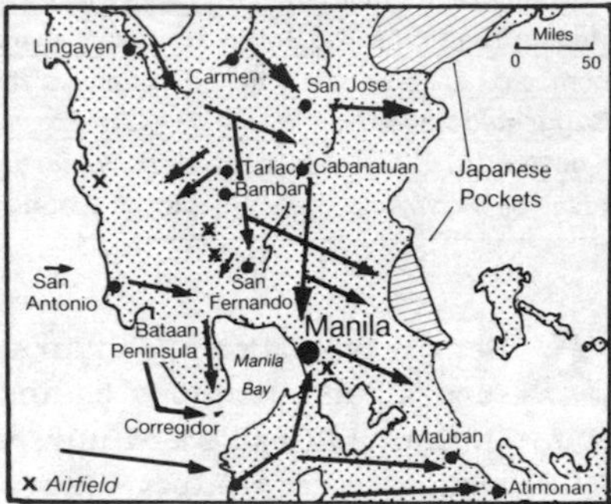

In the meantime reinforcements had reached the Japanese, and on 3 April Homma attacked again in strength. Breaking through II Corps' left flank, the Japanese gained ten miles in two days' fighting. I Corps' attempted counter-attacks were to small avail, and on 9 April II Corps finally disintegrated and King surrendered his 76,000 men unconditionally. The notorious 'death march' followed. Japanese forces now rapidly gained the upper hand on Mindanao, Cebu and Panay.

This left only the fortress island of Corregidor, 'the Gibraltar of Asia', defended by General Wainwright and some 13,000 men. They were subjected to an incessant artillery barrage, and although Fort Drum, 'the concrete battleship', survived the battering well, most troops were forced to seek cover in Malinta Hill tunnel. On 5 May a Japanese force landed on the north-east of the island, and the Americans inflicted 4,000 casualties but lost 1,000 men as well as Kindley Airfield. Reduced to three days' water, Wainwright surrendered unconditionally to General Homma on the 6th, followed by other detachments on the 10th and 18th.

Battle of Britain

Date: 10 July–12 October 1940.

Location: Air-space over mainly the south and south-east of England.

Object: The Luftwaffe was attempting to prepare the way for an invasion of the United Kingdom, and to break the will-power of the civilian population.

Opposing sides: (a) Air Marshal Sir Hugh Dowding, RAF Fighter Command; (b) *Reichsmarschall* Hermann Goering, commanding the Luftwaffe.

Forces engaged: (a) 55 RAF fighter squadrons. Total: at outset approx. 650 aircraft, 3,080 pilots; (b) German 2nd and 3rd Air Fleets. Total approx. 1,350 bombers and 1,480 fighters, approx. 10,000 aircrew.

Casualties: (a) 915 aircraft, 520 pilots killed; (b) 1,733 aircraft.

Result: The RAF saved Britain from likely invasion and the resilience of the people under air bombardment both strengthened its resolve and earned American admiration.

Suggested Reading: R. Hillary. *The Last Enemy* (London, 1942); P. Townsend. *Duel of Eagles* (London, 1970); L. Deighton. *Battle of Britain* (London, 1980); B. Pitt (ed.). *The Purnell History of the Second World War* vol. 1, No. 11 (London, 1966).

After the evacuation of Dunkirk, it was evident that Germany would turn all its attentions against Great Britain, particularly after Winston Churchill had scornfully rejected Hitler's offers of peace. The BEF's manpower had been saved, but at the cost of its equipment. The Royal Navy remained powerful, as did the RAF, and Churchill's wisdom in not committing all its fighter squadrons to the hopeless Battle of France was soon to be demonstrated. For although the German Air Force was superior in numbers it was in certain key respects deficient in quality. Great Britain had in the Spitfire and Hurricane two fighters of excellent design; her possession of a developed system of early-warning radar was another important advantage; best of all, the 3,000 or so RAF fighter pilots drawn from fourteen nations, not least the 147 Poles fighting in exile, were to prove of extraordinary ability.

To invade Great Britain (Operation 'Sealion'), the Germans had to gain air control over the English Channel as a preliminary to defeating the Royal Navy and sending the Wehrmacht over in force. The first task was to destroy the RAF. On 10 July the Battle of Britain opened when German bombers attacked British convoys in the Channel, an onslaught that reached a peak from 8 to 15 August. By this measure the Germans hoped to lure the RAF into battle, but to work this required German local air superiority. Thanks to the radar system, the composition of German incoming raids could be calculated before they crossed the French coast, and appropriate measures taken to meet them. Thus the 1,500 enemy sorties flown on 8 August and the 1,700 put in the air a week later failed to overwhelm the defenders. On the 15th the Germans lost some 76 aircraft. During the first phase the RAF lost 153 aircraft (but 60 pilots were

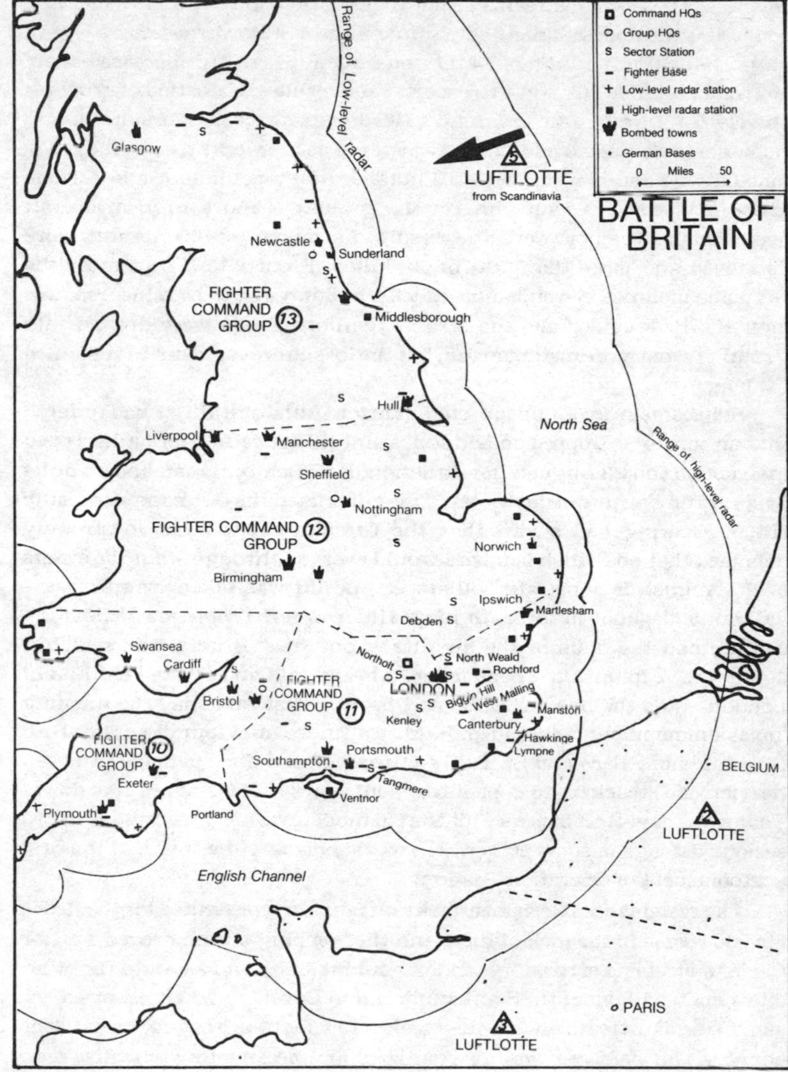

rescued), while the Germans lost at least twice as many (and almost all their aircrews) – although exact losses remain a contentious subject to the present day.

In mid-August the Germans switched their main attention to attacks on radar stations, RAF airfields and aircraft factories in the south of England – the defence of which was the particular responsibility of Fighter Command Group 11 under Air Vice-Marshal Park. 'Eagle Day' for the new offensive was 13 August. It was to prove a critical period for the British defences. The Germans realized that their Dornier Do 17s and Heinkel III bombers – and above all their slow Junker Ju 85 Stuka divebombers – were highly vulnerable to attack, and consequently greatly increased their Messerschmitt Me 109 and 110 escorts. The result was a period of growing anxiety for Dowding at Command Headquarters near Stanmore; many raids were intercepted and turned away, but as the weeks passed the radar installations and airfields began to take a heavy pounding, and serious losses of aircraft – many hit on the ground – and a drop in overall operational efficiency were the result. As many as 450 aircraft were destroyed and more than 100 pilots killed. From 1 to 5 September the Germans mounted eleven major attacks, and it began to be wondered how long the RAF could take the strain. Reinforcements were drafted into Group 11 from more distant areas, but the loss curve could not be sustained for long.

Help came from an unexpected quarter. Although Hitler had ordered that no bombs be dropped on London, a single Luftwaffe aircrew disobeyed instructions on 23 August. In retaliation, RAF Bomber Command made its first raid on Berlin two days later. This enfuriated the Germans, especially Hitler. Goering had sworn that the German capital was so strongly defended that no British bombers would ever get through – but the events of 25 August demonstrated otherwise. Berlin was taken by surprise – without a blackout in force. In fury, Hitler ordered reprisals against the capital, and the onus of the air attack on Great Britain was switched against the capital. On 7 September, a heavy raid struck the East End of London – and the famous '*Blitz*' had begun. That same day the warning 'invasion imminent' was issued. Raids continued, and four days later both Buckingham Palace and St. Paul's Cathedral sustained damage. An even heavier raid struck on 15 September – but at a cost of 56 planes shot down. That same day, RAF bombers hit the Channel invasion ports, and inflicted serious damage to some 200 craft. Two days later Hitler ordered the first postponement of Operation 'Sealion'.

The respite these German attacks on London represented for the RAF's airfields came in the nick of time, and the bombing-switch proved a major German strategic error, for 'London could take it' (and so could the other cities such as Plymouth, Southampton and Coventry which received the same German treatment in the weeks and months that followed). The country's air defences were reorganized, and became fully effective once more, as the Germans soon learned to their cost. For 23 successive days the Luftwaffe struck at London, but it was soon brought home to them that daylight raiding was becoming exorbitantly expensive. The RAF, backed by the barrage balloons and anti-aircraft guns of General Sir Frederick Pile which forced the Germans to fly high and thus bomb inaccurately, took an increasing toll. By late October German losses had reached 1,733 planes, and it was clear that British losses were capable of being made good by the aircraft industry. Our own losses totalled 915 aircraft, but a large proportion of the crews survived to fight again as they bailed out over friendly territory, while the German crews had no such advantage.

On 12 October Hitler had formally postponed Operation 'Sealion' until April 1941 – so the Battle of Britain was effectively won two weeks before this important decision. The Luftwaffe had failed to break the RAF and secure command of the air. Churchill rightly paid honour to the fighter pilots of the RAF with immortal words: 'Never in the field of human conflict has so much been owed by so many to so few.' Many have felt that Dowding was never accorded his just due as the mastermind and iron will behind the employment of Fighter Command. A major disagreement over air tactics with Air Vice-Marshal Leigh Mallory (whose 'big wing' concepts had helped win the air battle over London on 15 September) led to the eventual supersession of both Dowding and Park in a command decision that was ungenerous to say the least. For they, together with 'the Few' they inspired and led during three-and-a-half critical months, were the true architects and achievers of the notable air victory gained over southern Britain.

Beda Fomm

Date: 3–5 February 1941.

Location: Fifty miles south-west of Benghazi, Libya.

Object: Western Desert Force was intent on trapping the remnant of the Italian Tenth Army as they retreated from Benghazi.

Opposing sides: (a) Lieutenant-General Richard O'Connor, Western Desert Force; (b) Marshal Rodolfo Graziani commanding the Italian forces in Libya.

Forces engaged: (a) Parts of 7th Armoured and 6th Australian Divisions. Total: approx. 15,000 men; (b) Parts of three Italian divisions. Total: approx. 30,000 men.

Casualties: (a) approx. 50 Men; (b) 27,000 including 25,000 prisoners.

Result: The complete conquest of Cyrenaica and the destruction of an Italian army, its men and equipment. As the first major British land success of the Second World War, it strengthened national morale.

Suggested Reading: A. Moorehead. *African Trilogy* (London, 1956); C. Barnett. *The Desert Generals* (London, 1960); C. N. Barclay. *Against Great Odds* (London, 1956); B. Pitt (ed.). *The Purnell History of the Second World War* vol. 1, Part 15. (London, 1966).

Following the success of Operation 'Compass' at Sidi Barrani, General Wavell allowed O'Connor his head in following-up his victory to the uttermost despite his growing preoccupations with Eritrea, Abyssinia and Greece. After passing safely up the difficult coastal escarpment at Halfaya Pass, 7th Armoured Brigade took Sollum and Capuzzo, while 4th Armoured Brigade moved round Bardia to cut the Tobruk road. The attack on Bardia was given to the fresh 6th Australian Division, and after an assault on 3 January a further 40,000 prisoners were in the bag by the 5th. At this time Western Desert Force was redesignated XIII Corps. The 7th Armoured Division headed west again for Tobruk. Invested on 7 January, it was assaulted two weeks later, providing another 25,000 prisoners. It seemed that there could be no stopping O'Connor. Ahead lay the mountains of the Jebel Achdar and the most densely populated part of Italian Libya, through which ran the coast road towards Benghazi, Beda Fomm and distant Tripoli.

The Italians made a determined stand at Derna and Mechili, guarding the eastern approaches to Benghazi, but 7th Armoured Division drove off the Italian armour from the latter on 26 January, while 6th Australian Division closed up on Derna. A fortnight's pause ensued as O'Connor – with Wavell's encouragement – prepared for his boldest stroke of the campaign. Already his troops were operating at the end of a very tenuous line of communication stretching all the way back to Egypt, but Tobruk harbour was now in use by the Royal Navy which was bringing up supplies as well as bombarding Italian coastal positions from the sea. O'Connor's plan was for what was left of 7th Armoured Division's tanks to take the desert tracks south of Jebel Achdar towards Msus and Beda Fomm, with the intention of cutting the Tripoli coast road behind the retreating Italians, while the

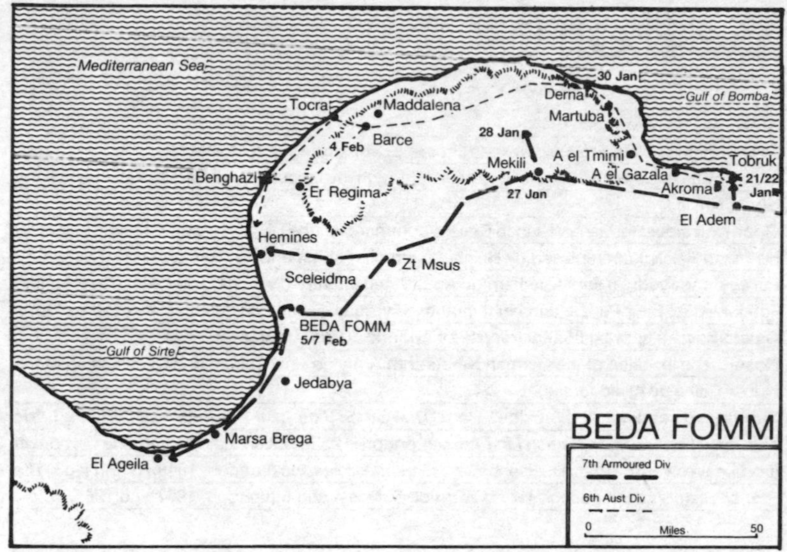

Australians pushed on for Benghazi along the coast road, serving as 'beaters'. On 1 February Wavell agreed to this bold plan.

His forces under pressure from the Australians, on 1 February Graziani ordered a full retreat towards Tripoli. For O'Connor the race was now on. On 3 February 4th Armoured Brigade struck west over unmapped terrain. A distance of 150 miles lay ahead (30 of them hard to cross) and many tanks and vehicles broke down or stuck in the soft sand. But at 1300 hours on the 5th, 'Coombes Force' (part of the 11th Hussars, 2nd Battalion the Rifle Brigade and a dozen guns) reached Antelat and thereafter Beda Fomm. The trap was set, but would it hold? On 6 February a second column of 7th Armoured came up from Sidi Saleh to reinforce Coombes as he was attacked by Italians from Benghazi (which fell that day to the Australians). Repeated attacks were beaten off, and on the 7th the Italians began to surrender. 7th Armoured had only 24 tanks serviceable at this juncture. The spoils of war included 25,000 more prisoners, 100 tanks and 105 guns. The Italian Tenth Army no longer existed.

Belfort

Date: 19 – 22 November 1944.

Location: In eastern France, between Saverne, Strasbourg and Mulhausen.

Object: The Allies were attempting to break through the Upper Vosges Mountains to reach the Upper Rhine.

Opposing sides: (a) General Jacob Devers commanding the US Sixth Army Group; (b) General Hermann Balck (later replaced by Heinrich Himmler) commanding German Army Group 'G'.

Forces engaged: (a) Five Allied armoured and ten infantry divisions. Total: 250,000 men and 750 tanks; (b) Four Panzer and eight infantry divisions. Total: 200,000 men and 350 tanks.

Casualties: (a) approx. 35,000 troops; (b) approx. 70,000 troops.

Result: The isolation of the German Nineteenth Army around Colmar and the reaching of the Upper Rhine by Allied forces.

Suggested reading: B. H. Liddell Hart. *The Other Side of the Hill* (London, 1952); L. de Tassigny. *History of the French First Army* (London, 1952); D. Glance. *The Lorraine Campaign* (Fort Leavenworth, 1985); D. Eisenhower. *Crusade in Europe* (London, 1948); B. Pitt (ed.). *The Purnell History of the Second World War* vol. 6, Nos 4 and 6 (London, 1967 and 1968).

As an insurance against possible stalemate in Normandy, to forestall a possible Communist take-over in southern France, and to bring maximum pressure on the Germans by ultimately mounting a 'broad-front' offensive along the Rhine all the way from Switzerland to the sea, the Allies had authorized a secondary invasion in southern France on 15 August 1944. The effect was to relegate the hitherto successful Italian campaign to secondary importance in the war as it was impossible to mount 'Anvil – Dragoon' and at the same time provide sufficient support for the battles north of Rome. But it was important to get General Jean de Lattre de Tassigny's French I Corps on to home soil without delay.

The US Seventh Army, headed by General Truscott's VI Corps, made rapid progress up the Rhône valley and into the foothills of the Alpes Maritimes. German resistance was sporadic, but General Friedrich Wiese's Nineteenth Army escaped from a trap at Montélimar (23–8 August). From 15 September the US Sixth Army Group was placed under command of Lieutenant General Devers, comprising Patch's US Seventh Army and the new French First Army under de Tassigny which had moved forward to link with Patton's US Third Army on the 11th near Dijon, where the Lorraine Campaign was raging. Over the next two months Patton attacked towards the Saar, at last taking Metz on 18 November, while Devers approached the Vosges in the teeth of determined resistance by the German First and Nineteenth Armies supported by the Fifth Panzerarmee. On 19 November de Tassigny – on the right – followed the classical military route through the Belfort Gap – reaching Mulhouse and the Upper Rhine in a single day's advance. Just 48 hours later the US Seventh Army successfully forced the Saverne Gap to the north, and on the 23rd the French General Leclerc's 2nd Armoured Division, leading the American thrust on the left,

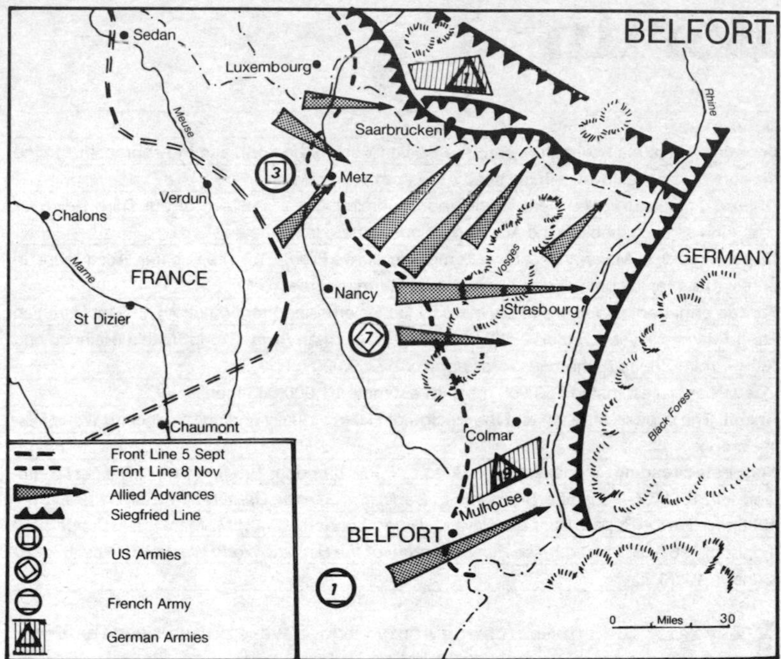

liberated the city of Strasbourg. The German Nineteenth Army found itself isolated in the Colmar pocket with orders from the Fuehrer to fight to the last. However, Eisenhower decided to switch the US Seventh Army to the battles raging in the Saar, and left the elimination of Wiese to the French. This proved a mistake, for the French were tired from their exertions since mid-August, and detachments had been sent to form a force in south-western France which further weakened their battle power. In consequence the German Nineteenth Army survived for some further time. But by mid-December the Colmar pocket was the sole German salient west of the Upper Rhine, dividing the Allied forces around Strasburg from those near Mulhouse. But France was almost clear of the enemy.

Berlin

Date: 16 April – 2 May 1945.
Location: From the Polish frontier to the Baltic Coast in the north and the approaches to the borders of Czechoslovakia in the south, the apex being Berlin.
Object: The Red Armies were intent upon completing the crushing of the Third Reich by capturing its capital before the Allies could arrive there from the west.
Opposing sides: Marshal Zhukov in command of two Fronts; (b) The Fuehrer, Adolf Hitler, in personal supreme command of all remaining German forces
Forces engaged: (a) Armies of the merged 1st Belorussian Front (Zhukov) and 1st Ukranian Front (Marshal Konev). Total: 2,500,000 men; (b) German Army Group Vistula (Heinrici) and Army Group Centre (Schörner). Total: approx. 1,250,000 men.
Casualties: (a) estimated 700,000 men; (b) estimated 1,000,000 men.
Result: The capture of Berlin and the suicide of Hitler, virtually ending the Second World War in Europe.
Suggested reading: J. Erickson. *The Road to Berlin* (London, 1984); C. Ryan. *The Last Battle* (London, 1966); E. F. Ziemke. *Stalingrad to Berlin: the German Defeat in the East* (Washington, 1968); H. Trevor-Roper. *The Last Days of Hitler* (London, 1945); M. MacIntosh. *Juggernaut* (London, 1967); B. Pitt (ed.). *The Purnell History of the Second World War* vol. 6, Nos. 6 and 9 (London 1968)

By early 1945 three Russian army groups were poised near the River Oder ready to attack Berlin, barely 50 miles away to the west. Marshal Georgi Zhukov's 1st Belorussian Front included Sokolovsky's 1st White Russian Army Group around Kustrin, which was ordered to force a passage over the river supported by attacks on its flanks. For the final great offensive, Zhukov was to head for Berlin itself, while to the north Rokossovsky's 2nd White Russian Group cleared East Prussia between Danzig and Stettin, and away to the south Konev's armies surged forward from near Breslau to thrust into Czechoslovakia to seize the upper Elbe.

On 16 April preceded by huge artillery and air bombardments, Red Army tanks thrust westwards from the Oder, shattering the defence offered by General Heinrici's Central Army Group. Four days later Russian advanced elements reached the eastern suburbs of the German capital. Two great pincer movements proceeded to isolate Berlin – Sokolovski from the north and part of the 1st Ukranian Front from the south – completing their task on the 25th. By this date Rokossovski was heading westwards towards the lower Elbe.

Hitler took himself to the deep bunker in the gardens of the Chancellery, and made bold plans for the relief of 'Fortress Berlin' by non-existent German armies. Zhukov's tanks and artillery crushed their way into Berlin's streets block by block, reducing almost everything to rubble in the process. The 26th saw their capture of Tempelhof Airport, and soon they were approaching the Unter den Linden and the Tiergarten district. Street-fighting was bitter, German army units being supplemented by fanatical Hitler Youth schoolboys. But the Russians could not be checked.

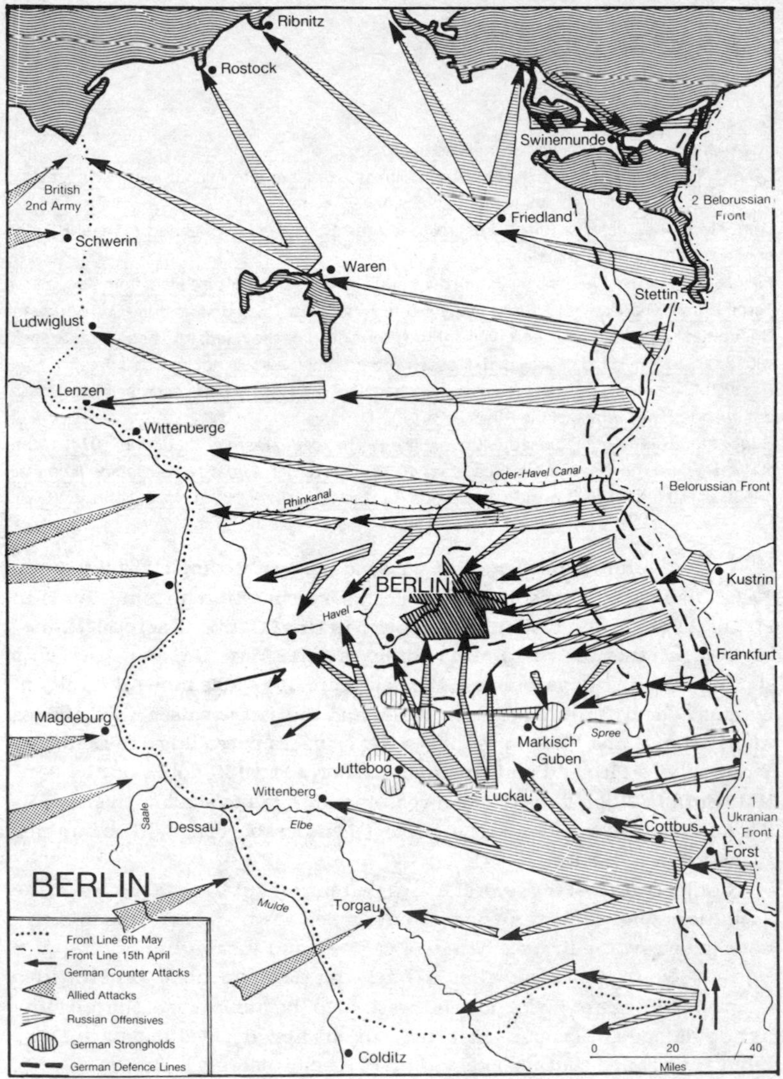

On 30 April Hitler, his new wife and the Goebbels family committed suicide, the Fuehrer's and Eva Braun's bodies being cremated immediately afterwards in the garden. Their remaining loyal followers now looked to their own salvation, and began to leave the bunker area. The Reichstag fell to the Russians on May Day, and the Red Flag was proudly hoisted on the highest point. Next day General Weidling surrendered the remaining 135,000 troops in the city. Thus a last titanic battle – which cost the Germans 6,000 aircraft and 12,000 tanks besides more than a million men – finally destroyed the '1,000 Year Reich'.

Bismarck

Date: 18–27 May 1941.

Location: The North Atlantic from the Denmark Strait to west of Brest.

Object: The Royal Navy was determined to eliminate the threat to Atlantic convoys posed by the powerful German battleship at large.

Opposing sides: (a) The British Admiralty and the Royal Navy; (b) Grand Admiral Raeder commanding the *Kriegsmarine*.

Forces engaged: (a) Admiral Sir John Tovey and elements of the Home Fleet from Scapa and Force H from Gibraltar; (b) Admiral Lütjens commanding the *Bismarck* and the *Prinz Eugen*.

Casualties: (a) HMS *Hood* sunk with 1,416 sailors killed or drowned; (b) The *Bismarck* sunk with 2,085 sailors killed or drowned. (Losses aboard other vessels not included here).

Result: The sinking of the *Bismarck* avenged that of HMS *Hood*, and restored British command of the surface of the Atlantic.

Suggested Reading: L. Kennedy. *Pursuit. The Sinking of the Bismarck* (London, 1974); Capt. S. W. Roskill. *The Navy at War* (London, 1960); O. Warner. *Great Naval Battles* (London, 1963); B. Pitt (ed.). *The Purnell History of the Second World War* vol. 2, No. 5 (London, 1967).

Grand Admiral Raeder's plans to send the newly completed 50,000-ton *Bismarck* in consort with the cruiser *Prinz Eugen* from Gdynia in Poland to challenge British naval power in the Atlantic (Exercise 'Rhine') began when they set sail towards Denmark on 18 May 1941. A neutral ship spotted them two days later and the news rapidly reached the Admiralty in London. The battleship *Prince of Wales* and the battlecruiser *Hood* at once sailed from Scapa Flow to reinforce RN cruisers patrolling the Denmark Strait between Iceland and Greenland. There, at 1930 hours on the 23rd HMS *Suffolk* sighted the German vessels and began to shadow them, while the Admiralty alerted Force H to protect a vulnerable convoy. The hunt for *Bismarck* had begun.

Contact was lost for several hours that night, but by 0400 hours on the 24th the capital ships were only twenty miles apart and back in sight. An hour later saw the first exchange of salvoes, and just eight minutes later *Hood* blew up and sank after a plunging German shell penetrated a magazine. *Prince of Wales* (also hit) retired to the jubilation of the still only lightly damaged German squadron. Lütjens now decided to detach *Prinz Eugen* and sailed south, shadowed by British cruisers.

The next contact was made by Swordfish torpedo-bombers from the aircraft carrier HMS *Victorious*, but their first raid early on the 25th achieved little damage. *Bismarck* now turned for France, and for a time threw off her pursuers, but the Admiralty correctly guessed her course and at 1810 hours Admiral Tovey (aboard *King George V*) turned east. He was now some 110 miles behind his quarry, but closing fast.

Thick weather concealed *Bismarck*'s precise position until a searching Catalina flying-boat had a lucky break at 1036 hours on the 26th, and the hunters – now joined by Force H and *Ramillies* – began to close in. Aircraft

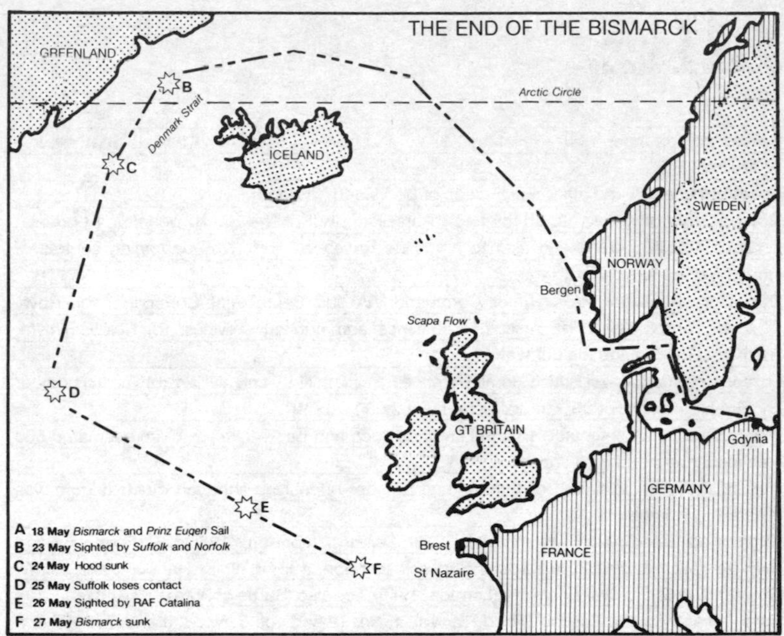

from Force H's *Ark Royal* maintained contact, and at 0845 hours a gallant Swordfish raid succeeded in damaging *Bismarck*'s steering-gear. The great vessel began to circle through heavy seas as desperate attempts were made by her crew to free the rudder. All night British destroyers harassed the crippled battleship as the capital ships closed in. At about 0830 hours on the 27th *King George V* and *Rodney* opened fire with their 16-inch guns. Two of *Bismarck*'s turrets were badly damaged and her main battle-control centre destroyed, and by 1000 hours she had ceased fire. At 1030 hours *Dorsetshire* was ordered to close in and fire torpedoes into the blazing vessel. Ten minutes later *Bismarck* heeled over and sank. HMS *Hood* had been avenged.

Blitz

Dates: 7 September 1940 – 21 May 1941; 21 January – 31 March 1944; 8 September – 17 March 1945.

Location: London and other major cities of the United Kingdom.

Object: The Luftwaffe was attempting to break the will of the British people by bombing densely inhabited areas and also to harm the British war effort by damaging centres of industry, ports and military targets.

Opposing sides: (a) RAF Fighter Command, AA and Searchlight Command, the Royal Observer Corps, the ARP, rescue, ambulance and nursing services; (b) *Reichsminister* Hermann Goering and the Luftwaffe.

Forces engaged: (a) All British Home Defence Forces, military and civilian; (b) The full bomber and fighter strength of the Luftwaffe, perhaps 2,000 aircraft.

Casualties: (a) an estimated 137,500 civilians killed and badly injured; (b) an estimated 600 German aircraft and their crews.

Result: the ultimate failure of the German bomber offensives although much damge was inflicted by bombing.

Suggested Reading: T. H. O'Brien. *Civil Defence* (London, 1955); S. Ferguson and H. Fitzgerald. *Studies in the Social Services* (London, 1954); W. K. Hancock and M. W. Gowing. *The British War Economy* (London, 1949); see also 'Battle of Britain', B. Pitt (ed.). *The Purnell History of the Second World War* vol. 1, No. 12 and vol. 5, No. 8, (London, 1967 and 1968).

Ever since the 1920s, much public concern had been devoted to the possibility of future air onslaughts against civilian populations in future major wars. The writings of the Italian General Giulio Douhet, especially his *The Command of the Air* (Rome, 1921), painted an apocalyptic picture of what was to be expected; wars would be decided by breaking the resistance and will-power of civilian populations by aerial bombardment with high-explosive, incendiary and gas bombs. There had been 103 raids on Great Britain during the First World War, causing 4,800 casualties and involving just 300 tons of bombs from Zeppelin and bomber attacks – but improvements in aircraft and their armaments during the two decades after 1918 had been considerable, and the *Blitz* experience of Guernica during the Spanish Civil War was taken to support the pessimistic popular view that '. . . the bomber will always get through'. In Britain the Home Office had set up an Air Raid Precautions Committee as early as 1924, and by 1938 extensive steps had been taken to plan the evacuation of children and pregnant women from likely targets and to set up nationwide air warning and ARP services, and provision for the issue of gasmasks to the entire population. Hospitals were told to expect twice as many psychiatric as injury cases, and by 1940 the London authorities had several million shrouds and cardboard coffins stored against Armageddon. In fact experience would show that Douhet underestimated both the possibilities of air defence and the resolution of civilian populations under fire, and greatly overestimated the killing-power of high-explosive bombs.

Nevertheless, the German bombing of Warsaw in September 1939 and Rotterdam in May 1940 were grim warnings of what might be meted out on a large scale to British cities.

Although there were a number of small raids against south coast ports and other objectives during 1939 and 1940, the *Blitz* proper dates from September 1940 when the Luftwaffe on Hitler's orders turned its attention for the first time to London.

For convenience the *Blitz* can be divided into a number of phases. First came the period of day raids against London, 7 to 15 September 1940, but the loss of 95 aircraft caused a switch to night bombing. This second phase lasted for 50 consecutive nights with raids of 200 or more aircraft being involved on each occasion. A particularly heavy raid came on 15 October, when 490 German aircraft dropped 70,000 incendiaries and 380 tons of high-explosive bombs during one night. But radar-guided night-fighters and the ring of anti-aircraft guns deployed around the capital by General Sir Frederick Pile hit back with determination. 'London could take it', and paradoxically civilian morale seemed to rise under air attack although serious damage was inflicted and casualties rose. Londoners slept in large numbers in tube stations for shelter.

The third phase of the German air onslaught started on 14 November, when new major urban targets – starting with Coventry, and then Birmingham (19 and 22 November) were added to London. These attacks continued regularly through the long winter of 1940–41, and into the next spring. Plymouth was particularly badly blitzed from 21 to 28 April, losing 1,000 killed and forty times that number made homeless during five nights of heavy raids. Bombing attacks were extended to include Liverpool and Hull. London, of course, still received regular attention. On the night of 10 May the Houses of Parliament were badly hit, the Commons's Chamber being totally destroyed. That night some 2,000 serious fires were caused by incendiaries, and there were 3,000 casualties. The raiders lost sixteen aircraft. But suddenly there was a pause, which extended into a respite. The reason? The main strength of the Luftwaffe was being moved eastwards, ready for the opening of the attack on the USSR on 22 June 1941.

The 'great *Blitz*' was over – but not enemy air activity over Great Britain as a whole. From early 1942 'hit-and-run' raids became frequent, and from April came a series of larger raids against cathedral cities in retaliation for RAF raids on Lübeck and Rostock. Next, from January to March 1944 came the 'little *Blitz*' – nothing like the 1940–1 ordeal – but bad enough. Compared to what Bomber Command and the USAAF were by now meting out to German cities these raids were puny.

German scientists had long been working on secret weapons, the 'V-Bombs', and it is fortunate none were ready before mid-1944. On the night of 12 June – a week after D-Day in Normandy – the first V-1 landed in England. The 'doodlebugs' caused much damage and loss of life over succeeding weeks – as bad in fact as in September 1941. Most of the attack was absorbed by London and the south-east, although some Heinkel-launched V-1s were sent against northern targets. Most flying-bombs came from French launching sites in the Pas-de-Calais by day and by night, and imposed a great strain on the civilian population in the areas affected. Eventually a huge concentration of AA guns was placed south of London, and large numbers of the menace were destroyed in the air. The challenge rapidly diminished following the break-out of Allied troops from

Normandy as the coastal sites were overrun. More than 6,000 V-1s were fired at England in all, 40 per cent of them hitting London.

But worse was to follow. On 8 September the first of more than 1,000 supersonic, long-range V-2s, each carrying a ton of explosives, hit London. These weapons arrived without warning, and a new evacuation of many people who had returned to London was ordered. The V-2 threat persisted for six months – London receiving half of the rockets. The worst casualties were sustained on 8 March 1945 when more than 230 casualties were caused by one missile. In all, the V-1s and V-2s caused 34,342 casualties, including 8,928 fatalities. Only when the Allies crossed the Rhine in strength in late March was this dread threat lifted.

It has been calculated that from first to last the Germans dropped or launched 71,000 tons of bombs against Great Britain. In all they caused more than 146,000 civilian casualties, more than 80,000 of them in the Greater London Area. After the capital, Birmingham and Liverpool were next worst hit, losing more than 5,000 each. Men and women suffered equally, and 15,358 children under 16 became victims. Among these losses the 6,800 police, firemen, ARP members, doctors, nurses and other civilian services (2,380 being killed) deserve special mention. But the national resolve to see the war through to victory never faltered.

Caen

Date: 7 June – 25 July 1944.

Location: A key road and rail centre in eastern Normandy, France, with *bocage* to the north, and more open ground to east and south apart from Bourguébus Ridge. The battle covered Caen, Bayeux and Villers-Bocage.

Object: Montgomery intended to lure German forces to the Caen sector and thus aid the Americans to break-out from the bridgehead to the west.

Opposing sides: (a) Field Marshal Montgomery (under Eisenhower) commanding 21st Army Group; (b) Field Marshal Rommel (under Rundstedt) commanding Army Group B.

Forces engaged: (a) British Second Army – ten infantry, three armoured and one airborne divisions, and six armoured brigades. Total: approx. 150,000 men; (b) German Seventh Army and Panzer Group West – six infantry and seven Panzer divisions. Total: approx. 100,000 men.

Casualties: (a) 37,000 killed and wounded; (b) 117,000 Germans lost.

Result: The bulk of the German armour was attracted to the British sector and into an attritional battle which aided Bradley to break out farther west on 25 July. Much Anglo-American contention continues over the battle.

Suggested reading: C. Wilmot. *The Struggle for Europe* (London, 1952); H. Essame. *The Battle for Normandy* (London, 1965); H. P. Willmott. *June, 1944* (London, 1984); J. D. P. Keegan. *Six Armies in Normandy* (London, 1983); M. Hastings. *Normandy 1944* (London, 1984); B. Pitt (ed.). *The Purnell History of the Second World War* vol. 5. Nos. 5 and 9 (London, 1968).

Despite the facts that the Germans were slow to react to D-Day, and their Fifteenth Army was left in the Pas-de-Calais, their troops – although far from élite in many cases – fought outstandingly well and denied the Allies Caen and contained the bridgehead for far longer than had been hoped. The communications centre of Caen – guarding the road to Paris – became the crucible of a huge and devastating battle.

Montgomery – according to his account – deliberately set about drawing the weight of the German forces, particularly their armour, to the Caen sector. Americans disagree, claiming that events forced the attritional battles upon British Second Army. Whatever the truth of this, Bayeux fell to the British on 7 June, but to take Caen would need another four weeks of heavy and costly fighting.

A projected large German armoured counter-attack on 9 June failed to materialize owing to air attack destroying its headquarters staff, but soon the Germans had four good Panzer divisions near Caen. The British launched three successive battles to capture the city. The first, Operation 'Perch' (7–15 June) attempted to encircle Caen from the west with XXX Corps, but failed near Villers-Bocage owing to strong German reaction. The second attempt was delayed by appalling weather from 18 to 21 June (which also destroyed one Mulberry harbour and badly damaged the second, complicating the supply build-up still further). Operation 'Odon' (25–28 June) saw VIII Corps make a strong thrust from the north between Caen and Tilly which effectively pre-empted the last German attempt to

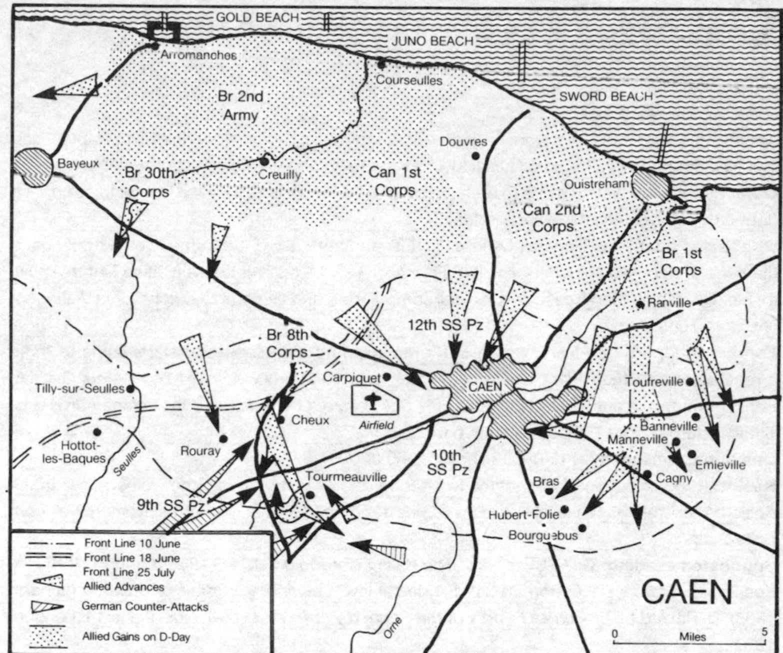

smash the bridgehead. This achieved, Montgomery called off the attack. Meanwhile the Americans had occupied Cherbourg only to find its port far too damaged for early use.

Next, at 2100 hours on 7 July, 2,560 tons of bombs were dropped on Caen causing much damage and French suffering, but permitting British troops to occupy the devastated city by the 10th. For the next three weeks Montgomery continued to draw German attention. From 18 to 20 July, Operation 'Goodwood' – an attempt to break-through east and south of Caen – foundered on strong German defences anchored on fortified villages and above all Bourguébus Ridge, and sustained heavy losses. Thus, by the time the Americans were ready to break-out at St-Lô, all of seven Panzers and six other divisions were still in the Caen area with 600 tanks, leaving only nine weak divisions and 100 tanks in the west.

Cassino

Date: 17 January – 22 May 1944.

Location: The main battles were fought around Monte Cairo and along the River Rapido, and in part over the Rivers Liri and Garigliano, in west Italy, some 70 miles south-east of Rome.

Object: The Allies were striving to break through the Gustav Line to reach Rome; the Germans hoped to hold the Allied advance indefinitely.

Opposing sides: (a) General Dwight D. Eisenhower, Allied Supreme Commander, and Lieutenant-Generals Mark W. Clark (US Fifth Army) and Sir Oliver Leese (British Eighth Army); (b) Field Marshal Albert Kesselring, overall commander, and General Heinrich S. von Vietinghof (German Tenth Army).

Forces engaged: (a) At first one Allied armoured and six infantry divisions rising to three armoured and thirteen infantry divisions. Total: approx. 300,000 men; (b) At first four German Panzer and five infantry divisions, later only one Panzer Grenadier and five infantry divisions. Total: reducing from 100,000 to 80,000 men.

Casualties: (a) approx. 115,000; (b) approx. 60,000.

Result: It took the Allies four months to conquer the area, but at last they joined up with the Anzio beachead and reached Rome on 4 June 1944; the Germans fought extremely well from first to last.

Suggested reading: G. A. Shepperd. *The Italian Campaign, 1943–1945* (London, 1968); A. Kesselring. *Memoirs* (London, 1954); F. Majdalany, *Cassino – Portrait of a Battle* (London 1963); B. Pitt (ed.). *The Purnell History of the Second World War* vol. 4, Nos. 9 and 14 (London, 1967).

The long, bitterly fought battle for Cassino was one of the hardest battles of the Second World War in the west. Four major battles were needed to capture the Cassino massif and its famous monastery, and thus open up Route 6 – the road to Rome. Monastery Hill (435 metres high) was the key to this immensely strong natural position, the western end of the German Gustav Line stretching across the Italian peninsula, overlooking as it did the town of Cassino and the key road, as well as dominating the Rapido and Liri valleys. The defences had been improved by General von Senger-Etterlin over a period of three months, and the tough XIV Panzer Korps and élite paratroop and infantry battalions made it a very hard nut to crack indeed.

Preliminary operations against the Gustav Line began in early January 1944 when 3,000 Allied bombers began a series of attacks on German lines of communication. On 15 January US II Corps captured Monte Trocchio, gaining thereby a good observation post. Then, on the 17th, the first battle of Cassino began. By the plan, the Free French forces were to attack Santa Croce, while US II Corps (with part of US 1st Armored Division) struck against Cassino town and San Angelo, with the British X Corps moving on Minturno – all this activity intended to serve as a prelude to Operation 'Shingle' (the amphibious landing at Anzio behind the Gustav Line's right flank, scheduled for 22 January). In the first phase, the British

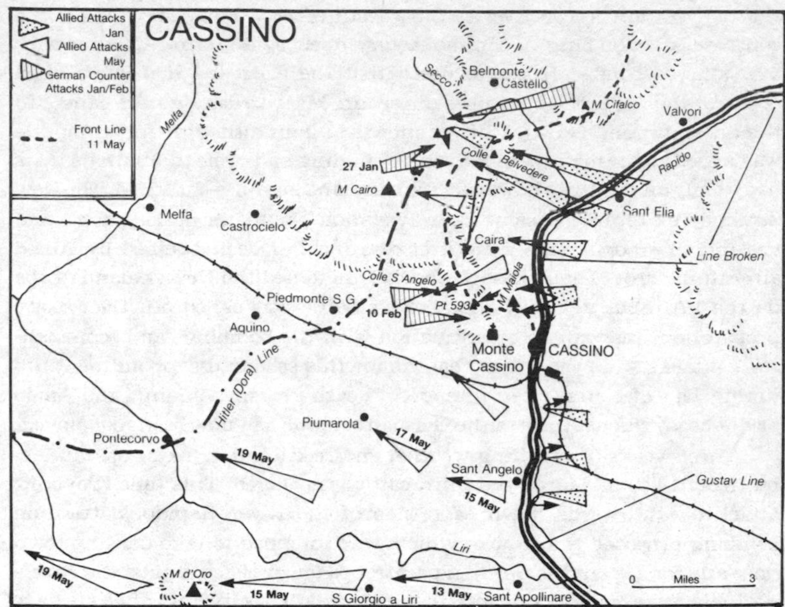

X Corps under General McCreary successfully passed over the mouth of the River Garigliano to take Castelforte on 17 January, but from the 20th determined German counterattacks took eleven days first to contain and then beat-off. Meanwhile in the second phase, the US II Corps under General Keyes launched US 36th Division against San Angelo supported by US 34th Division's attack on Cassino town, with the armour ready to exploit the hoped-for break-through. In fact the 36th's crossing of the Rapido failed on the 20th, while the 34th came close to taking both Cassino and its monastery by a *coup de main* on the 24th. But German resistance stiffened, and regained much lost ground by early February. The 2nd New Zealand Division relieved the badly battered US 36th on 6 February, and the US 34th's heroic attempts to take the dominating monastery position failed when only 300 yards from the objective. When the 4th Indian Division took over from the weary Americans in this sector, two regiments had only 840 survivors from a joint original strength of 3,200 men. However, the French Expeditionary Corps under General Juin had eventually made good progress on its sector from 20 January, taking Santa Croce. Having thus achieved success on the flanks but having failed in the centre, the first battle petered out. Anzio, meantime, had long been contained by the Germans.

The second battle of Cassino lasted from 15 to 18 February. General Freyberg's New Zealanders were put under command of US Fifth Army, and 4th Indian Division and 2nd New Zealand Division prepared to assault the Monte Cassino massif via Snakeshead Ridge, and to take Cassino railway station respectively. But first, on 15 February, came the controversial bombing of the monastery itself by 254 aircraft, dropping 576 tons of bombs. It was claimed that the Germans had established observers on the roof – but this is uncertain. Massive damage was caused to the ancient monument for little immediate gain although Allied morale was raised as the massive overlooking building had come to dominate their lives. Only on the 16th, however, were the land assaults launched. The New Zealanders captured Cassino railway station – but later pulled back – and the Indian troops made little progress, having been bombed by Allied aircraft in error. The British 78th Division joined the New Zealand Corps on the 17th, but next day the abortive battle was called off. Over-hasty preparation, inadequate co-ordination with the bombing, and too small-scale attacks were the major reasons for this second disappointment. Its timing had of course been intended to ease pressure against the Anzio bridgehead, whence most of the German armour had now been redeployed.

Three weeks of appalling weather enforced a lull in major operations, but from 14 to 22 March the third battle was waged. This time Freyburg attacked southwards down each side of the River Rapido. Saturation bombing preceded the attacks which were intended to take Cassino town once and for all, but the German paratroops fought back amidst the rubble – which tanks could not negotiate – with great ferocity, and after six days of attritional battle the New Zealand Corps had to be taken out of the line. So another failure had to be admitted.

The preparations for the fourth and final battle were immense. British Eighth Army was redeployed in great secrecy. By the plan, the Polish Corps was to attack Monastery Hill from the north, while British XIII Corps struck over the Rapido to cut Route 6 and isolate the town. Further south the French and US II Corps were to attack south of the River Liri on each side of San Andrea. The Germans were fooled into expecting a major break-out attempt from Anzio, and this absorbed all their attention and reserves. Thus when the great attack on Cassino began early on 12 May it achieved both total surprise and a three to one superiority – the classical recipe for success in the offensive – on a narrow front. Both senior German commanders were away on leave. Some 2,000 Allied guns rained down fire and the attacking forces moved off. Some German units were caught being relieved in the line, and soon progress was being reported on all sectors. The French reached and took the Liri/Garigliano confluence on the 13th, and an air attack destroyed German Tenth Army's headquarters. Two days later the Americans reached Spigno, breaching the German defences on the coastal side. On the 16th, Kesselring, realizing the battle was lost, ordered a withdrawal from Cassino. The 17th saw XIII Corps cut Highway 6, and the second Polish assault began against the monastery itself. At last, on the 18th, this objective – so long denied the Allies – fell to the Poles. By the 22nd the Germans were in full retreat, their discomfiture being compounded when on the 23rd the break-out from Anzio began. The road to

Rome at last lay open before the long-delayed Allies, and soon the Italian capital was occupied. But the D-Day landings in Normandy outshone these notable achievements, and soon five divisions would be withdrawn to prepare Operation 'Anvil', the complementary invasion of the South of France.

Crete

Date: 20 May – 1 June 1941.

Location: The main fighting on this Mediterranean island between Greece and Turkey took place around Heraklion, Retimo and Galatas.

Object: The Germans were determined to complete their capture of Greek territories and possessions, and thus ensure their domination of the Balkans.

Opposing sides: (a) General Löhr commanding Fleigerkorps XI and VIII; (b) Major-General B. C. Freyberg commanding British, New Zealand, Australian and Greek forces.

Forces engaged: (a) German paratroops, glider-borne, air-landed and seaborne troops. Total: 23,000; (b) Commonwealth troops (32,000) and Greek forces (10,000), 21 tanks. Total: 42,000.

Casualties: (a) 7,000 killed and wounded; (b) 17,320 casualties (including 12,000 taken prisoner).

Result: The German conquest of Crete (albeit costly) improved their strategic position in the eastern Mediterranean.

Suggested Reading: C. H. R. Buckley. *The Battle for Greece and Crete* (London, 1952); J. H. Spencer. *The Battle for Crete* (London, 1962); B. Pitt (ed.). *The Purnell History of the Second World War* vol. 2, No. 3 (London, 1967).

The rapid German conquest of the Greek mainland (6–28 April) forced the British forces to evacuate by sea to Crete and Egypt – an operation carried out by the Royal Navy with a high degree of success. It would clearly only be a matter of time before the Germans turned their attention to the island of Crete. Its capture would provide the Axis with useful air bases from which to strike at Egypt, and would deny the Allies similar facilities for bombing the Balkans, especially the Roumanian oilfields around Ploesti.

Originally garrisoned by a single brigade, the island's defences were not very developed, but General Wavell ordered General Freyberg's 2nd New Zealand Division and a number of Australian and British units – perhaps 21,000 men – to join the defenders following the evacuation from Greece. Some 10,000 Greek infantry were also brought in by sea. But there were only sixteen 25pdr field guns, sixty anti-aircraft guns and 21 armoured vehicles available, while the Axis enjoyed almost complete air superiority. Freyberg used the little time he had to prepare a defence plan – designed to deny the enemy the naval bases at Suda Bay and the three airfields situated at Maleme, Retimo and Heraklion.

The German plan was to drop seven parachute battalions early on 20 May to take Maleme and Canea in the west, and three more on Retimo and Heraklion, following six days of heavy air bombardment. The paratroops would be followed by transport aircraft carrying mountain infantry, and two sea-borne convoys would bring over tanks and guns. The key assault was given to General Kurt Student commanding the XI Airborne Corps.

The paratroops sustained severe casualties on all sectors, but Student flew in reinforcements, and after 36 hours of savage fighting made himself

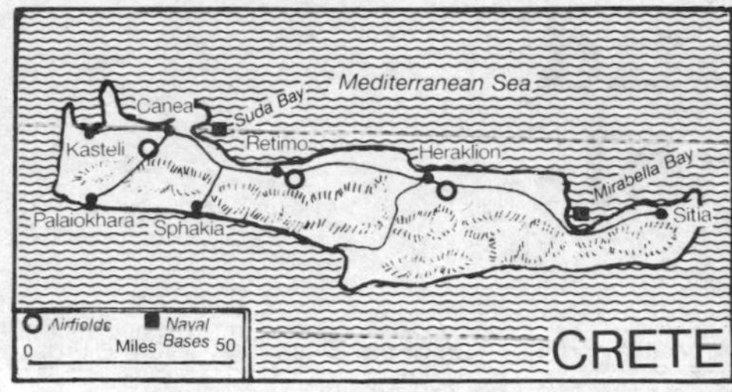

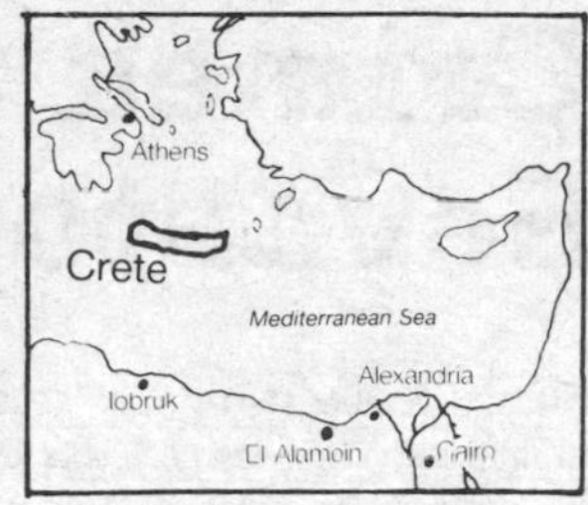

master of Maleme airfield. The defenders were forced back to Canea and Suda under remorseless pressure. At sea, however, the Royal Navy sank or scattered the two German convoys. The effects of constant air attacks and poor radio communications made Freyberg's task increasingly difficult, and so an evacuation through Sfakia on the south coast and Heraklion on the north was ordered on 27 May. Retimo fell as the evacuations commenced. More than 18,000 troops were lifted from the ports, but nine British warships were sunk in the process. The last troops to escape were picked up on 1 June and the operation ended. Some 12,000 became prisoners-of-war.

The Germans had become masters of Crete albeit at a heavy cost to Student's paratroops. This was the last occasion on which the Germans mounted a large-scale airborne assault.

Crimea and Sevastopol

Date: 29 October 1941 – 3 July 1942.

Location: The Crimean peninsula juts into the northern side of the Black Sea, with the great city and naval base of Sevastopol at its south-western tip.

Object: The German forces were determined to take the Crimea and Sevastopol to complete their conquest of the north coast of the Black Sea in the Soviet Union.

Opposing sides: (a) Field Marshal Gerd von Rundstedt (initially) commanding the German Army Group South; (b) Marshal Semen Budenny (initially) commanding the Soviet Odessa Special Military District, South and South West Front Red Armies.

Forces engaged: (a) General Erich von Manstein commanding the German Eleventh Army. Total: eventually fifteen divisions; (b) The Russian garrison of the Crimea. Total: an estimated eleven divisions.

Casualties: (a) approx. 80,000 troops; (b) approx. 250,000 troops.

Result: The completion of the German conquest of the Crimea, and its holding until final liberation by the Russians in May 1944.

Suggested reading: E. von Manstein. *Lost Victories* (London, 1958); J. Erikson. *The Road to Stalingrad* (London, 1982); A. Clarke. *Barbarossa* (London, 1965); B. Pitt (ed.). *The Purnell History of the Second World War* vol. 2, No. 16 and vol. 3, No. 6 (London, 1967).

At the outset of 'Barbarossa' von Rundstedt's Army Group South made considerable progress through the Ukraine, capturing Kharkov in late October and (temporarily) Rostov. The front having bypassed the Crimea, von Rundstedt ordered General von Manstein and the Eleventh Army to attack the Peninsula from the north by way of the fortified Perekop Isthmus while other German forces attacked Kerch to the east.

Manstein made short work of the Perekop defences, breaking through on 8 November 1941, and soon overran the whole of the Crimea except for the area surrounding Sevastopol itself, where Russian resistance was determined and a 245-day siege began. Kerch was also captured, but the strong Red Army winter counter-offensive regained it in December, as well as Rostov. Manstein remained besieging Sevastopol throughout the hard winter months, and latterly extended his operations to include renewed pressure on the Kerch Peninsula.

With the coming of spring 1942, Manstein was reinforced to fifteen divisions, including two Panzers and five Roumanian formations. On 7 May a massive attack on the Kerch defences led to their collapse by the 13th, but some of the Red Army defenders and other troops (possibly 86,000 in all) escaped over the straits to the Taman Peninsula in the Caucasus region. But in all the Russians had lost 150,000 men. Manstein wasted no time in returning his full attention to Sevastopol and the west of the Crimea, deploying captured large Russian guns to increase fire-power.

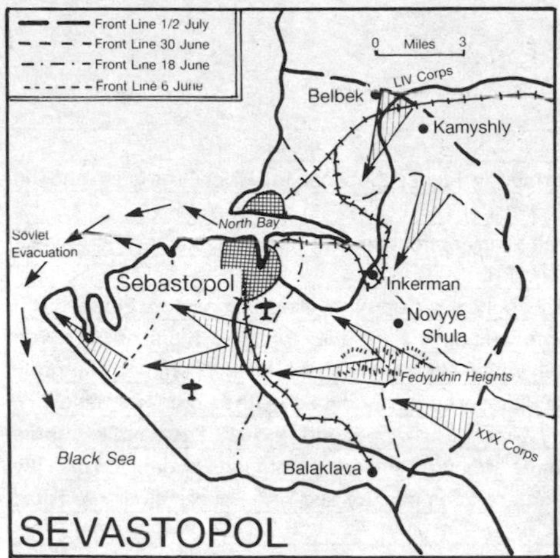

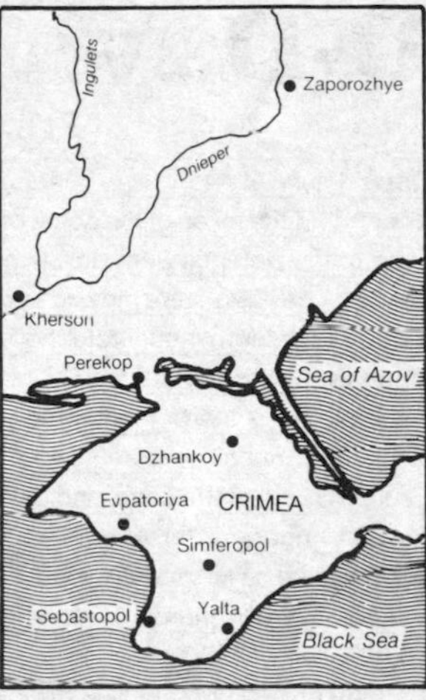

The Germans also brought up naval forces to seal off Sevastopol from the seaward side, and subjected the Russian positions and city to a 5-day air, sea and land bombardment. On 3 June, heavy German assaults were launched. On the 7th, the LIV Corps broke through near Belbek in the north, and pressed on to take Inkerman, while XXX Corps forced a gap from the east near Balaclava. But Russian resistance became stronger rather than weaker as they were forced back into the city, and only when reinforcements from the German Seventeenth Army were made available was progress resumed. On 18 June the Germans broke through to North Bay overlooking the Russian naval base installations. Still the Russians fought back with ferocity, but as their ammunition reserves dwindled so they were forced to the south side of the bay on the 23rd. By the 29th the Germans had a bridgehead, and next day entered Sevastopol. Russian resistance ended on 3 July. Some 90,000 prisoners were taken.

D-Day

Date: 6 June 1944.

Location: Fifty miles of the coast of Normandy, France, between the River Orne (east) and the base of the Cotentin Peninsula (west).

Object: The Allies were striving to create a major bridgehead in German-occupied north-west Europe in order to inaugurate the Second Front.

Opposing sides: (a) General Dwight D. Eisenhower, Supreme Allied Commander Europe, with General Sir Bernard Montgomery commanding the assault; (b) Field Marshal Geyr von Rundstedt, Supreme Commander West, with Field Marshal Erwin Romel commanding Army Group B north of the Loire, and General Hausser commanding Seventh Army in Normandy.

Forces engaged: (a) Allied 21st Army Group (British Second and US First Armies); three airborne and seven infantry divisions, three armoured and two commando brigades. Total: (by 8 June) 175,000 men; (b) Germans: parts of three infantry and one Panzer divisions. Total: 80,000 men.

Casualties: (a) 12,500 Allied troops; (b) German casualties not known.

Result: The establishment of a successful bridgehead in France, but no final objectives were taken. D-Day led to the liberation of western Europe.

Suggested reading: C. Wilmot, *The Struggle for Europe* (London, 1952); C. Ryan. *The Longest Day* (London, 1960); H. P. Willmott. *June 1944* (London, 1984); B. L. Montgomery. *Normandy to the Baltic* (London, 1946); B. Pitt (ed.). *The Purnell History of the Second World War* vol. 5, Nos. 1 to 4 (London, 1968).

D-Day saw the breaching of Hitler's vaunted *Festung Europa* by means of a huge combined operation involving the British and American forces. Its purpose was to form a bridgehead from which the Allies could break out to liberate France and the Low Countries, and thereafter force the Rhine to compel Germany's unconditional surrender.

Massive preparations preceded the invasion of France, going back in many instances to late 1941 when the first full-scale Allied planning began. To aid the assault from the sea, much cunning was put into Operation 'Fortitude' – the deception plan – which succeeded in duping the Germans into expecting the major attack to be in the Pas-de-Calais area, and continued to do so for another 40 days after 6 June. Similarly, much ingenuity went into devising secret weapons of many types, ranging from Mulberry harbours (transportable over the Channel in prefabricated sections), Pluto (the underwater fuel pipeline), to the 'funnies' – a whole range of special armour developed for 49th Armoured Division: amphibious D-D Tanks, flails, road-layers, 'dustbin' heavy mortar tanks, armoured bull-dozers and the like. Rocket ships were developed capable of putting down dense patterns of missiles. And, for a full month before D-Day, the Allied air forces pounded railways and radar sites – taking care to concentrate their efforts behind the Pas-de-Calais to avoid revealing the true area of intended attack. To move the vast armies required more than 3,000 vessels, and many aircraft for three parachute divisions (two, smaller, American and one, large, British) had to be found, including

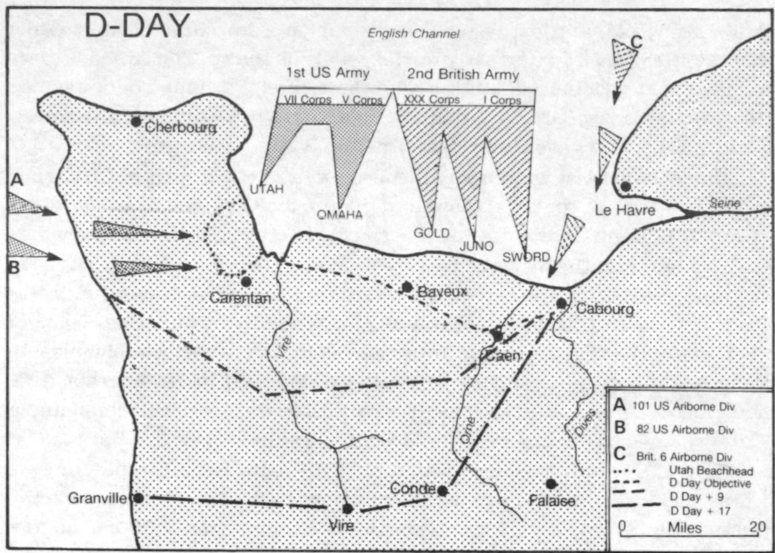

gliders, ready to seal-off the flanks of the invasion area on the night before the sea assault.

Owing to the nature of the defences Rommel had rapidly developed since late 1943, Montgomery had insisted on the area of assault being doubled, with five divisions in the first wave instead of just three as originally envisaged. General Omar Bradley's US First Army was to land in the west of the bridgehead on Utah and Omaha Beaches respectively, while General Sir Miles Dempsey's Second Army British landed on Gold, Juno and Sword Beaches nearer to the River Orne. The British paratroops were to seize the Orne bridges and destroy those on the neighbouring River Dives, while the American 82nd and 101st Airborne Divisions (each one brigade in strength) secured Ste-Mère-Eglise and the exits behind the western beaches. The date was settled by the need to have an early-setting full moon with maximum darkness just before dawn – the first to show the transport aircraft their drop-zones, the latter to permit the naval shipping and landing craft to close with their beaches unseen. The landings were to commence at half-tide so as to avoid the high tide undersea beach obstacles. This meant that there would be a one-hour delay in the troops coming ashore from west to east, and, even worse, the presence of the redoubtable 21st Panzer Division at Caen meant that the troops to reach the eastern-most beaches would not only be the last ashore but also the most exposed to German armoured counter-attack. To allow for this, the Juno and Sword divisions were provided with extra anti-tank formations, while a complete 'spare' assault division was held in reserve.

All was ready for embarkation when a westerly gale blew up in early June. The Germans believed this would put off any invasion danger for at least two weeks, and many units were put on a low state of alert while Rommel went back to Germany for his wife's birthday. The Allied leaders were worried men indeed, but Eisenhower backed the opinon of one senior RAF meteorologist (Group-Captain Stagge) that a lull would occur between 5 and 7 June, and gave the critical order on 3 June – 'We go!'

Immense activity thereupon uncoiled like a released spring. On the late evening of the 5th the paratroops and gliders took off, and by early on the 6th their landings were beginning – smoothly on the British sector where vital bridges and the Merville battery were secured on schedule, less so in the American areas where the drops were very scattered. Nevertheless the Germans – except at one place – were taken wholly by surprise. Then, at 0630 hours the first sea-borne forces landed at Utah – fortunately missing their beach by a mile and as a result landing with ease. Further east, however, at Omaha, the tale was different. Here the American commander had disdained to use the profferred British 'funnies', lost most of his D-D tanks in the rough seas and found difficult exits from the beach; even worse, the local German commander had ordered a full invasion practice for that night. The result was near-disaster, more than 2,000 casualties being sustained there and at the neighbouring Pointe du Hoc battery – stormed at immense cost by US Rangers only to find the big guns not in position. The reserve battle groups had to be diverted to Omaha, and even at the end of the day only the most tenuous of bridgeheads had been established there.

Meanwhile, at about 0730 hours the British landings had begun to the east. These went comparatively smoothly, and despite the fears of German armoured attack, all three were well established by early afternoon when the first German tanks appeared. Even with all the special preparations for meeting them, one Panzer battle group forced its way through to the cliffs near Lion-sur-Mer, and only withdrew overnight – proof of how much damage might have been inflicted had the 21st intervened during the morning phase. This unforeseen delay probably saved many casualties. By late afternoon the British had reached Arromanches (site for one of the two Mulberry prefabricated harbours), had joined up with the 6th Airborne, and were on the outskirts of Bayeux inland. However, no final objectives were achieved by Dempsey; the three beaches were only finally linked on the 7th and above all Caen had not been reached as hoped.

However, the situation was better than on the US Second Army's sector: Omaha remained isolated and only four miles by one-and-a-half in extent by nightfall; and the troops from Utah only gradually linked up with their scattered paratroops inland, but by midnight their bridgehead measured nine miles deep by four wide. Nevertheless, the Allies were ashore in force although unloading was soon twelve hours behind schedule. Fortunately German reaction had proved slow, hindered by the French Resistance and the effective Allied air and sea bombardments. But all would hinge on the forthcoming 'Battle for the Bridgehead' around Caen.

Dunkirk

Date: 26 May – 4 June 1940.

Location: On the Channel coast, east of Calais.

Object: The evacuation of the British Expeditionary Force trapped against the sea by German forces.

Opposing sides: (a) General Lord Gort commanding the BEF and French and Belgian units; (b) Generals Gerd von Rundstedt and Fedor von Bock commanding the German Army Groups 'A' and 'B'.

Forces engaged: (a) Nine British and five French divisions. Total: approx. 250,000 British and 130,000 French troops; (b) Ten German armoured divisions with infantry. Total: approx. 210,000 troops.

Casualties: (a) 68,000 British (whole campaign) and 40,000 French (Dunkirk only); (b) approx. 156,000 Germans (whole campaign).

Result: The BEF saved its men (and many French), but lost its equipment.

Suggested Reading: A. Horne. *To Lose a Battle* (London, 1969); D. Divine. *The Nine days of Dunkirk* (London, 1959); H. Guderian. *Panzer Leader* (London, 1952); A. Gouthard. *The Battle of France, 1940* (London, 1958); B. Pitt (ed.). *The Purnell History of the Second World War* vol. 1, No. 9 (London, 1966).

The staggering success of the armoured elements of Army Group 'A' in forcing a way through to the Channel coast near Abbeville in just five days from their assault-crossing of the Meuse near Sedan meant that the French Seventh and First Armies, together with the BEF, were cut off from the main French armies holding the line of the River Somme. Even worse, the rapid advance of Army Group 'B' into Belgium had brought that country's government to the point of surrender by 28 May.

Aware that a Belgian collapse would enable von Bock to capture the Channel coast and thus surround the Allies in the northern pocket entirely, Lord Gort had been in close touch with Churchill's government in London. The general had already ordered rear elements including military hospitals to make for Dunkirk, and the first fighting men were taken on board shipping there on the 26th. Next day, Gort was informed that he was to take the BEF out of overall French command and to regard the saving of as many of his forces as possible as his sole responsibility.

In overall command of the naval aspects of the evacuation, Operation 'Dynamo', that was about to begin was Admiral Ramsay, whose headquarters were in Dover Castle. His logistical problems were made even more difficult by the Luftwaffe's superiority in the skies, and the speed of the German advance. Plans to use Boulogne and Calais had to be abandoned in rapid succession as first the former fell to the Germans on 24 May, followed by the latter – after a heroic defence by 1st Battalion the Rifle Brigade and other units which fought literally to the 'last round' – two days later. But at least this earned a little time for the retreat into the extemporised perimeter enclosing a 25-mile stretch of coastline between Gravelines and Nieuport, containing the port of Dunkirk. But enemy air and artillery could command every road within the area, and some believed that all would be over within two days.

Dunkirk was a large port with about 100 acres of docks and harbours, but as a result of protracted enemy bombing the town was ablaze and many shore facilities badly damaged. The only practicable taking-off points were the two moles – but neither was really suited for berthing ships alongside. But that was the only solution available – except the utilization of the wind-swept beaches should this prove possible.

The defensive perimeter stretched in a rectangle some 45 miles in extent, incorporating the inland towns of Bergues and Furnes (Veurne). The French 68th Division held the western end, while the British 46th, 1st, 50th, 3rd and 4th Divisions would man the remainder as far as Nieuport. The remainder of the French XVI Corps (four divisions) and the British 5th and 23rd Divisions were to be positioned within along the Dunkirk-Furnes road, whilst General Lord Gort was to establish GHQ at La Panne overlooking the coast. Step by step the German Eighteenth, Sixth and Fourth Armies closed in on the defences, and it was only thanks to the valour of British 2nd and 5th Divisions that a gap was kept open between Comines and Ypres through which the greater part of the BEF and a third of the French First Army were able to pass over the River Yser and reach the Dunkirk sector.

The major evacuation began on Sunday 26 May, although town and port were already ablaze. German reaction was slow except on Guderian's south-western sector, where 9th Panzer Division rapidly approached the River Aa. The 27th and 28th saw further German delays by Army Group 'B' although the Allied sector was rapidly shrinking, and a large force around Lille was cut off by a German double-envelopment. Many troops were embarked from the moles on these days and carried safely to England. But from the 29th this became increasingly difficult as German bombers switched all their attentions against the port, beaches and naval approaches. Overhead the RAF struggled to protect the area, but they were too outnumbered to make much impression. Shipping was badly damaged, including hospital ships.

Despite the worsening situation, discipline was maintained in an exemplary fashion by the BEF. All vehicles were ordered to be abandoned at the canal line outside the town; there they were immobilized and rendered useless to the enemy. The weary troops then joined the long lines of their comrades stretching down to the water's edge, awaiting their turn in a boat ferrying troops out to the waiting ships. Periodically attacked by dive-bombers or strafing fighters, or bracketed by shells from the German artillery, their stoicism was impressive.

The vast bulk of the lifting was performed by the Royal Navy, in particular by the destroyers, which lost six sunk and nineteen damaged. However the legend of the 'little ships' – the fishing boats and pleasure craft that participated in the great national effort – is not to be wholly discounted. Indeed, they provided much of the shore-to-ship lift, and suffered

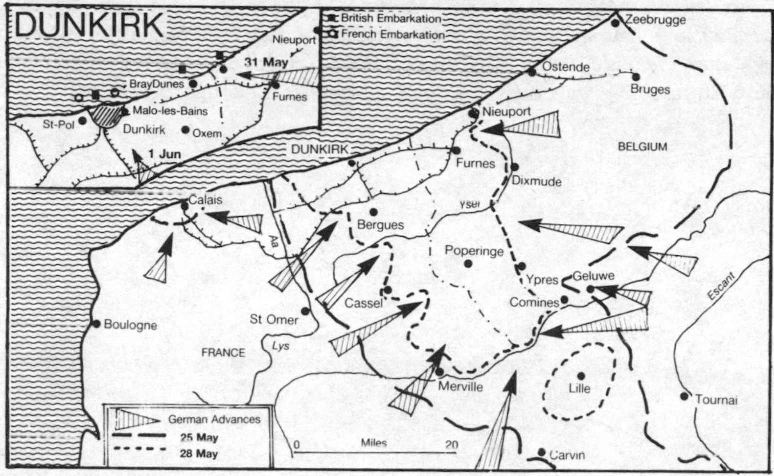

accordingly. On 30 May they reached their apogee, carrying 30,000 of the 53,823 troops brought safely to England. They suffered serious losses. Of the 1,000 vessels of all sorts taking part in the evacuation, by its end 243 ships had been sunk.

On 31 May the operation was reaching its climax. The eastern end of the perimeter was redrawn along the Belgian frontier, and Lord Gort and General Brooke left for England, handing over command of the rearguard to Major-General Alexander. On 1 June, there were only the 46th, 1st and 50th Divisions of the BEF still ashore. By now the air onslaught had become so heavy that only night-time evacuation from the Dunkirk moles could be authorized. When ships sailed they were packed to danger point with soldiers, above and below decks. At last, at 2330 hours on 2 June, Captain Tennant, RN could signal to Dover, 'BEF evacuated'.

The story was not yet quite over. The French rearguard still remained in action, holding off the German attacks. The Royal Navy mounted a rescue operation to try and bring off 30,000 Frenchmen on 3 June. This was thought to be the total requirement – but at the last moment many more French troops poured down to the port than had been anticipated. Some chaos ensued, and although the Royal Navy performed its commitment some 40,000 troops had to be left behind to become prisoners-of-war. The last British ship left Dunkirk at 0340 hours on 4 June. Five hours later Dunkirk surrendered.

A mood of exultation swept Great Britain, but, as Winston Churchill warned the people in a broadcast, '. . . wars are not won by evacuations'. Although 338,226 British and French troops had been brought home safely (and further numbers escaped from west coast French ports during the next two weeks) there was no disguising that the campaign had been a failure. At and near Dunkirk stood the forlorn remnants of 2,472 guns, 68,879 vehicles, 20,548 motorcycles and more than half a million tons of ammunition and stores. A breathing-space had been won for Great Britain while the Germans turned to complete the conquest of France by 22 June, when an armistice came into force. But a huge defeat had been sustained, and England lay wide open to invasion for several dangerous months.

Eben Emael

Date: 10–11 May 1940.

Location: At the junction of the Meuse and the Albert Canal, near Liège.

Object: The fort's capture – and that of three neighbouring bridges – was vital for the invasion of Belgium by General von Bock's Army Group 'B'.

Opposing sides: (a) Lieutenant Rudolf Witzig commanding the Parachute Sappers of Koch Storm Detachment; (b) Major Jottrand commanding the Belgian garrison.

Forces engaged: (a) 85 German sappers in eleven gliders; (b) 750 Belgian garrison troops manning twelve emplaced guns and numerous machine-guns.

Casualties: (a) Six killed and fifteen wounded; (b) 23 killed and 59 wounded, approx. 700 prisoners-of-war.

Result: The capture and holding of the fort (and of two of the three bridges by No. 1 Company of 1st Parachute Regiment) opened Belgium to invasion.

Suggested Reading: A. Horne. *To Lose a Battle* (London, 1969); B. Pitt (ed.). *The Purnell History of the Second World War* vol. 1, No 7 (London, 1966).

As the German forces prepared to attack in the West, Army Group 'B' was ordered to invade Belgium and Holland simultaneously to distract Allied attention from the impending major blow further south by Army Group 'A' through the Ardennes Forest. Although Belgium clung on to its neutrality until the last moment, the Germans knew that the defences of the Meuse/Albert Canal sector north of Liège were strong, and might delay their initial attack seriously. The key to these was Fort Eben Emael, completed in 1935; a strong, mainly subterranean, complex of gun positions and other posts adjoining a 120-foot drop into the Albert Canal. By reputation it was the strongest position in Europe.

From November 1939 a special force of German volunteers was trained in great secrecy near Hildesheim under Captain Koch. Every detail was rehearsed on models, and practice assaults carried out on Czech fortifications. Special hollow cavity explosive charges were prepared for the *coup de main*, and the enthusiasm of the engineers and paratroopers was high.

At 0430 hours on 10 May, the eleven Junker Ju 52 tug aircraft took off from airfields near Cologne. The landing was timed for five minutes before the start of the main land attack over the frontier. When the tows were cast off two gliders went astray (including Lt. Witzig's), but the remaining nine landed on top of the fortress, achieving complete surprise, Sergeant-Major Wenzel assumed command of 55 men in his lieutenant's absence, and began to carry out the planned tasks. First they attacked anti-aircraft posts, and within ten minutes nine defended installations were overwhelmed. Nine Belgian guns were destroyed together with their cupolas – the larger pieces having charges exploded down their barrels. Witzig managed to arrive three hours later, to find the surface of the fort in the hands of his men after some tough fighting. Fortunately, however, the Belgians had planted no mines over the area.

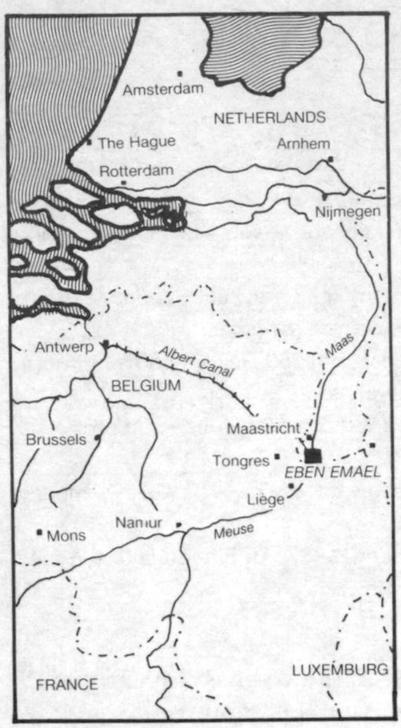

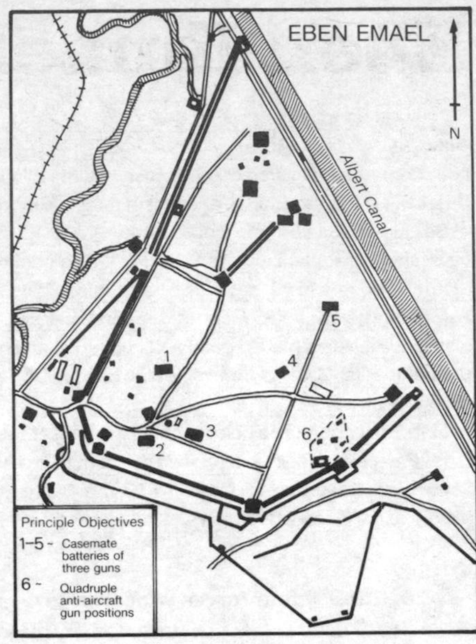

The German assault-engineers now began to penetrate into the shafts and tunnels of the underground fortress, using more explosive charges to disable casemates. Meanwhile Captain Koch's paratroops had captured two of the key bridges nearby. Belgian artillery was soon shelling the fort, but no serious attempt – beyond one reconnaissance in force – was made to recapture the fortress. German troops from the frontier linked up with the bridge parties that afternoon, but not until 0700 hours on the 11th was Eben Emael reached by relief detachments who crossed the canal in rubber boats under heavy fire. At midday the last Belgians in Eben Emael capitulated, and the garrison marched out into captivity. This notable feat of arms opened the way for the Germans into Belgium, and dealt a serious blow to Allied morale at the very outset of the campaign. Koch and Witzig were both promoted and decorated, with a number of their paratroopers and assault-engineers, by Hitler in person. Just 30 hours had sufficed to breach the Belgian main defences.

Etna (and the Invasion of Sicily)

Date: 9 July – 17 August 1943.

Location: The main landings took place between Licata and Syracuse; the major action was fought on the southern and western slopes of Mount Etna.

Object: The Allies were seeking to complete their conquest of the island of Sicily – the German and Italian troops to prevent or delay this.

Opposing sides (a) General Sir Harold Alexander (under Supreme Commander General Eisenhower) in overall command of Lieutenant General Patton's US Seventh Army and Lieutenant-General B. L. Montgomery's British Eighth Army; (b) General Guzzoni commanding the Italian Sixth Army and associated German forces under Colonel-General Hans Hube.

Forces engaged: (a) Four US infantry, one US armoured and one US airborne divisions; five British infantry, one British airborne and one Canadian divisions. Total: approx. 160,000 troops landed; (b) Eight Italian and four German divisions including two Panzers (later reinforced by a further armoured and a paratroop division). Total: approx. 350,000 troops (one-third German).

Casualties: (a) approx. 19,000 killed and wounded; (b) approx. 164,000. (including 32,000 Germans and many prisoners-of-war).

Result: The conquest of Sicily, and its use as a springboard for the subsequent invasion of the Italian mainland. The Axis, however, managed to evacuate more than 100,000 men across the Straits of Messina.

Suggested reading: G. A. Shepperd. *The Italian Campaign, 1943–1945* (London 1968); B. L. Montgomery. *El Alamein to the River Sangro* (London, 1950); R. Lamb. *Montgomery in Europe, 1943–45: Success or Failure?* (London, 1983); Carlo d'Este. *Bitter Victory – the Battle for Sicily, 1943* (London, 1988); B. Pitt (ed.). *The Purnell History of the Second World War* vol. 4, No. 6 (London, 1967).

Profiting from their completion of the liberation of North Africa, and eager to fill gainfully the time that must elapse before the invasion of north-west Europe in 1944, the Allies rapidly planned an amphibious assault on Sicily to clear once and for all the sea-lanes through the Mediterranean from Axis air attack and to carry the war for the first time on to enemy home territory. Following a month-long aerial bombardment, the invasion took place on the night of 9/10 July 1943. It involved 3,000 ships and 3,700 Allied aircraft, and was in fact larger in terms of men landed in the first wave than on D-Day in the following year. Although the British airborne landing was something of a disaster (many men being drowned), the invasion was a success despite stormy weather, and an Allied bridgehead was soon established in the south-east of the island. But from the first there was rivalry between Patton and Montgomery.

Within two weeks of the invasion, the US Seventh Army broke out and cleared the west of the island, taking many prisoners. Less dramatically,

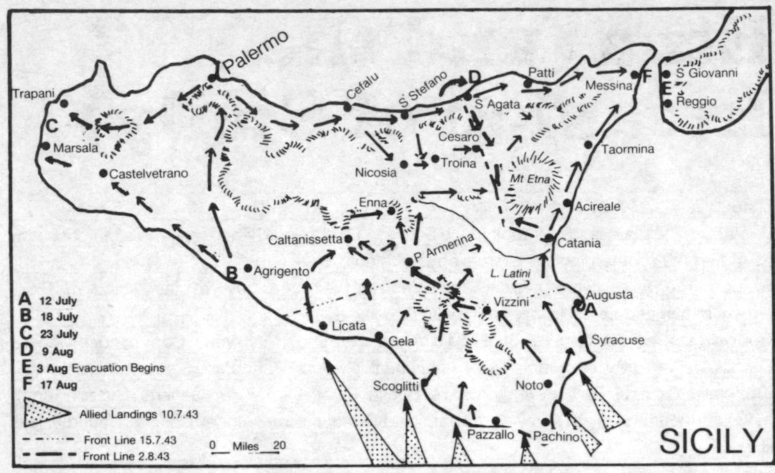

British Eighth Army struck north to Catania against stiff resistance from German units, who had been substantially reinforced from Italy by 27 July, concentrating their forces in the north-east of the island, alongside the remnants of three Italian divisions still fighting.

The German positions taken up on the rough southern foothills of the Etna massif were the key to the possession of Sicily, denying the Allies use of the airfields on the Catanian Plain, and safeguarding the links between Messina and southern Italy. General Montgomery launched the Canadians and the 78th Division against Leonforte and Catenanuova in an attempt to outflank the German position. German resistance around Centuripe was strong, however, and it took three days' savage fighting to press them back over the River Salso towards Adrano, the key to Etna.

The Americans meanwhile were driving on Messina along the north coast road. The Eighth Army continued its attacks, and on 4 August launched an all-out assault against Adrano, which was cleared on the 7th. Skilful demolitions slowed the pursuit of the retreating Germans, but although Messina fell on the 16th, many Germans escaped across the Straits.

Gazala

Date: 26 May – 21 June 1942.

Location: Thirty miles west of Tobruk in the Western Desert, Libya.

Object: Auchinleck hoped to use the Gazala Line as a jumping-off point for a new offensive, but he was pre-empted by Rommel, who outflanked the position with his armour in a bold move.

Opposing sides: (a) General Erwin Rommel commanding the Axis forces; (b) General Claude Auchinleck, CinC, Middle East.

Forces engaged: (a) The Desert Afrika Korps and Italian forces. Total: approx. 560 tanks, 704 aircraft, approx. 113,000 troops; (b) Lieutenant-General Neil Ritchie's Eighth Army. Total: 849 tanks, 320 aircraft, approx. 125,000 troops.

Casualties: (a) approx. 60,000 Axis troops; (b) including Tobruk, approx. 88,000 Allied troops.

Result: The destruction of the British 'Gazala Line' and the German capture of Tobruk – leading to a renewed invasion of Egypt.

Suggested reading: M. Carver. *Tobruk* (London, 1964); R. Lewin. *Rommel as Military Commander* (London, 1968); W. G. F. Jackson. *The North African Campaign* (London, 1974); R. Parkinson. *Auchinleck of Alamein* (London 1977); B. Pitt (ed.). *The Purnell History of the Second World War* vol. 3 No. 5 (London 1967).

The pursuit of Rommel after his defeat in Operation 'Crusader' ended at El Agheila in early January 1942. A temporary pause settled over the Western Desert as Allied attention switched to disasters in the Far East and southern Russia, both of which attracted much of the available aid. Rommel used the respite to absorb reinforcements, and in a sudden attack on 21 January proceeded to regain much lost ground, retaking Benghazi eight days later. A new lull followed, destined to last until May.

The Eighth Army fell back towards Gazala, and began the construction of a line from the Mediterranean coast to Bir Hacheim in the desert. Behind it General Ritchie began the reorganization of Eighth Army's armoured divisions of General Norrie's XXX Corps into self-contained Armoured Brigade Groups as a first step towards the mounting of the new offensive that Churchill was continually urging upon Auchinleck. Meanwhile Rommel absorbed a large tank convoy in February and began to lay his own plans for a major attack, although it was not until May that Hitler – who was obsessed at this time over Malta – authorized an offensive towards Tripoli.

The attempt to create a fixed position in the desert so close to Rommel's forward positions was optimistic; the open desert flank, some 50 miles from the coast, invited envelopment, although a supporting line of 'boxes' (unfinished in mid-May) running east to El Adem and Sidi Rezegh were intended to provide pivots for an armoured battle. The main north-south position comprised an extensive mine-marsh set within which were a series of self-contained 'boxes' (all-round defence positions) each holding a brigade of General 'Strafer' Gott's XIII Corps. Shortages of mines were overcome by raising some of the minefields of the Tobruk defences, which were entrusted to the 2nd South African Division. It was anticipated that any Axis attack would come along the coast road. Insufficient steps were taken to achieve proper armour-infantry integration, and above all to keep XXX Corps concentrated.

Rommel was never noted for complying with his opponents' sanguine expectations. His highly flexible plan was to mount a feint towards Gazala while the Desert Afrika Korps (two Panzer and one Light divisions) and the Italian XX Corps swung in a broad southerly sweep to pass round Bir Hacheim (held by the 1st Free French Brigade) and thence advance north towards the coast seeking a decisive armoured battle. Meanwhile the Italian Trieste Division was to penetrate the mine-marsh near '150 Brigade Box' south of the centre point of the Gazala Line, creating a gap for Rommel's supply convoys. Finally, he envisaged a drive on Tobruk. The plan was bold and full of risks; its execution was destined to be brilliant, but not without grave crises.

On the afternoon of 26 May the attack began. The Italian X and XXI Corps stiffened by Group Cruwell advanced boldly on the coastal positions held by the 1st South African and British 50th Divisions. Meanwhile, far to the south, Rommel was in person leading his armour in their great sweep through the desert to turn the flank of the Gazala Line. By early on the 26th he was past Bir Hacheim, scattering two Motorized Brigades, and capturing Retma before wrecking 4th Armoured Brigade, and then repulsing 22 Armoured Brigade towards Knightsbridge. However, a crisis was developing elsewhere: Italian attempts to capture Bir Hacheim and to create the minefield gap both failed. By nightfall on the 27th the Germans were short of both petrol and water, but Rommel pressed ahead regardless to El Adem, gambling on Ritchie's being unaware of his mounting problems. Then, on the 29th, Rommel in person returned to south of Bir Hacheim to find his blocked convoys, and brought them up through a sandstorm to relieve his parched, static forward formations.

At this juncture, Rommel changed his plan, and withdrew his armour into a highly unorthodox defensive position in 'the Cauldron', east of the mine-marsh, with '150 Brigade Box' in the centre (taking this position only on the 31st). Setting up a gun-ring to protect his armour and opening two lanes west through the mines for his supplies, he calmly lay low for four days, challenging a bemused Ritchie to counter-attack. When Operation 'Aberdeen' at last materialized on 5 June it was made in insufficient strength and poorly co-ordinated, and only resulted in the loss of 108 British tanks – making a total of 228 since 26 May. Sending Bayerlein south with a force to attack staunchly-held Bir Hacheim (a task that only succeeded when General Koenig evacuated the position on the night of 10/11 June), Rommel prepared his next blow, satisfied that the Gazala Line had now virtually ceased to exist. The Eighth Army was staggering, but not yet defeated.

On 11 June Rommel struck north out of the Cauldron with his 124 remaining tanks towards XXX Corps' centre and El Adem. A skilful

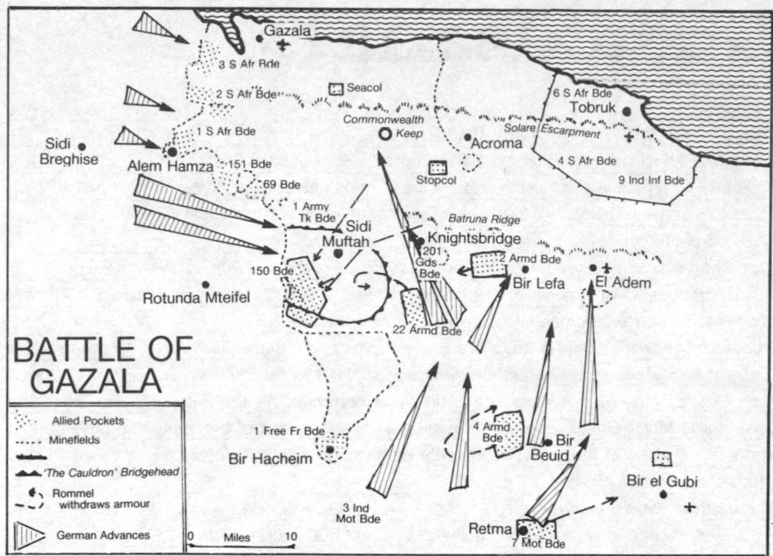

ambush wrecked 7th Armoured Division's cohesion, and in the two-day tank battle that ensued he destroyed or damaged a further 320 British tanks. Greatly alarmed, Auchinleck flew up from GHQ in Cairo. He soon approved Ritchie's intention to abandon what was left of the Gazala position and to fall back to hold a new line from Tobruk to El Adem, trusting on approaching reinforcements to permit this to hold firm.

On 14 June the 'Gazala Gallop' began: the remaining positions in the Gazala Line were abandoned, and the South Africans and 50th Division made their way back, the latter by breaking out to the west initially before continuing round Bir Hacheim and driving east. By the 17th Rommel had captured Sidi Rezegh and El Adem – so the new line collapsed – and next day Eighth Army HQ was back at Sollum over the Egyptian border.

Tobruk was now isolated: General Klopper's South Africans were holding positions behind depleted minefields without air cover. Rommel was ready by the 20th – and struck the south-east corner of the perimeter in strength. By 0700 hours the town was occupied. Next day, after trying to destroy the massed stores, Klopper surrendered with 33,000 men, and Rommel captured 1,400 tons of fuel and 5,000 tons of supplies. On the 22nd a jubilant Hitler notified Rommel of his promotion to Field Marshal. It was a deserved reward. The Eighth Army was now in a state of total crisis. Churchill faced – and survived – a vote of censure in the House of Commons, but Roosevelt rallied to his old friend with the promise of extra aid. Rommel swept east to Sidi Barrani inside Egypt and then advanced on Mersa Matruh, where Ritchie turned at bay. On the 25th Auchinleck took over command in person, relieving Ritchie. A lull descended once more. A virtuoso performance by Rommel was over, and the omens looked ill for the future of Eighth Army.

Guadalcanal

Date: 7 August 1942 – 7 February 1943.

Location: An island in the Solomon Islands group, east of New Guinea.

Object: The Americans wished to prevent the island's use as a Japanese air base in the South Pacific Ocean and to secure a foothold in the Japanese area of conquest in south-east Asia for future exploitation.

Opposing sides: (a) Vice Admiral Robert L. Ghormley (later Vice Admiral William F. Halsey), in overall command of American amphibious forces in the South Pacific area; (b) Admiral Shigeyoshe Inouye commanding Japanese forces at Rabaul.

Forces engaged: (a) Rear Admiral Frank J. Fletcher and a carrier task-force escorting Major General Alexander A. Vandegrift's reinforced US 1st Marine Division. Total: 23,000 troops (mid-October); (b) Vice-Admiral Gunihi Mikawa commanding the Japanese 8th Fleet and (eventually) Major-General Haruyoshi Hyukatake in command of the Japanese Seventeenth Army. Total: 20,000 troops (subsequently reinforced). NB, No details given here of naval strengths, which fluctuated.

Casualties: (whole campaign): (a) 1,500 killed, 4,800 wounded and 24 US vessels sunk; (b) 25,000 killed and wounded, 24 vessels sunk and 600 aircraft destroyed.

Result: The first defeat of a Japanese Imperial Army on land in the Second World War – and as such an important psychological and strategic success for the Americans and their allies.

Suggested reading: G. Kent. *Guadalcanal* (New York, 1972); S. W. Kirby. *The War against Japan* vol. 2 (London, 1958); D. Macintyre. *The Battle for the Pacific* (London, 1966); S. Sakai. *Samurai* (London, 1974); B. Pitt (ed.) *The Purnell History of the Second World War* vol. 3, Part 11 (London, 1967).

Following their great naval victory at Midway, the Americans had regained a large measure of the initiative, and learning that the Japanese were developing an airfield at Guadalcanal in the southern Solomons, they rapidly prepared an amphibious operation. This, based on New Zealand, was code-named Operation 'Watchtower', and envisaged the capture of Guadalcanal and Tulagi islands by the US 1st Marine Division suitably escorted and protected by forces of the US Navy.

Although this was the Marine Corps' first combined operation of the war, and neither their equipment nor their state of training was complete, it began remarkably successfully. On 7 August 1942 the assault landing achieved surprise, and little immediate opposition was encountered. At that date the Japanese garrison was barely 2,000 men. The airstrip was captured the same day and renamed Henderson Field.

To capture Guadalcanal was one thing; to hold it quite another. Six months' of hard fighting by land and sea would follow before Japan admitted failure – including seven sea engagements as both sides strove to bring reinforcements to the jungle-clad island and, in the case of the Japanese 8th Fleet, to avenge Midway.

Admiral Mikawa sent off a first reinforcement from Rabaul, but the ship carrying the troops was torpedoed. A Japanese naval force, however, engaged the escorting American force under Rear Admiral R. K. Turner

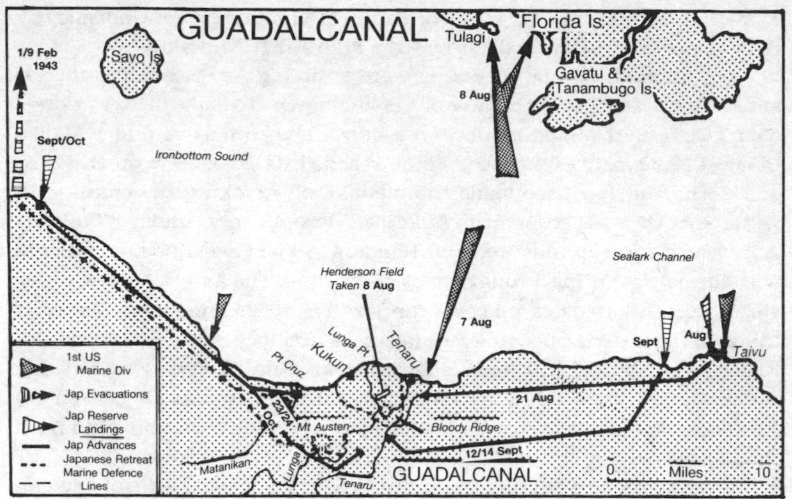

off Savo Island overnight on 9 August (Admiral Fletcher had already withdrawn his carriers as being too exposed to Japanese air attack), and sank four cruisers and a destroyer for minimal loss before withdrawing. Thereupon Turner withdrew the rest of his force and the transports, leaving the Marines to their own devices for the time being.

General Vandegrift was able to hold the area around the airstrip, the Japanese fortunately believing him to be far stronger than was in fact the case. In mid-August they put ashore some 800 troops – who were destroyed at Alligator Creek. Marine Corps aircraft (eventually 100) were now operating from Henderson Field from 20 August. But almost nightly the 'Tokyo Express' of destroyers brought further enemy reinforcements in penny-packets. The arrival of a far larger force – some 1,500 men – escorted by a strong task force commanded by no less a seaman than Yamamoto, led to the naval battle of the Eastern Solomons on the 24th. The engagement was inconclusive: the Americans sank one light carrier (missing the two large ones) but sustained serious damage to one of their own (while the *Yorktown* was torpedoed a week later, taking three months to repair). However, Yamamoto withdrew.

By 12 September the Japanese had 9,000 troops on Guadalcanal, and General Kawaguchi made a strong attack against Lunga Ridge (the key to the American perimeter). The Marines eventually drove them off by the 15th with the loss of 2,000 men for only 200 sustained after a desperate fight. Meanwhile the struggle at sea continued, and on 15 September the Americans lost the carrier *Wasp* as it helped convoy the US 7th Marine Regiment which was successfully put ashore on the 18th. Next, on 11–12 October, came the naval battle off Cape Esperance – during which both sides placed further reinforcements ashore, the Japanese now having two divisions on the island. For their part, the Marines had been brought up to more than 23,000 men. On the 20th, Admiral Nimitz replaced Ghormley by Halsey, and soon after Fletcher by Rear Admiral T. Kinkaid.

On Guadalcanal fuel shortages were crippling American air-support, and the battle of logistics became of grave concern. To make matters worse, on 20 October the Japanese began a new all-out offensive under Major-General Haruyoshi Hykutake, which reached its peak between the 23rd and 25th. The Japanese made the mistake of attacking piecemeal, and suffered 2,000 killed whilst American losses were under 300. The American perimeter survived and Henderson Field remained operational with the help of air fuel brought in by submarine. The Americans were now able to take the offensive, and over the next five weeks Vandegrift managed to extend his perimeter to keep Japanese artillery fire off the airfield. Elements of the US 2nd Marine Division were now arriving on Guadalcanal, and on 9 December the 1st Division was relieved as Major General Alexander Patch of the Army Americal Division took over command from Vandegrift.

November had seen much activity at sea. The naval battle of Guadalcanal (12–15 November) cost the Japanese two battleships and a heavy cruiser, while the Americans lost two admirals killed, one heavy cruiser, two light cruisers and five destroyers sunk in a three-phase battle, two of which were fought at night. However, Vice-Admiral Tanaka managed to get some 4,000 reinforcements ashore (about half the force he was conveying). The tide of the naval struggle was now slowly moving in the American favour; and when, on 30 November, another Japanese force bringing troops was turned back at the action off Tassafaronga, again a night-engagement, the balance began to tip the American way. Both sides, however, continued to receive more troops on the island during December.

On 19 January General Patch began a two-division attack towards Cape Esperance, and yard by yard the tenacious Japanese were forced to concede ground. Already, in Japan the premier, General Tojo, had decided to evacuate the island. Although Halsey did his uttermost to force Yamamoto to major battle, this did not come about. From 1 to 7 February, the Japanese Navy succeeded in taking off 13,000 surviving troops. Thus the long battle for Guadalcanal ended in an American victory, which had cost both sides grievous losses of naval shipping and the Japanese some 20,000 soldiers on land. Strategically, there can be no denying that the battle marked the turning-point in the war in the South Pacific region. The Americans and their allies no longer regarded the Japanese soldier as a superman, while they were in a better position to sustain their naval losses than were their opponents.

Hiroshima and Nagasaki

Date: 6 and 9 August 1945.

Location: Hiroshima is a city on the south coast of Honshu Island, Japan; Nagasaki is a city and port on the west coast of Kyushu island, Japan.

Object: The American Government of President Truman decided to use the first atomic weapons as a means to force the Japanese Government to surrender unconditionally, and thus avoid a long, costly conquest of mainland Japan. Such an event would also end the Second World War in Allied victory; complementing that already achieved against Hitler in Europe in May 1945.

Opposing sides: (a) President Harry S. Truman and his Allies; (b) The Emperor Hirohito and the Japanese Government headed, since Tojo's resignation in July 1944, by Prince Konoye but in effect dominated by its military members.

Forces engaged: (a) One US B-29 Superfortress, 'Enola Gay', commanded by Colonel Paul Tibbets, on 6 August; a second Superfortress, escorted by an observer aircraft, on 9 August; (b) Not applicable; there was no Japanese attempt to intercept either raid.

Casualties: (a) Nil; (b) 71,379 killed directly at Hiroshima; an inestimable further number eventually died of injuries or radiation-induced diseases, and continue to do so. An estimated 60,000 killed directly at Nagasaki, and many later deaths and innumerable wounded.

Result: The first atomic bomb did not persuade the Japanese Government to surrender; the dropping of the second weapon led directly to the unconditional surrender agreed on 14 August. The formal instrument of surrender was signed aboard USS *Missouri* in Tokyo Bay on 2 September. The Second World War in the Far East had ended in victory for the Allies, including Russia, which declared war on Japan on 8 August.

Suggested reading: R. J. C. Butow. *Japan's Decision to Surrender* (Stamford, 1954); L. Cheshire. *The Face of Victory* (London, 1962); J. Ehrman. *Grand Strategy* vol. 6 (HMSO, London 1956); *US Strategic Bombing Survey* Nos. 3, 13, 14, 60 and 93; B. Pitt (ed.). *The Purnell History of the Second World War* vol. 6, Nos. 15 and 16 (London, 1968).

By the spring of 1945 Japan was defeated beyond redemption, but her government, dominated by its military members, refused to face up to the inevitable. Although certain negotiations were instituted through Switzerland and Moscow (the USSR was not a belligerent in the Far Eastern War until 8 August), the Japanese refused to contemplate any idea of unconditional surrender. The Emperor Hirohito had ordained on 22 June that his ministers were to end the war as soon as possible – but frenzied chauvinism still gripped the military high command.

American strategic bombing of Japan was already at its height. On 19 March Tokyo was subjected to a fire-bomb raid by 234 B-29s which destroyed sixteen square miles of the capital and, in the firestorm, killed 83,793 people. By mid-June four more major cities lay in ruins. By August nine million Japanese had been rendered homeless as the US 20th and 8th Air Forces (the latter newly redeployed from Europe) continued their

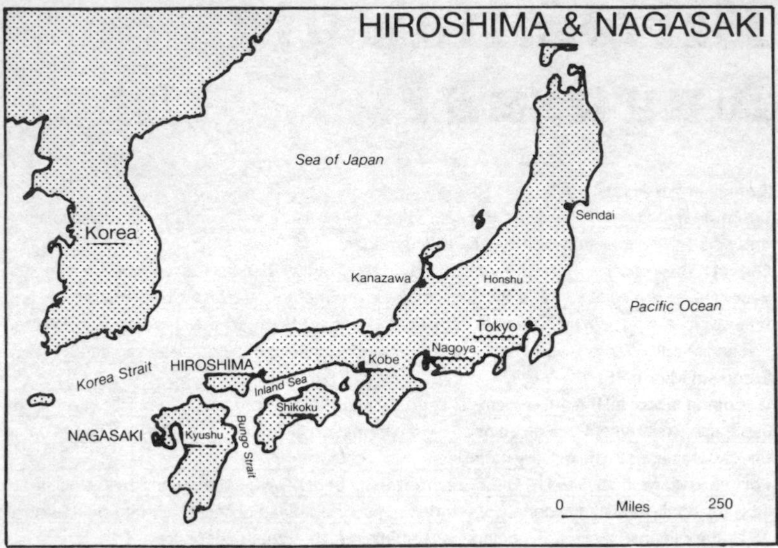

operations, losing a total of 343 aircraft and 243 aircrews. US and British carrier-based aircraft added a further element to reinforce the main effort based upon the airfields of the Marianas.

On 16 July the US successfully tested an atomic device in the New Mexico desert. Truman accepted his Chiefs of Staff's recommendation that Hiroshima, Japan's seventh city (population 343,000 besides 150,000 military personnel), the centre of much war industry and resources, should receive the first atomic bomb. A formal summons to surrender was passed to Japan on 27 July, but was ignored. Accordingly, on 6 August, following a routine raid by four B-29s intended as a distraction, 'Enola Gay' dropped its bomb with horrific results. Still the Japanese Government refused to capitulate. A second bomb was accordingly dropped on Nagasaki (population 250,000) three days later. The Japanese Government thereupon – despite an attempted *coup* by fanatical officers – surrendered; the recorded message spoken by Emperor Hirohito was broadcast to the Japanese nation on the 14th (or 15th by Japanese dating). The decision to use these devastating new weapons for the first two (and to date only) times in history, remains the subject of much controversy and debate to the present day. But they indubitably brought the Second World War in the Far East to its unmourned conclusion.

Kasserine and the Mareth Line

Dates: 14–22 February, and 20–25 March 1943.

Location: In Tunisia, north-west Africa, about 110 miles south-west of Tunis and much the same distance north-west from Gabès.

Object: The Germans were hoping to force a passage through the Kasserine Pass to reach the town of Tebèssa over the Algerian frontier, which was an important Allied supply point, and thereby pre-empt any Allied offensive eastwards towards Sfax on the Mediterranean coast, thus splitting the Axis forces in two.

Opposing sides: (a) Field Marshals von Arnim and Erwin Rommel jointly commanding the Axis forces in Tunisia; (b) Lieutenant-General Dwight D. Eisenhower, Allied Supreme Commander in North-West Africa.

Forces engaged: (a) General Rommel commanding 10th and 21st Panzer divisions and other troops, supported by the Luftwaffe; (b) Major General Lloyd R. Fredendall commanding the US II Corps, and other Allied elements drawn into the battle from other parts of Lieutenant-General Kenneth Anderson's British First Army; Lieutenant-General Bernard Montgomery and Eighth Army.

Casualties: Kasserine only: (a) approx. 2,000 men; (b) 2,816 killed and wounded and 2,459 taken prisoner and missing (US II Corps only); flanking forces, approx. 5,000 more.

Result: The last notable Axis success in North Africa which temporarily shook American confidence, but failed to achieve Rommel's objective as he lost the subsequent battle of the Mareth Line.

Suggested reading: M. Blumenson. *Kasserine Pass* (London, 1968); P. Carell. *The Foxes of the Desert* (London, 1960); R. Lewin, *Rommel as Military Commander* (London, 1968); B. H. Liddell Hart (ed.). *The Rommel Papers* (London, 1953); B. Pitt (ed.). *The Purnell History of the Second World War* vol. 3, Part 14 (London, 1967).

Operation 'Torch' began in north-west Africa four days after the end of second Alamein. Under Eisenhower's overall command, three landings in strength were successfully made at Casablanca, Oran and Algiers. A race for Tunis ensued, but German reinforcements were rushed in from Sicily and France, and at the year's end British First Army was facing von Arnim's Fifth Panzerarmee in a stalemate in Tunisia amidst difficult terrain and wet weather. Rommel, meantime, had conducted a long retreat, abandoning Tripoli to the pursuing Eighth Army, to take up a strong position in the Mareth Line facing east.

Von Arnim was soon planning to improve his position in the eastern dorsale, and fighting flared from Christmas Day. The Germans made considerable gains, and were soon planning a further, larger, offensive rather more to the south once Rommel was in a position to transfer his attention – and his armour – from the Mareth Line. By the plan, von Arnim was to strike for Kasserine with 10th and 21st Panzer divisions, while Rommel led up a detachment of the Afrika Korps via Gafsa in a second

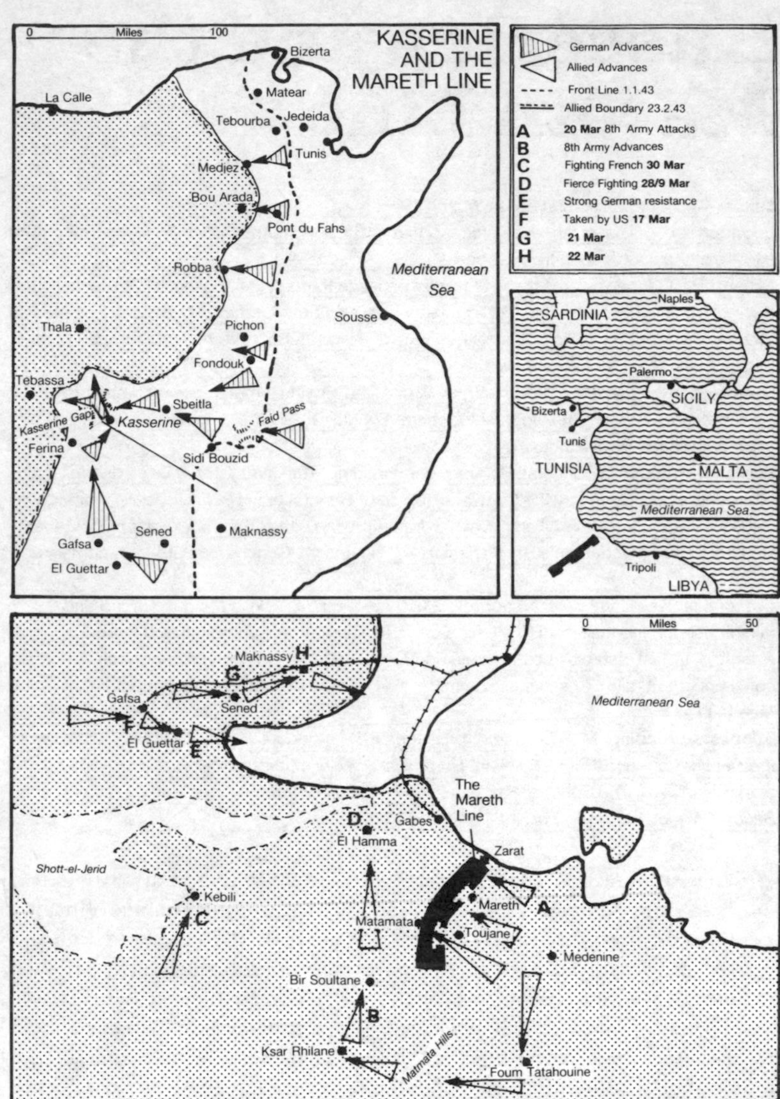

pincer attack to join him at the Pass, before striking for Tebessa – the key Allied supply and communications centre.

On 14 February von Arnim launched a double-blow which took Sidi Bou Zid and then held it against US 1st Armored Division's counter-attack the next day. The 15th also saw Rommel strike through Gafsa and sweep northwards. After three days of heavy fighting the Germans were masters of both Sbeitla and Kasserine, and the US II Corps was in disarray.

On 19 February Rommel attacked again, but failed to co-ordinate this with von Arnim. He nevertheless made progress towards Tebessa and Thala, but was gradually slowed by growing Allied resistance. Von Arnim, meanwhile, was taking up a defensive position further north.

General Sir Harold Alexander took over command and forbade any further withdrawals. He sent 6th Armoured Division south in the nick of time to reinforce the American line and thwart Rommel's intended break-through. By the 22nd Rommel had decided to retreat back to Mareth, and three days later the shaken Allies retook Kasserine and Sidi Bou Zid.

On 6 March Rommel launched the 10th, 15th and 21st Panzer divisions from the Mareth positions intent upon capturing the British supply dumps at Médenine. He met heavy resistance and lost a third of his armour by nightfall, so pulled back. The Eighth Army had lost only 130 casualties and not a single tank. On 12 March Rommel was recalled to Germany by Hitler.

By this date the Eighth Army had been reinforced by Free French forces under General Leclerc. On the 20th a heavy artillery bombardment presaged a major assault along a 20-mile front. On the coast XXX Corps mounted a frontal attack, while inland General Freyberg's New Zealand Division of X Corps conducted a celebrated wide envelopment march covering some 200 miles. By the 26th this manoeuvre had turned the flank of the German positions at El Hamma, and British 1st Armoured Division ground its way forward into the enemy rear areas. Under attack from two directions simultaneously, General Messe fell back to the Gabès – Gafsa road with the merged Italo-German First Army, having lost some 70,000 casualties. On 6 April Montgomery assaulted Gabès, taking 2,000 captives in six hours, and driving the Axis forces still farther to the north. On the 7th British and American patrols met, and the scene was set for the final defeat of Germany and Italy in North Africa.

Kiev

Date: 9–23 September 1941.

Location: On the River Dnieper, south-east of the Pripet Marshes, in the Ukraine, USSR.

Object: The Wehrmacht, on Hitler's orders, was determined to eliminate the Red Army forces of Kiev Special Military District (or South-West Front) in order to secure the Ukraine's rich resources.

Opposing sides: (a) Generals Heinz Guderian and Paul von Kleist commanding the armoured elements of the German Army Groups Centre and South; (b) Marshal Semen Mikhailovich Budenny (replaced by Marshal Semen Konstantinovich Timoshenko) commanding the South-West Front.

Forces engaged: (a) The Second and First Panzergruppen, 28 armoured and mechanized divisions). Total: approx. 300,000 Germans; (b) Elements of 5th, 26th, 21st and 37th Red Armies totalling some 50 divisions. Total: approx. 676,000 Russians.

Casualties: (a) approx. 100,000 men; (b) More than 500,000 Russians killed or captured (initial battles only).

Result: The destruction around Kiev of two-thirds of the Russian South-West Front in the greatest German victory of the Second World War.

Suggested reading: Alan Clarke. *Barbarossa* (London, 1965); J. Erickson. *The Road to Stalingrad* (London, 1975); Heinz Guderian. *Panzer Leader* (London, 1952); V. I. Chuikov. *The Beginning of the Road* (New York 1963); B. Pitt (ed.). *The Purnell History of the Second World War* vol. 2, No. 9 (London, 1967).

As part of Operation 'Barbarossa', von Bock's Army Group Centre made rapid progress against the Red Army, and three successive pincer-attacks by Hoth's and Guderian's Panzergruppen culminated in the capture of 300,000 Russian soldiers, 2,500 tanks and 1,400 guns in the Minsk pocket in late June. By 11 July the Germans were over the River Dnieper at Shklov, and five days later the trap was closing around Smolensk. Further south, however, Timoshenko had mounted a counter-offensive on 15 July to the east of the Pripet Marshes against Guderian's flank and spearhead near Rogachev in an attempt to save his compatriots at Smolensk. This failed, but it reinforced Hitler's growing caution about an immediate drive on Moscow. Meanwhile von Rundstedt's Army Group South had been making famous progress deep into the Ukraine, and by 11 July he was within ten miles of Kiev, where determined resistance was encountered. Sweeping on to the south, Rundstedt prepared to take out the Uman pocket, while Guderian was preparing to close the Smolensk trap, when on 23 August Hitler ordered priority to be given to eliminating the Kiev salient.

Despite objections, Second Panzergruppe and Fourth Army were swung south to support von Rundstedt, who sent von Kleist's armour north, crossing the Dnieper at Kremenchug, to close the trap behind Kiev. An attack by Yeremenko near Gomel on 30 August was repulsed. By 9 September Guderian was 100 miles north-west of Kiev at Nezhin, and Kleist was 60 miles south-east near Pereyaslav. Wishing to avoid the

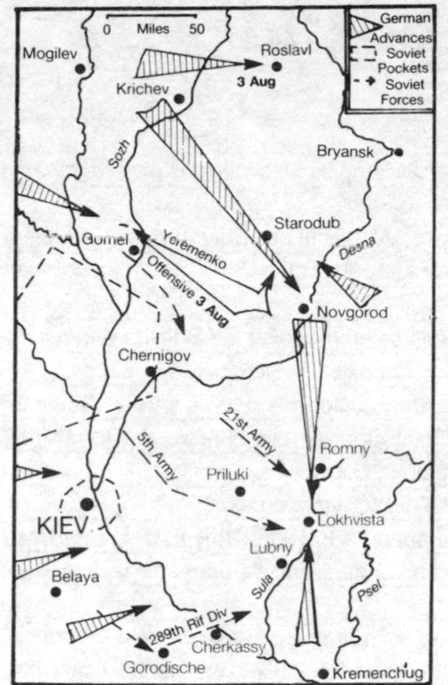

developing trap, Budenny (backed by his senior political officer Kruschev) ordered withdrawal from Kiev, but Stalin forbade this and replaced Budenny with Timoshenko, who took over command on 13 September. On that date the Russians might still have escaped to the east towards Poltava through a 20-mile gap, but Stalin refused Kirponos permission until the 17th. By then it was too late. Two days earlier elements of Guderian's and Kleist's armour had joined up at Lokhvitsa, and the ring was closed. By the time the Russians tried to break out towards the River Psel the German grip had been strengthened. Some 150,000 Russians managed to escape, but for the rest there was little hope. Kiev itself fell on the 19th, and the Germans had mopped-up final pockets of resistance by the 23rd. Two-thirds of the Red Army's strength in the south-west had been eliminated in the greatest military disaster in Russian history. But the German advance on Moscow had been delayed.

Kohima-Imphal

Date: 8 March to 22 June 1944.

Location: In Assam in north-east Burma, amidst the hilly jungles of the Indo-Burmese border region.

Object: The Japanese wished to forestall an anticipated Allied offensive and thus secure their hold on Burma by destroying its logistical bases of Kohima and Dimapur, and also to offset the mounting list of naval and land defeats in the Pacific.

Opposing sides: (a) Lieutenant-General Sir William Slim commanding the British Fourteenth Army; (b) General Renya Mutaguchi commanding the Japanese Fifteenth Army.

Forces engaged: (a) General Scoones's IV Corps (three, later five, divisions) and General Stopford's XXXIII Corps (approx. two divisions). Total: approx. 200,000 troops; (b) Three divisions (later reinforced to five). Total: approx. 150,000 troops.

Casualties: (a) 16,700 killed and wounded; (b) 53,000 killed and wounded.

Result: The greatest defeat on land suffered by the Japanese Imperial Army to this date. This finally secured the approaches to India's north-eastern frontiers, and prepared the way for the reconquest of Burma.

Suggested reading: E. A. Brett-James and Lt-Gen. Sir Geoffrey Evans. *Imphal* (London, 1962); S. E. Kirby. *The War against Japan* vols. 3 & 4 (London, 1956); W. Slim. *Defeat into Victory* (London, 1956); A. Swinson. *Kohima* (London, 1966); B. Pitt (ed.). *The Purnell History of the Second World War* vol. 4, Nos. 15 & 16 (London, 1967).

On 15 January 1942 the Japanese invaded Burma, and by mid-June the remnants of Burcorps were completing a retreat of 1,000 miles to the hills of Assam on the Indian frontier, having lost most of Burma to the enemy including its important oil fields. As Slim wrote: 'We, the Allies, had been outmanoeuvred, outfought and out-generalled.' For the defence of the Indian frontier region he could call on resources from India and some help from Chinese Nationalist Armies fighting under the prickly American commander, 'Vinegar Joe' Stilwell – striving to keep open the Burma Road into China, virtually the only lifeline for that embattled country. It was soon cut. The situation looked black indeed.

For fifteen months Slim – aided by Lord Louis Mountbatten, Allied Supreme Commander, South-East Asia – fought to rebuild the morale and battle-strength of the redesignated British Fourteenth Army. They managed to overcome their men's 'Forgotten Army' complex, and eventually Slim commanded no less than 500,000 men of many races. Further defeats in the First Arakan Campaign were offset by the success (limited but significant) of Orde Wingate's First Chindit operation deep behind the Japanese lines, which proved that Allied troops were capable of undertaking successful jungle operations. The battle against malaria was also waged with success.

The Japanese High Command was aware that an Allied counter-offensive was being planned, and although they had earlier decided against an attack upon Imphal set amidst the inhospitable and communication-starved Assam hills, in January 1944 they issued orders for a pre-emptive

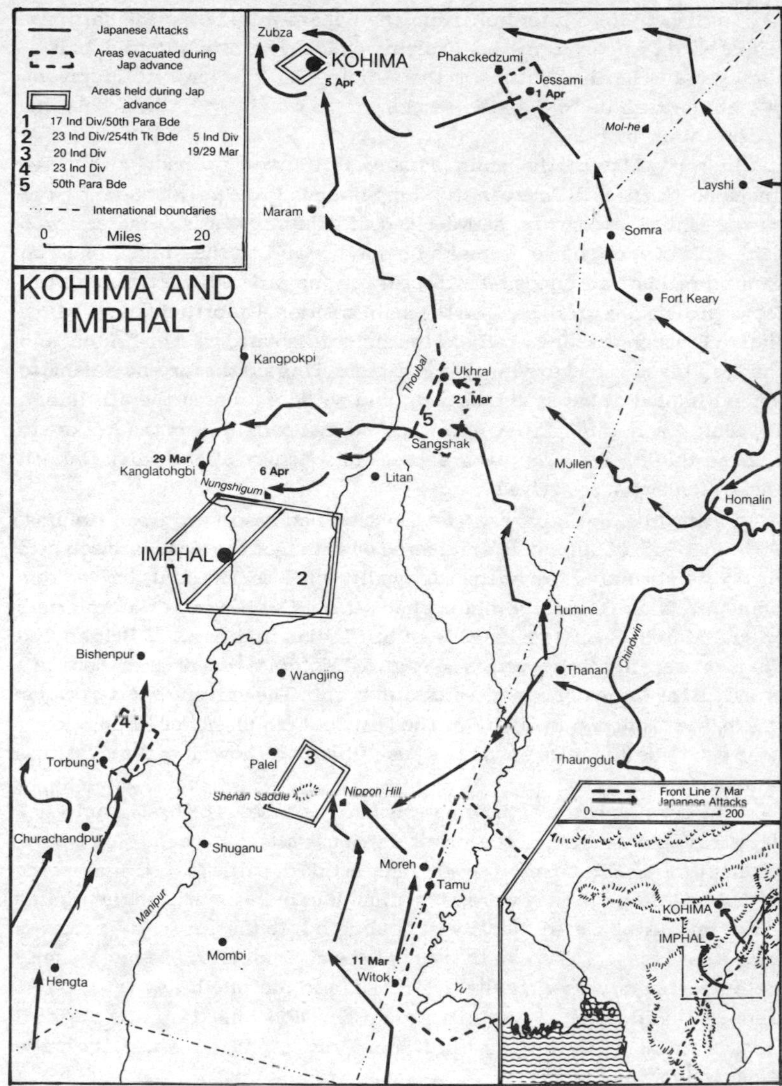

offensive to take Tiddim, Kohima and Imphal in order to smash Fourteenth Army's logistical bases and close the single all-weather road linking Burma with India. It is doubtful whether they ever intended to 'march on Delhi', but a major demonstration of Japanese strength on India's north-east frontier within range of Calcutta and Bengal would, it was thought, compound the problems already being encountered within India, where large-scale public disorders, passive resistance and non-cooperation campaigns were in progress in support of Mahatma Gandhi.

To divert Slim's attention from their main intentions, the Japanese launched an offensive in the Arakan, which was brought to a halt at Ngakyedauk in the 'Battle of the Admin. Box', where air-supply by parachute permitted a defensive victory to be won by the Allies. This was important for morale.

In early March, the main Japanese offensive opened, with three divisions of Fifteenth Army in the van. Slim had to defend a 300-mile front on the central sector, and had decided, if a Japanese attack materialized before his own offensive, to make his main stand on the Imphal plain on ground of his own choosing. Accordingly he ordered the two outlying forward divisions to fall back on the main position. Unfortunately, the 17th Indian Division withdrew rather late, and was isolated west of Tiddim, and the 23rd Division had to be sent to its rescue. This left the forces available to defend Imphal at barely 3,000 men, and so Slim ordered the 5th Indian Division – men, guns, mules and jeeps – to be flown-in from the Arakan to redress the balance. This was successfully achieved, and later the 4th Indian Division also arrived.

Meanwhile, the Japanese 31st Division had descended upon Kohima, 80 miles north of Imphal. Despite ferocious attacks, the local garrison held on to its shrinking perimeter doggedly until relief could arrive from Dimapur, where General Stopford had set up XXXIII Corps Headquarters in late March. Soon 161 Brigade of 5th Indian and parts of British 2nd Division were fighting towards beleagured Kohima. Part arrived there on 4 April just as the major Japanese assault began. The fighting was ferocious: the 'battle of the tennis-court' at the District Commissioner's bungalow – with each side dug in on opposite sides – illustrates how close the rival lines were drawn.

The ensuing battle of Kohima was in two phases. The first, from 4 to 7 May, saw the repulse of the worst Japanese attacks. Then, on 11 May, elements of XXXIII Corps arrived, and the tide of battle turned against the Japanese. Although they were very difficult to prise loose from their gains – the Japanese believed literally in holding out to the last man – progress was steadily made. Then, in the second phase, from 18 to 22 May, General Sato's command was virtually destroyed, and, despite heavy rains on 22 June, the 2nd Division and 5th Indian Division linked up at Kangpoki Mission Station, and the sieges of Kohima and Imphal were over, the battle effectively won.

Meantime the main battle had long been joined in and around the plain of Imphal. Although it was cut off from land support, air-supply and reinforcement – and evacuation of the wounded – were continued throughout the battle. This proved to be the largest use of air-portability in war to date. During the three months' struggle, 6,000 tons of supplies (including 12,000 bags of mail, 27,000 eggs and 43 million cigarettes, besides 835,000 gallons of fuel) and two whole divisions of troops were flown in, and 43,000 non-combatants and 13,000 casualties evacuated: an immense achievement by any standard – and only made possible by having overall command of the air and brilliant planning at every level.

The Japanese fought with customary tenacity, but little by little superior numbers began to tell. By early June the rival armies were locked in complex layered combat – or 'salami tactics' as they were called; in the north were Stopford's two divisions in and around Kohima; between them and Imphal were interposed two Japanese divisions; around Imphal and Pahel were four more British major formations, and south of them another Japanese division and an additional brigade. In the end, outnumbered by two to one, the Japanese cohesion snapped, and Mutaguchi pulled back to the River Chindwin in great disorder. The Japanese had lost most of their transport and guns, and at least 53,000 men. Five Imperial Japanese divisions (the original three had been joined by the 18th and 54th during the battle) had been virtually destroyed. A turning-point had been reached in the Burma war, and a great defensive double victory had been won. The morale of Fourteenth Army soared accordingly, and soon General Slim was planning his 'campaign on the wet' – pressing on after the Japanese through the violent rains of the monsoon.

Kursk

Date: 5–16 July 1943.

Location: A city 150 miles north of Kharkov in the Soviet Union.

Object: The German High Command aimed to eliminate the large salient extending on three sides of Kursk, and to achieve a major success on the central front that would overshadow earlier disasters such as Stalingrad.

Opposing sides: (a) Marshal Georgi Zhukov commanding a large group of six Soviet armies; (b) Field Marshal Günther von Kluge commanding large parts of Army Groups Centre (his own) and South.

Forces engaged: (a) One tank army and five combined-arms armies including 20,000 guns, 3,600 tanks and 2,400 aircraft. Total: 1,300,000 Russians; (b) Seventeen Panzer and 21 infantry divisions comprising 10,000 guns, 2,700 tanks, 2,000 aircraft. Total: 900,000 Germans.

Casualties: (a) approx. 120,000 men; (b) approx. 100,000 men and 980 tanks.

Result: The failure of the last great German offensive in Russia, leading to renewed Red Army attacks at all points from Leningrad to the Crimea.

Suggested reading: J. Erickson. *The Road to Berlin* (London, 1983); E. von Manstein. *Lost Victories* (London, 1958); F. W. von Mellinthin, *Panzer Battles (1939–45)* (London, 1955); B. Pitt (ed.). *The Purnell History of the Second World War* vol. 4, No. 5 (London, 1967).

Following the disaster of Stalingrad, the Germans had lost the initiative to a marked degree. Manstein managed to extricate Army Group 'Don' back to the River Donetz, but the first great Russian success of exploitation was the recapture of Kharkov in mid-February 1943. The Soviets then attacked southwards to drive a wedge between von Manstein and Army Group 'B' – which they succeeded in doing on 19 February. But this crisis brought out the best in von Manstein, probably the ablest of all Hitler's generals, and in a telling counter-attack of eight days' duration he defeated Colonel-General Popov's group of armoured divisions, trapping them between the refurbished Fourth Panzerarmee and the First Panzerarmee. Subsequently, the Germans reoccupied Kharkov on 11 March. This success created the 100-mile southern flank of the Kursk salient. The deep mud of spring then imposed a pause on both sides.

During late May, von Kluge and *OKH*'s Chief-of-Staff, General Zeitzler, put an ambitious plan before the Führer for a huge double-envelopment operation designed to trap and destroy the Russian forces holding the Kursk salient. Many senior advisers – including Model and Guderian – were strongly opposed to the concept, claiming that the Germans would be insane to attempt a major offensive in 1943, but Hitler – after some hesitation – decided that the gamble should be attempted.

The plan for Operation 'Zitadelle' called for a southwards drive by General Walther Model's Ninth Army (part of Army Group Centre) from the vicinity of Orel, to break through the northern side of the pocket near Ponyri before penetrating to the rear of the city of Kursk. Meanwhile, from the south, through and to the west of Belgorod, General Hoth's Fourth

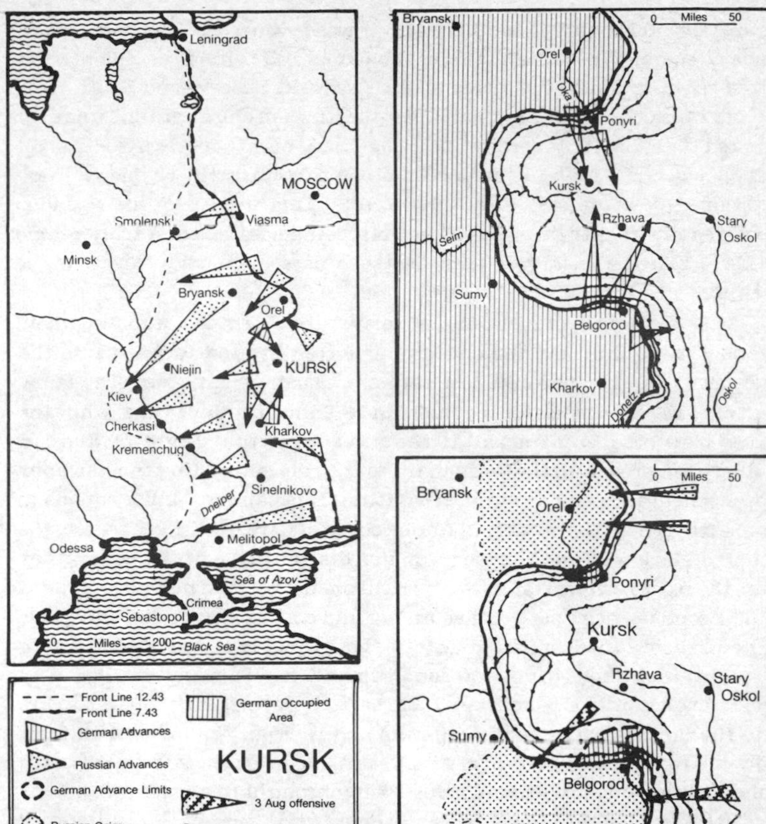

Panzerarmee (now part of Army Group South) would strike in two columns smashing through the Russians of the Voronezh Front to bypass Rzhava and link up with Ninth Army near Kursk. From the outset, scheduled for early July, the German Second Army would hold the western side of the salient, distracting Russian attention. Hoth was given nine Panzer divisions, and Model eight, between them including 2,700 tanks and assault guns. Much faith was placed in the new Mark VI Tiger battle-tank, with its 88mm gun and very strong frontal armour. Ninety of this formidable weapon were entrusted to Ninth Army. The Luftwaffe was to make an all-out effort to gain superiority over the battlefield.

However, in the event this plan came as no surprise to the Russians. The Lucy spy-ring in Switzerland gave warning in good time of what was to come, and Zhukov could make his defensive preparations. These were thorough in the extreme. The northern sector of the salient was entrusted to General Konstantin Rokossovsky commanding the divisions of the Red

Army Central Front. The southern sector was given to the Veronezh Front, under General Nikolai Vatutin. On the flanks and behind the salient were (from north to south) the forces of the Bryansk, Reserve and South-West Fronts respectively. Within the salient, the Russian engineers and infantry worked fanatically to create no less than eight successive lines of minefields and anti-tank defences. Some 20,000 artillery pieces were positioned in readiness, with 3,600 tanks. The Red Air Force was also deployed in strength, all of 2,400 aircraft being assembled. A truly titanic battle – indeed the largest tank battle to date in history – was in the making.

After a number of last-minute delays, the Germans launched their offensive on 5 July. As the enveloping forces ground forward into the Russian lines, they began to lose tanks in alarming numbers. The Pzkw Mark IVs were no match for the Russian 76.2mm anti-tank guns, while the mines blew off many tracks. At the same time, the weight of Russian artillery fire prevented the German infantry from supporting their armour closely enough by day or night, permitting Russian tank-killer squads to range freely over the battlefield under cover of darkness. Even worse, the vaunted Mark VI Tigers proved a major disappointment. Although they were the most powerful tanks on the battlefield, they had not been supplied with secondary machine-gun armament and consequently were incapable of neutralizing the Russian infantry. These quickly learnt – after seeing their anti-tank shells bounce off the German frontal armour – to lie low in their trenches until the monsters had roared by, and then to emerge to fire into the far less well-armoured flanks and rears of the tanks with their infantry rockets at close range. As a result, Model's attack from the north only made six miles of ground before being brought to a halt.

The story for the Germans was little better in the south. On the very first day, Hoth's tanks –six miles into the Russian anti-tank belts – were held up by torrential rain, which turned a stream they were about to cross into a swamp. For three days they could make no progress, but lost many vehicles to Russian fire. By 12 July the Fourth Panzerarmee had at last managed to hack out an area 20 miles deep by 40 wide, but on neither flank had the planned German break-through materialized, and time was passing. Overhead, the Luftwaffe similarly failed to overcome the Red Air Force.

At last, on 12 July, Hoth was facing the eighth and last line of Russian defences. Gathering 600 tanks, he ordered them forward – only to find them facing Vatutin's reserve, the intact Fifth Tank Army. For eight hours a terrible tank battle raged over the Russian plains, but as nightfall brought a lull there was no denying that the Russians were still masters of the field. Meanwhile, on the 12th in the north a new development had been Colonel-General Popov's armoured counter-attack against Orel. This, too, made significant progress and once again the Russians were wresting the initiative from the tiring Germans.

After digesting all the reports, on 13 July a bitterly disappointed Hitler ordered the abandonment of Operation 'Zitadelle'. It was hoped that at least enough damage had been inflicted on the Russians to earn a respite. Heavily although the Red Army had suffered, there was no question of any pause. Offensive after offensive began along the 1,000-mile battle-front, and the Germans were forced to redeploy what was left of their massed Panzer divisions to try to hold their weakening line. In the opinion of Major-General J. F. C. Fuller. 'It is in no way an exaggeration to say that the defeat at Kursk was as disastrous to the Germans as had been their defeat at Stalingrad.'

Leningrad

Date: 8 September 1941 – 25 January 1944.

Location: At the eastern extremity of the Gulf of Finland.

Object: The starvation into surrender of the second most important city of the USSR.

Opposing sides: (a) Marshal Kliment Efremovich Voroshilov in command of the forces of the Soviet Union, with General Mikhail Khozin (initially) as commandant of Leningrad; (b) Field Marshal Wilhelm Ritter von Leeb (until January 1942), then successively, Field Marshal Ernst Busch and General Georg von Küchler, in command of the German Army Group North.

Forces engaged: (a) 42nd and 55th Red Armies and units of the Baltic Fleet. Total approx. 250,000 Russians; (b) Sixteenth and Eighteenth German and the Finnish Karelian Armies. Total: approx. 350,000 Germans and Finns.

Casualties: (a) Approx. 1,800,000 Russian soldiers and civilians; (b) approx. 200,000 Germans and Finns.

Result: After horrendous suffering, the German and Finnish siege of the city was broken off after 31 months.

Suggested reading: Alan Clarke, *Barbarossa* (London, 1965); J. Erikson. *The Road to Stalingrad* and *The Road to Berlin* (London, 1975 & 1983); H. Salisbury. *The Nine Hundred Days* (London, 1975); B. Pitt (ed.). *The Purnell History of the Second World War* vol. 2, Nos. 10 and 14 (London, 1967).

As the Wehrmacht swept into Russia, Army Group North was under orders to conquer the Baltic States and seize the great city of Leningrad. On 26 June, Finland declared war on Russia, and their Karelian Army under Field Marshal Mannerheim slowly began to move its twelve divisions towards Leningrad from the north. Von Leeb's Army Group North captured Riga on 1 July, and two months later, the occupation of the Baltic States achieved, Hoeppner's Fourth Panzergruppe was within 90 miles of Leningrad near Luga. Voroshilov ordered his battered forces back into the city, and mobilized its population to dig defences. The first German shells fell upon Leningrad on 4 September, and four days later the encirclement was complete.

The defences took the strain, but with only one month's food within the city everything depended on maintaining a tenuous line of communication with the outside world. Thousands of civilians were dying weekly as winter asserted its grip, and when the line of supply through Tikhvin was severed on 9 November it seemed that the end was near. However, by herculean efforts a new lifeline road from Zaborie to Novaya Ladoga was completed by 6 December, and from there supplies and reinforcements were driven over the ice of Lake Ladoga into Leningrad. But it was a tenuous supply route at best.

In February 1942 the Russians attempted to attack the German Sixteenth Army near Lake Ilmen, but were driven back. On Hitler's orders, von Manstein was brought north from the Crimea to lead a new assault on Leningrad during the summer, but this failed. A new Russian attempt to break-through on the Volkhov Front to link with a break-out attempt by

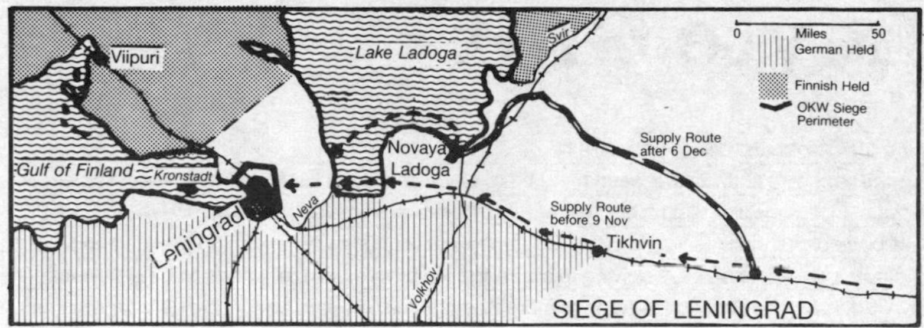

55th Army and the Neva Task Force, failed during August and September. During the second winter of the siege a new Russian counter-attack also failed in January 1943. Meantime there had been two changes in German command as Hitler expressed his rage at the failure to take the city. More were to follow during the following year. Eventually, in mid-January 1944, four Red Armies united in a new all-out effort, along a 120-mile front from Lake Ilmen to Leningrad. General Meretskov's Volkhov Army, assisted by Govorov's Army of Leningrad managed to link-up on 25 January after desperate fighting. The reopening of the Moscow to Leningrad highroad marked the raising of the siege. Battles raged on as the Red Armies pressed back Army Group North, as well as the Finns, who were eventually granted an armistice in September. The tide of war had thus been turned in the north, but at a terrible cost to both sides.

Leyte Gulf

Date: 2 October – 31 December 1944.

Location: Leyte Gulf lies between Mindanao, Leyte and Samai islands in the Philippine archipelago in south-east Asia; the sea battles raged over a vast area of ocean around the Philippines, but the land fighting was concentrated around the American bridgehead on Leyte.

Object: The Japanese were striving to challenge the progressive reconquest of the Philippines by US forces; the Americans to gain supremacy at sea, on land and in the air over southern Asia.

Opposing sides: (a) General Douglas MacArthur and Admiral Chester W. Nimitz commanding US forces in southern Asia; (b) General Tomoyuki Yamashita and Admiral Jisaburo Ozawa commanding the Japanese.

Forces engaged: (a) General Krueger's US Sixth Army and Admiral Kinkaid's US 7th Fleet and Admiral Halsey's US 3rd Fleet. Total: variable, but at least 150,000 troops and 148,000 sailors; (b) General Sosasku Suzuki's Japanese 35th Army and Admiral Soemu Toyoda commanding the Japanese Combined Fleet. Total: approx. 350,000 troops and 42,800 sailors.

Casualties: (a) 15,584 troops and 3,800 US sailors; (b) 74,000 troops and 10,500 Japanese sailors.

Result: Effectively the winning of the war in the Pacific against Japan; the virtual destruction of the Japanese Combined Fleet was decisive; the capture of the central Philippines was an important advance on land.

Suggested reading; J. Ehrman. *Grand Strategy* vol. 5 (London, 1956); D. MacArthur. *Reminiscences* (New York 1954); S. E. Morison. *Leyte* (New York, 1960); S. L. Falk. *Decision at Leyte* (New York, 1972); B. Pitt (ed.). *The Purnell History of the Second World War* vol. 5 No. 16 (London, 1968).

As the Americans closed in on Japanese-held territories in southern Asia, the naval war rose to a new climax. Island after small island was retaken after horrendous fighting by the US Marine Corps – Saipan, Guam, Tinian, Morotai and Angaur – all would be in American hands by late October 1944. Meantime the bombing of the Marianas in June had demonstrated the growing American superiority in the air, while the US surface fleet's naval preponderance was rapidly growing – some 112 naval vessels (including seven fleet and eight light carriers, and seven battleships among them) to the Japanese 55 (including five fleet and four light carriers and five battleships), while American submarines were wreaking havoc on the Japanese mercantile marine which never adopted a full convoy system. American naval aircraft totalled 956 to the Japanese 573. The writing was becoming apparent on the wall.

The naval battles off the Marianas took a further toll of shrinking Japanese resources. In September Admiral Halsey's carrier aircraft raided the Philippines, and at the Quebec Conference Roosevelt and Churchill agreed to an invasion to liberate Manila and Luzon. As a preliminary to this attack (scheduled for late October), four US carrier groups attacked Formosa, destroying 500 more Japanese aircraft for the loss of 76. For the attack on Leyte – the chosen invasion area for the reconquest of the central

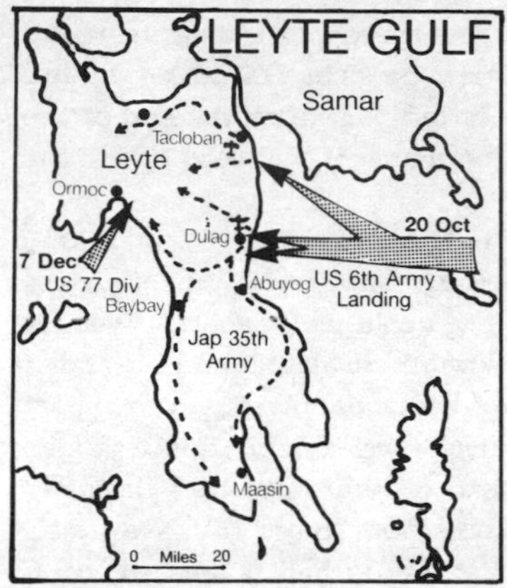

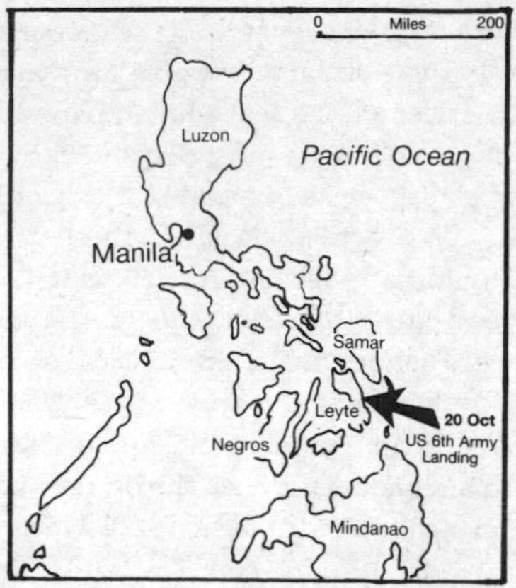

Philippines – the Americans assembled almost 740 ships including all of seventeen carriers. On 20 October the landings began, meeting only light opposition, and within 48 hours 132,000 troops and over 200,000 tons of stores were safely ashore.

As expected, Admiral Toyoda rose to the bait. Out from the Inland Sea came two Japanese fleets: Vice-Admiral Kurita from Borneo with five battleships (assisted by two more) and 31 more vessels of war, while from Japan sailed the able Vice-Admiral Ozawa, with four carriers strongly escorted. American submarines took a toll, sinking the heavy cruiser *Atago* on the 23rd while an air strike sank *Mushashi*. Halsey was now seeking Ozawa and the Japanese carriers, while Kurita and Nishimura were bearing down on Kinkaid's task forces. At the Surigao Straits the six battleships and eight cruisers met Kurita in a classic battle which left the Japanese definitely worsted, with two capital units sunk.

Early on the 25th Halsey was 300 miles north of Leyte, but the centre of action was destined to be off Samar far nearer to Leyte – where Kurita was sailing determined to win a major victory. The battle of Samar took place 40 miles off-shore from the American beach-head. Rear Admiral Sprague's escort carriers and destroyers were the first Americans Kurita encountered, and although massively outnumbered the Americans attacked and sustained some losses to destroyers. But then Sprague called down a massive air strike from all three US carrier groups, and Kurita withdrew after sinking one light American carrier, mistaking destroyers for cruisers and escort carriers for fleet carriers. The same day also saw the first *Kamikaze* suicide raids (named after the 'Divine Wind' which had saved Japan from invasion by Kublai Khan in 1281 by destroying his fleet), which scored hits on three US carriers, sinking the USS *St-Lo*.

Later on the 25th Halsey found action at last against Ozawa in the battle of Cape Engano, and by dusk all four Japanese carriers were sunk. Halsey failed to block Kurita's escape route via the San Bernardino Channel

– and a great opportunity was thereby lost. But there was no disguising the fact that the Japanese plan for a major naval success had failed abysmally. The loss of the last four Japanese fleet carriers signalled the end of the naval war, won most decisively by the Americans. It had been one of the greatest series of naval battles in history.

Meanwhile, on land, the battle for Leyte was raging. Some 45,000 Japanese were striving to hem in the Americans, but by 1 November no less than 101,600 Americans of the US Sixth Army under General Krueger were ashore. Such a numerical superiority would have to tell in the end.

But a further series of *Kamikaze* raids badly damaged four support American carriers, and a little later the fleet carrier *Lexington* was also severely damaged. As the US fleet hit at Japanese reinforcements, the latter reacted violently, and on 25 November three more major US naval units were badly damaged. On land, General Yamashita had taken over command, and a combination of his skill, bad weather and difficult ground made the American campaign hellish. But by the end of the month 183,000 Americans were ashore facing 35,000 surviving Japanese, and most of Leyte was in American hands for the loss of 2,260 killed.

There is no denying that the *Kamikaze* pilots caused grave losses to American supply and reinforcement convoys. The threat they represented effectively created a new form of air warfare which it took all the US anti-aircraft firepower to survive, never mind contain or defeat. The toll of lost or severely damaged shipping mounted – but the sources of Japanese aircraft and young pilots keen to seek a martyr's death began to dwindle, and by mid-January 1945 there were few of either left in the Philippines.

As this unforeseen and critical struggle was being waged at sea, on land the US Sixth Army was closing in on Manila. A last-ditch garrison of 20,000 troops under Rear-Admiral Iwabachi conducted a vicious defence of the capital city's naval base, ignoring General Yamashita's orders to evacuate. Before the Americans could claim victory, most of the city had been razed. Soon American columns were fanning out to recover island after island. Luzon had taken 173 days and more than 37,000 casualties to liberate (and a further 2,000 sailors were lost at sea mainly to the *Kamikaze* onslaught), but it would not be until after the Japanese surrender in August 1945 that Yamashita would surrender at the head of his remaining 50,000 troops. But General MacArthur's oath in the dark days of 1942 that he would 'return' to the Philippines had been fulfilled.

Malta

Date: April 1941 – June 1943.

Location: Malta and Gozo, central Mediterranean islands, south of Sicily.

Object: The Axis wished to neutralize the islands which were strategically placed close to their sea-links between Italy and North Africa, and also served as a half-way staging-post between Gibraltar and Alexandria.

Opposing sides: (a) General Sir William Dobbie, and later Field Marshal Lord Gort, commanding the British and Maltese defence forces; (b) Field Marshal Albrecht Kesselring, German Commander in the Mediterranean.

Forces engaged: (a) The Army garrison and varying amounts of RN and RAF support; (b) Large numbers of Aeronautica and Luftwaffe fighters and bombers operating from Sicily and Libya.

Casualties: (a) approx. 4,000 military personnel and 6,000 civilians; (b) approx. 600 Axis aircraft shot down.

Result: The successful defence of Malta was an epic of the Second World War, and operations from it caused severe damage to the Axis campaigns in North Africa.

Suggested Reading: C. Shores & B. Cull. *Malta – the Hurricane Years 1940–41* (London, 1987); G. Hogan. *Malta – the Triumphant Years, 1940–43* (London, 1978); P. Shankland & A. Hunter. *Malta Convoy* (London, 1961); E. Bradford, *Malta 1940-43* (London, 1985); B. Pitt (ed.). *The Purnell History of the Second World War* vol. 3, No. 5 (London, 1967).

The islands of Malta were strategically important as both a naval arsenal and as an air base, whose possession made it possible for the Allies to cover important convoys travelling by the Mediterranean route to Alexandria and Suez and at the same time posed a severe threat to German and Italian sea-routes linking Naples and Palermo with Tripoli. Although a planned airborne invasion (Operation 'Hercules') never materialized, the islands were subjected to a long bombing ordeal which they successfully withstood, earning the award of the George Cross from King George VI for their patience and sustained gallantry under fire.

The first air attack was on 11 June 1940, just after Italy's entry into the war when the sole air defences amounted to three out-dated Gladiator biplanes, *Faith*, *Hope* and *Charity*, but the main air onslaughts came from April to November 1941, and February to November 1942. During these periods Malta was truly besieged from the air, and it was only with the greatest difficulty that supplies and munitions were passed in to the garrison and population. The Luftwaffe was fully involved in the battle from December 1941 as an Air Fleet based on Sicily began a daily series of raids under Kesselring's direction. These numbered up to 300 aircraft at a time, and by May 1942 some 2,470 air raids had been mounted. After Crete's losses, plans for an airborne invasion were scrapped despite Kesselring's strong advocacy.

A critical moment came in March 1942 when a relief convoy from Alexandria lost all four freighters, but a little later RN aircraft-carriers managed to fly-in 126 Spitfires which soon put an end to Axis daylight

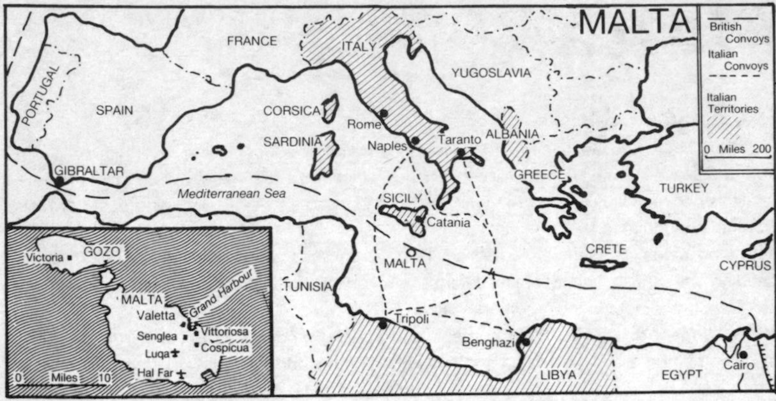

raids. In June all but two ships out of seventeen were sunk *en route* for Malta, and it needed a huge naval operation to get five out of fourteen supply vessels into Valletta harbour in August, including the crippled tanker *Ohio* whose fuel was vital for the maintenance of the air defence.

Meanwhile from Malta RN submarines and fast surface-craft, supplemented by RAF fighter-bombers, were waging a highly effective offensive against Axis Africa-bound convoys. In October 1941 two-thirds of Rommel's supplies never reached North Africa. In July 1942 three out of four Axis tankers were sunk – and their loss starved Panzerarmee Afrika of vital fuel in the critical battles against Eighth Army for the Western Desert later that year. Thus Malta played key offensive as well as defensive roles in the Middle East, and the courage of its people fully deserved the distinction awarded to it in recognition.

Manchuria

Date: 9–17 August 1945.

Location: South of the Rivers Argon and Amur around the cities and communication centres of Tsitsihar, Harbin and Mukden in Manchuria.

Object: The Red Army was determined to occupy Manchuria and compel a local Japanese surrender in the very last days of the Second World War, having only declared hostilities with the Empire of Japan on 8 August 1945 following the dropping by the USA of the first atomic bomb on Hiroshima two days previously. Stalin was determined to be in at the kill to share the spoils of war.

Opposing sides: (a) The Red Army's Manchurian Front commanded by Marshal Vasilevsky, chief of the united Far East command; (b) General Yamada Otozo, commanding the Japanese Kwantung Army.

Forces engaged: (a) Armies of the Trans-Baikal Front (Marshal Malinovsky), the 1st Far Eastern Front (Marshal Meretskov) and the 2nd Far Eastern Front (General Purkayev). Total: 1,600,000 men (5,550 tanks, 28,000 guns, 4,370 aircraft); (b) The Kwantung Army (Group). Total: 1,040,000 men (1,155 tanks, 5,360 guns, 1,155 aircraft).

Casualties: (a) 8,219 killed, 22,264 wounded; (b) An estimated 83,737 killed and 594,000 made prisoners-of-war.

Result: The conquest of Manchuria in a *Blitzkrieg* campaign and the occupation (by early September) of the Kurile islands.

Suggested reading: M. Glantz. *August Storm: the Soviet 1945 Strategic Offensive in Manchuria,* 2 vols. (Fort Leavenworth, 1983); C. J. Duffy. *The Soviet Offensive in Manchuria,* August 1945 (Sandhurst, 1987) – and accompanying reader; B. Pitt (ed.). *The Purnell History of the Second World War* vol. 6, No. 16, (London, 1968).

The significance of this rarely described Russo-Japanese campaign (often overlooked as it in part took place in the days following the end of the Second World War and was in any case dwarfed by the implications of the two explosions of US atomic weaponry that preceded and accompanied its opening) lies in its scale and above all its speed. Compared to the ponderous mile-by-mile Russian advance through Poland and Germany to Berlin and the Elbe in 1944–5 – which has tended to be regarded subsequently as archetypal of Soviet aspirations and capabilities in any future major conflict in Europe – this was a *Blitzkreig* worthy of a Manstein or a Guderian. It is also significant that the Manchurian campaign is widely studied for its lessons throughout the modern Soviet Army, and is for that reason, as well as for its intrinsic interest as a major example of operational art, receiving more and more attention in American and British staff colleges. It is likely to present the prototype of what the Soviet Union might hope to achieve in any major sub-nuclear conflict in Central Europe, and as such merits attention. Forewarned may be forearmed – and even (or especially) in this day of *glasnost* and *perestroika* it behoves NATO to keep up its guard.

From November 1943 the USA and Great Britain were exerting pressure on Stalin to bring Russia into the war against Japan. Although in

1939 there had been a short but sharp campaign in Mongolia between Red Army and Imperial Japanese troops, this had not led to general hostilities either then or later. But it was only in April 1945 that Russian planning for a Manchurian offensive began – as it became evident that the war against Hitler was rapidly drawing to its close thus releasing Russian resources. Stalin appointed Marshal Alexsandr M. Vasilevsky to head a united Far East Command – including all of eleven combined-arms armies, one tank army, three air armies and as many air defence armies. Opposed to them were General Yamada Otozo's Kwantung Army – strong in numbers but fragile in morale, particularly after the Emperor's order to cease hostilities, containing as it did some 300,000 unreliable Manchukuo troops owing allegiance to the Japanese puppet ruler, 'the Last Emperor' (of China). Soviet superiority in tanks, guns and aircraft was also impressive, and naturally their men's morale was high following the smashing of Hitler's Third Reich and the occupation of Berlin. Many of Otozo's best troops had in any case been drafted to the Pacific war.

Aware that Japanese forces were over-extended on the Chinese front (which had absorbed the attention of two-thirds of the Japanese Imperial Army since 1937), General Okamura began to pull back his forces northwards between May and August to reinforce the Kwantung Army as it became clear that a Russian offensive was possible against Manchuria. General Chiang Kai-shek made this withdrawal difficult by cutting the corridor into Indo-China from 30 May, and one month later 100,000 Japanese had been trapped around Canton, and while falling back through North China were greatly harassed *en route* for Manchuria by the US 14th and 10th Air Forces.

At last, on 8 August, Moscow declared war on Japan following the dropping of the Hiroshima atomic bomb, intent on getting into the war, however belatedly, in order to acquire important territorial gains at Japan's expense. Next day, the massive Russian forces swept into Manchuria from the north. Making good use of poor weather Marshal Rodion Y. Malinovsky's army group made the major attack, advancing eastwards from Outer Mongolia on a broad front. In support, Marshal Kirill A. Meretskov's army group pressed south from the line Khabarovsk to Vladivostok, while between these fast-moving pincers General Maxim Purkayev's group of armies advanced south from the River Amur.

Despite the confusion reigning within their forces over the Emperor's order to lay down their arms, the Kwantung Army fought with typical Japanese *élan* and ferocity. However the Russian 6th Guards Tank Army achieved a great success by penetrating the Khingan Mountains – supposedly trackless – against minimal opposition (an interesting parallel to the German penetrations through the 'impassible' Ardennes in 1940 and 1944). Opening at 0100 hours on 9 August, Colonel-General Kravchenko's advance was fast, rushing the Khorokhon Pass by early on the 11th. The two-pronged advance ground to a halt on the plain beyond, having far out-

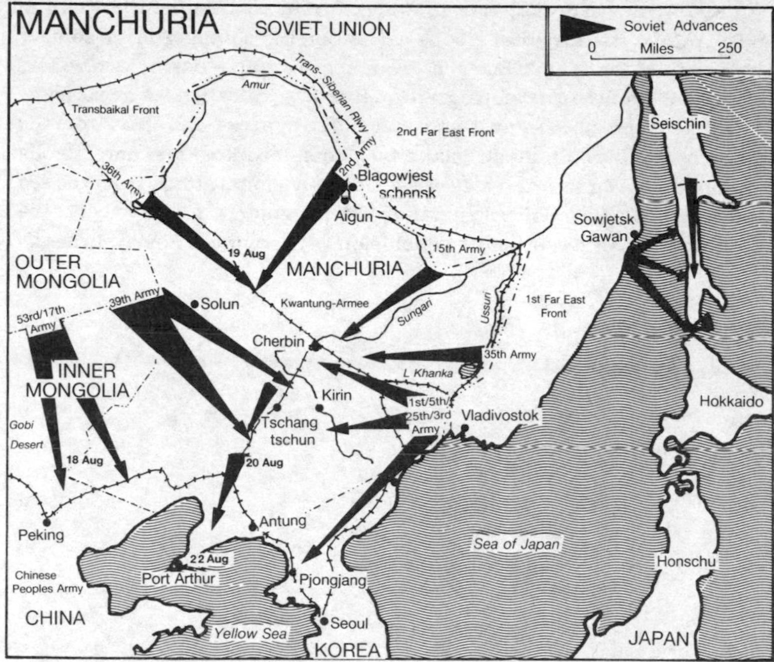

distanced its fuel supplies, but Marshal Malinovsky was equal to the crisis and used 400 aircraft to airlift fuel forward to the stranded tanks. The advance was resumed on the 13th, and eight days later the 6th Guards Tank Army had occupied both Changohun and Mukden.

Meanwhile General Pliev's 39th Red Army was encountering savage fighting on the Russian left flank. His two columns comprised both tanks and cavalry and moved some 92 miles apart, crossing the desert regions at a rate of up to 60 miles a day. The Japanese held out around Kalgan until the 21st – when Pliev crossed the Great Wall of China and soon made contact with Mao Tse-tung's Communist Chinese 8th Route Army.

It fell to the 5th Red Army and the 1st Red Banner Army (parts of Maretskov's force of 37 divisions) to fight the only set-piece battle of the campaign against the Japanese 1st Area Army defending the headquarters town of Mutankiang. On 15 and 16 August, the 5th Red Army carried out an envelopment from the east while the 1st Red Banner Army closed in from the north. The Japanese defence cracked after two days' heavy fighting, and 48 hours later began to surrender on this sector.

The most spectacular advance of all was that carried out by General Purkayev's pair or armies – the 2nd Far Eastern Front. Advancing on three axes past difficult marshland, the two main columns advanced on Harbin and Tsitsihar. Crossing the Amur on a wide front on 9 August, the Russians were held by Japanese strongpoints until the 13th, but then the

15th Red Army headed for Harbin, supported by the Amur River Flotilla. On 21 August the advanced troops carried on the shipping made contact with troops of the 1st Far Eastern Front near Harbin – having covered no less than 500 miles in a campaign of twelve days' duration – a great feat.

The Japanese now began to surrender area by area – and apart from the seizure of southern Sakhalin Island by a combined land and amphibious attack (11–25 August), and a 49-vessel, one-divisional attack from the sea against the northern Kurile Islands (18 August – 3 September), the lightning campaign came to its conclusion with complete Soviet success.

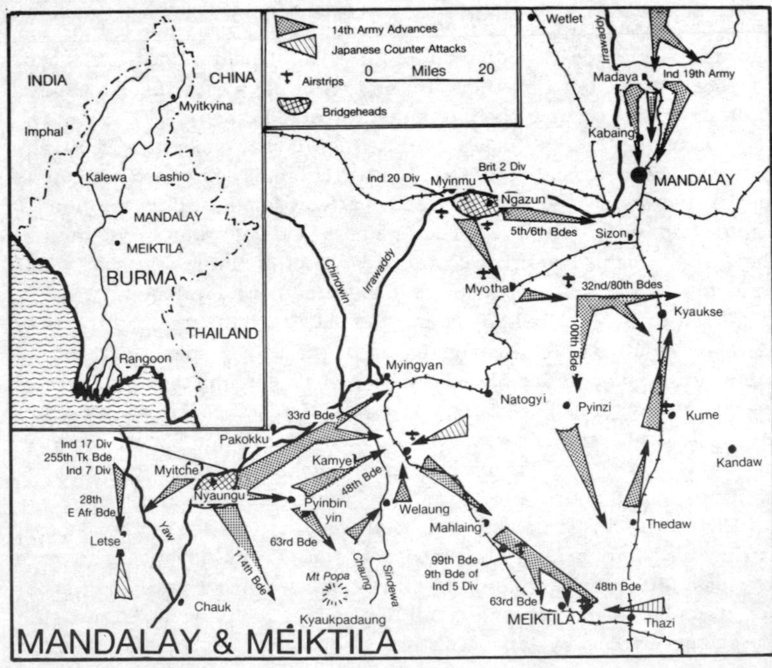

Mandalay-Meiktila

Date: 14 January – 31 March 1945.

Location: Central Burma, along the Irrawaddy River and on the plain to its south and east.

Object: The Allies were determined to defeat the main Japanese forces in central Burma and thus ensure the safety of the new Ledo road-link with China to the north and also facilitate the reconquest of the rest of Burma.

Opposing sides: (a) General Sir William Slim commanding the British Fourteenth Army; (b) General Hyotaro Kimura commanding the three armies of the Japanese imperial forces.

Forces engaged: (a) British XXXIII Corps and IV Corps, two armoured brigades and six infantry divisions, and General Stilwell's Northern Area Combat Command (commanded by Generals Wedemeyer and Sultan), two Chinese Divisions. Total: approx. 250,000 troops; (b) One Tank Regiment and five and a half infantry divisions (General Katamura's reinforced Japanese Fifteenth Army). Total: approx. 60,000 troops.

Casualties: (a) estimated 35,000 troops; (b) estimated 45,000 troops.

Result: The total defeat of Kimura's forces, and the opening up of Central Burma to the Allies and the pursuit of the Japanese to Rangoon.

Suggested reading: S. W. Kirby. *The War Against Japan* vol. 4 (London, 1956); J. Masters. *The Road Past Mandalay* (London, 1961); W. Slim. *Defeat into Victory* (London, 1956); B. Pitt (ed.). *The Purnell History of the Second World War* vol. 6, No. 5 (London, 1968).

Following the great defensive victory of Kohima-Imphal, the Allies began to plan an offensive. The need to secure the route of the Ledo or 'New China Road', still under construction to relink Nationalist China with India by land, was a major inducement to carry the war into Central Burma without delay and drive the Japanese south. General 'Vinegar Joe' Stilwell's Northern Area Combat Command (mainly Chinese in composition) was almost ready to march on Myitkina, aided by the famous formation 'Merrill's Marauders', while behind him the engineers and a huge labour force slaved to build the vital all-weather road-link to China on which the material support of Chiang Kai-shek's forces in large measure depended. The 'Old Burma Road' was also eventually reopened on 27 January 1945 as the Japanese were pushed back in north Burma.

Slim pursued the remnant of the Japanese Fifteenth Army back to the valley of the River Chindwin by September. Defying advice, the commander of British Fourteenth Army decided to give the foe no rest during the impending monsoon, but with Supreme Commander Lord Louis Mountbatten's full support overrode Lieutenant-General Sir Oliver Leese's (the Army Group Commander's) misgivings and campaigned on 'in the wet'. The new Japanese commander, Hoyatoro Kimura, had received some reinforcements, and hoped in due course to lure Slim over the Irrawaddy. He would get his wish but not in the form he desired. So it was that through late November Slim fought his way forward to force three crossings over the Chindwin by 3 December – the Japanese falling back before him. The Allies were aided by the complete air superiority General George E. Stretmeyer's Eastern Air Command had established before the monsoon broke. Then, in mid-December, the British XV Corps advanced down the Arakan coast to take Akyab, while Slim planned his next major move. He had by now realized that the Japanese did not intend to fight west, but east, of the great Irrawaddy – so the daunting prospect of an opposed river-crossing had to be faced.

By the new Fourteenth Army plan, British XXXIII Corps was to force a crossing north and west of Mandalay to attract Japanese reserves, while, at the right moment, British IV Corps, moving up concealed by the Gangaw valley, was to cross the Irrawaddy much farther south near Pakokku – there to march on the Japanese supply and communications centre of Meiktila (the support-base for the Japanese 15th and 33rd Armies with a complex of six airfields) far in rear, it was hoped, of the main fighting. Everything would depend on surprise if the 'hammer and anvil' concept was to succeed. Although signals deception worked well, the withdrawal of 75 Dakotas to help with a crisis in China did not assist Slim's preparations, but somehow all was achieved – including the building of many barges for the crossing. Already Slim's lines of communication stretched behind him for more than 560 miles to the railhead of Dimapur. Much logistical extemporisation was called for: 'We do the impossible immediately; miracles take a little longer,' was the slogan.

By the second week of January the preliminary moves and build-up of supplies was complete – and still the foe had no idea of what was about to befall. On 9 January 1945, forward patrols of 19th Division (part of XXXIII Corps) reached the Irrawaddy near Thabeikkyin, while IV Corps approached Pakokku. Slim now had better air support, and could finalize his plan. First over the river would be 19th Division, north of Mandalay, supported by 36th Division and NCAC beyond. The second XXXIII Corps crossing would be west of Mandalay by 20th Division, later supported by the 2nd. Third and last – synchronized if possible with 20th Division's crossing, IV Corps' 7th Division would pass over south of Mandalay. Slim was confident that the Japanese would not be able to block all three attempts. The first operation began on the 14th and, as was expected and hoped, attracted most of Kimura's attention as two Japanese divisions and the artillery of two more moved north. On the 22nd General Gracey was at Monywa, and 20th Division's crossings began on the night of 12/13 February. It was bitterly opposed by the Japanese 33rd Division, but when 2nd Division came in on the act on the 25th at Ngazun, ten miles east of 20th Division, the Japanese position became untenable. Meanwhile IV Corps was fast approaching Pakokku, covering 350 miles of road to do so. On 3 February 7th Indian Division captured the town, and prepared for the major river crossing. There was no sign of an enemy, so on the night of 13 February the transfer began, taking seven hours to complete. Enemy forces were reported to be in Pagan, but turned out to be only units of the Indian National Army, who surrendered at once. Slim's deception plan had worked; no major enemy counter-attack had taken place.

By this time all of Kimura's attention had been absorbed by the double threat to Mandalay posed by XXXIII Corps. All of eight Japanese divisions were now involved, plus one and a half of renegade Indian troops. Slim called up 5th Indian Division to redress the balance. The 17th Division entered 7th Division's bridgehead with 255 Tank Brigade, and on the 21st the move on Meiktila began. Four days later Thabutkun airstrip was rushed, and that permitted 99 Brigade's fly-in to begin on the 26th, together with fuel for the tanks. Meiktila, garrisoned by 3,300 Japanese under General Kasuya, put up a strong defence. The crisis had come: Kimura was facing XXXIII Corps while Kasuya concentrated against IV Corps. At the worst possible moment it was proposed to withdraw NCAC's Chinese troops and their supporting Dakotas, but Slim won a postponement of this until April. Then, on 3 March, Meiktila fell, including its airfield.

The trap had now closed behind Kimura. In desperation he sent Lieutenant-General Honda with parts of four divisions to regain Meiktila, and a series of violent Japanese counter-attacks had to be beaten back. Then 5th Indian Division was flown in at the critical moment on the 17th. The main airfield changed hands twice that day, but by the 29th it was unquestionably in British hands – and Kimura was truly doomed. On 1 April British 36th Division arrived from the north to relieve the exhausted 19th Division, and this permitted the Chinese to be pulled back. All this time the battle for Mandalay was intensifying: on 15 March Mandalay Hill and Fort Dufferin were massively attacked, and on the 21st the Japanese in Mandalay surrendered. The road to the south and Rangoon lay open before Slim; a great, decisive victory had been won.

Midway

Date: 4–6 June 1942.

Location: The Midway Islands are in the central Pacific Ocean, 1,100 miles west of Oahu (Pearl Harbor).

Object: The Japanese were seeking to extend the line of Pacific islands under their control by taking Midway so as to safeguard their main conquests in Asia.

Opposing sides: (a) Admiral Chester Nimitz commanding the American Pacific Fleet; (b) Admiral Isoruku Yamamoto commanding the Japanese Imperial Combined Fleet.

Forces engaged: (a) 76 warships including three fleet carriers, and the Midway land-based air defence forces. Total: approx. 250 carrier aircraft and 109 land-based; (b) 162 warships including four fleet and two light carriers, and twelve troop transports. Total: approx. 280 carrier aircraft, and 51,000 troops.

Casualties: (a) One fleet carrier, one destroyer, 132 aircraft, 307 men; (b) Four fleet carriers, one heavy cruiser, 275 aircraft, 3,500 men.

Result: In one of history's most decisive naval battles, the Japanese advance over the Pacific was checked and turned back, the USA regaining the strategic initiative at sea. Fatal blows to the Japanese were the loss of four fleet carriers in a battle fought wholly by aircraft.

Suggested reading: S. E. Morrison. *History of United States Naval Operations in World War Two* vol. 2 (Boston, 1962); H. P. Willmott. *The Barrier and the Javelin* (Annapolis, 1984); B. Pitt (ed.). *The Purnell History of the Second World War* vol.3, No. 4 (London, 1967).

Pearl Harbor had won the Japanese a great advantage in the Pacific region, but in Admiral Nagumo's failure to destroy the American aircraft carriers lay the seeds of future defeat. On 7 and 8 May 1942, the battle of the Coral Sea had thwarted a Japanese intention to seize Port Moresby – the first naval battle carried out wholly by carrier aircraft, the capital ships never coming within gunnery range. The Americans lost the carrier *Lexington* and had the *Yorktown* badly damaged, but the Japanese lost many more naval aircraft and sustained serious damage to one carrier, *Shokaku*, in what was essentially a drawn battle. Just one month later, however, a decisive naval engagement was to occur.

The initiative was again in the hands of the great Japanese admiral, Yamamoto. Believing (wrongly) that the Americans would not be able to pit aircraft carriers against him, he drew up a complex plan for a naval-supported invasion of the Midway Islands. To shield this, a diversionary attack against the Aleutian Islands was to be mounted by 21 ships, including two light carriers – which, it was hoped, would distract Admiral Nimitz's attention. Meanwhile Vice-Admiral Kondo would sail with the invasion force, 37 vessels including one light carrier of the Second Fleet, escorting twelve large troop transports, to attack Midway. Nagumo's First Carrier Strike Force – four fleet carriers – was to give air cover for the Midway attack, while two screens totalling eighteen submarines kept a close watch on Midway for any sign of the Americans sailing to intercept either the Aleutians or Midway-bound squadrons. Finally, the main force under Yamamoto – seven battleships, five cruisers and twelve destroyers –

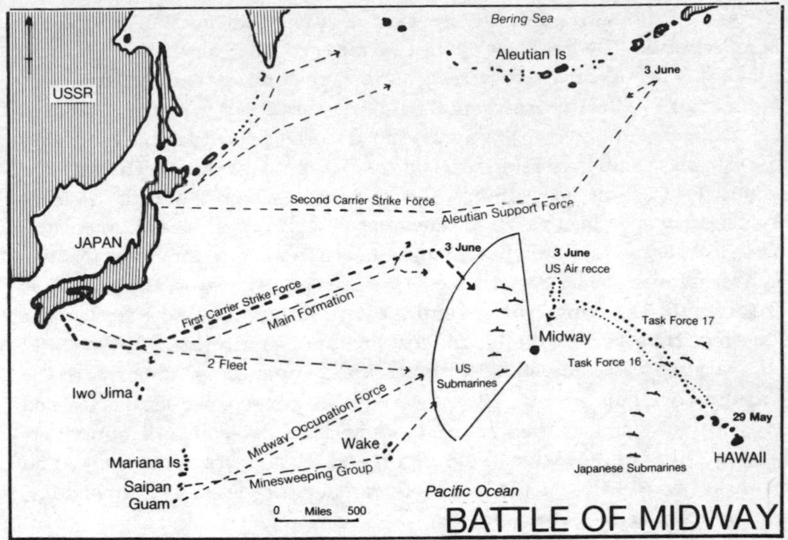

would place itself in a central position ready to give battle to the American fleet, once Nimitz's counter-move became apparent. But the various elements were too widely separated.

Possession of radio-intercepts and deciphered codes gave Nimitz a good overall idea of what was to happen. From the outset he determined to leave the Aleutians' defence to the North Pacific Fleet (Rear Admiral Robert A. Theobald), and ordered his main force to sea – divided into two Task Forces: No. 16 (Rear Admiral Raymond Spruance) including the carriers *Hornet* and *Enterprise* and No. 18 (Rear Admiral Frank J. Fletcher, including the rapidly repaired carrier *Yorktown*), to protect Midway. Nimitz exercised strategic command from the island itself.

The Japanese Northern Force under Admiral Hosogaya captured two islands in the Aleutians on 3–7 June, but the main American naval forces remained steadfastly north-west of Midway, which Yamamoto, Nagumo and Kondo were rapidly approaching by late on the 3rd. At 0430 hours on the 4th, Nagumo launched his first raid against Midway, and prepared a second strike armed with torpedoes and armour-piercing bombs ready to attack naval targets. Almost simultaneously, American land-based aircraft took off from Midway to meet the in-coming raid. The Japanese had the better of the mêlée that followed, and broke through to inflict serious damage on Midway, while the Americans failed to damage the Japanese carriers. Nagumo had been informed that a second raid on Midway would be needed, and at 0700 hours ordered his second-strike aircraft to be re-armed with suitable bombs. This was half-completed when news was received from a reconnaissance aircraft that ten American ships were closing from the north-east. No carrier was identified, so Nagumo concentrated on defeating the American air attack with all his fighters.

At 0820 hours the Admiral received positive identification of a carrier being with the US force, just as the rearming of his aircraft for the island attack was being completed. His fighters were circling ready to land, and, worst of all, the first aircraft sent to Midway were about to return. Placed in a considerable quandary, Nagumo decided to give priority to the returning aircraft and thereafter attend to the American naval threat. His carriers changed direction accordingly. As a result, when the first wave of American dive-bombers arrived they missed their prey. The next wave was more fortunate – and soon the Japanese carriers were under attack by dive-bombers, torpedo-carriers and escorting fighters. However, the protective fire from the escorting cruisers and the Zero fighters was so effective that the Americans scored no hits, and lost 35 out of 41 aircraft.

Nagumo was well-pleased with this apparent success, and ordered the rearming of all his aircraft. His carriers' decks were consequently crowded with aircraft when, at 1025 hours, the American dive-bombers found their targets. Five minutes later *Kaga, Akagi* and *Soryu* were all sinking – and the naval war in the Pacific had been transformed. Disaster, not victory, was now facing the Japanese.

Only the carrier *Hiryu* remained operational. Shortly after midday, its aircraft found the *Yorktown*, and over the next two-and-a-half hours scored a number of telling hits. At 1500 hours, Admiral Fletcher ordered the carrier to be abandoned, and transferred his flag to a cruiser. Meanwhile the flights from *Enterprise* had located *Hiryu*, and by 1700 hours she in her turn had been battered into a smoking wreck (and was scuttled). Attempts to save the badly damaged *Yorktown* came to an end on 6 June when she was torpedoed by a Japanese submarine, and sank.

Meanwhile, Yamamoto was striving to bring the Americans to surface-action, in which he would have enjoyed a considerable superiority. Admiral Spruance (to whom Fletcher had handed-over full command after the evacuation of the *Yorktown*), however, manoeuvred with great skill, pursuing the Japanese by day and avoiding their ambushes by night. As fuel was running low, Yamamoto had ordered a retreat towards Japan early on the 6th, and a number of further American air strikes were launched which caused some damage to the Japanese fleet. Spruance called off the pursuit, his fuel in turn running low, and headed for Pearl Harbor.

The Americans lost only two vessels (USS *Yorktown* and its towing destroyer) to the Japanese four fleet carriers and one heavy cruiser sunk. The Japanese had lost twice the number of aircraft and, worse, their skilled aircrews who were irreplaceable; more, they had lost the war at sea – and naval warfare had been changed for ever.

Moscow

Date: 8 October 1941 – 30 April 1942.

Location: West and south of the capital of the USSR.

Object: Hitler was pressing for the capture of the Soviet capital in the hope that this would lead to Stalin's fall and the possible collapse of Soviet resistance.

Opposing sides: (a) Marshal Stalin in command of the forces of the Soviet Union, and Marshals Timoshenko and (later) Georgei Zhukov commanding the West Front; (b) Field Marshal Walter von Reichenau (under Hitler) until 7 December, CinC, Wehrmacht in Russia.

Forces engaged: (a) Marshal Zhukov and the forces massed to defend Moscow, 100 divisions. Total: 1,000,000 Russians; (b) Field Marshal Fedor von Bock, and (later) Field Marshal Günther von Kluge, commanding the Army Group Centre of 60 divisions. Total: 750,000 Germans.

Casualties: (a) 680,000 Russian troops; (b) 340,000 German troops.

Result: The German failure to capture Moscow, and the success of the Russian counter-offensive, marked one of the most significant turning-points in the war on the Eastern Front.

Suggested reading: Alan Clarke. *Barbarossa* (London, 1965); J. Erickson. *The Road to Stalingrad* (London, 1975); D. P. Chaney. *Zhukov* (New York, 1972); B. Pitt (ed.). *The Purnell History of the Second World War* vol. 2, Nos. 10 & 11 (London, 1967).

After the great success at Kiev, Hitler ordered the resumption of the drive on Moscow, 200 miles away, by Army Group Centre. Great stress was laid on the need to take the Soviet capital before the full onset of winter, but time lost earlier in the year was not to be made up.

The first phase of the new offensive began on 8 October, when Guderian's Second Panzergruppe seized Orel, Chern and Tula in turn – coming to within 100 miles of Moscow. At the same time, Hoth's Fourth, and (from the northern sector) Hoeppner's Third Panzergruppen had eliminated some 600,000 Russian troops by a bold envelopment at Vyazma by 13 October, and pressed on for the Line of Mozhaysk (running from Kaluga to Kalinin) barely 50 miles west of the objective. The Third Panzergruppen (now commanded by Reinhardt) occupied Kalinin two days later while Guderian took Kaluga on the 21st. The Soviet Government (but not Stalin) left Moscow for the Volga as von Kluge closed to within 40 miles of the city. But then heavy rains brought the German advance to a halt.

The first hard frosts permitted a new phase to open on 16 November. Six days later leading German elements were at Istra, fifteen miles from Moscow. At Tula, 100 miles to the south, another large Russian force was surrounded. Meanwhile, in the north, Guderian fought to within sight of Moscow, and the 258th Infantry Division entered the suburbs, but were repulsed by armed factory workers in early December. Within sight of success, the combination of hard frosts, petrol shortages, and fanatical Russian fighting for the Moscow Defence Line, ground the Germans to a halt. On 5 December, a furious Hitler abandoned the Moscow offensive until the following spring, and began a wholesale purge of his commanders.

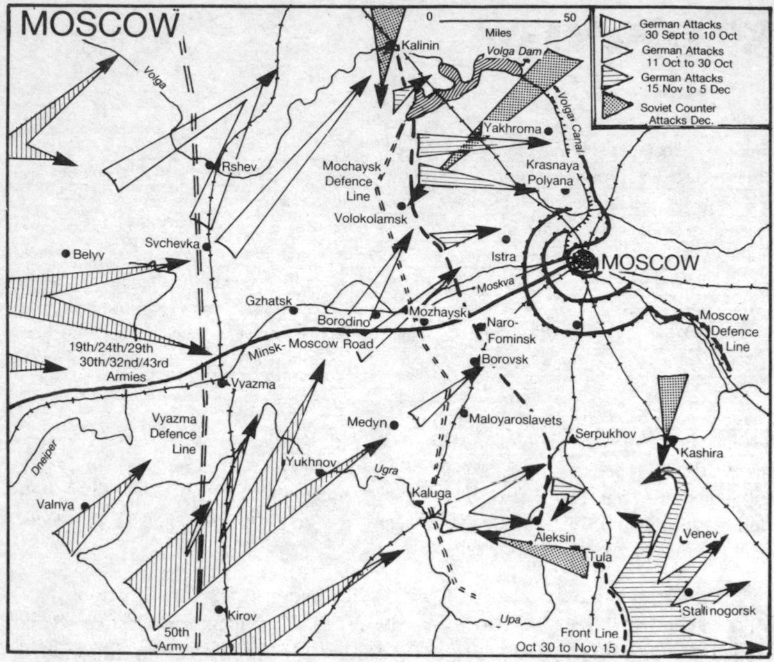

On 6 December Stalin appointed Zhukov in Timoshenko's place, and the new commander lost no time in launching a massive Red Army counter-offensive – and so started the final phase of the Battle of Moscow. Ski-troops assaulted Guderian's command post at Tula on 9 December, followed by massed divisions, and regained some ground, Hitler promptly replaced Guderian by Schmidt, refusing any permission to retreat. But the Russians, more used to winter warfare, continued to regain ground. A herculean battle raged around Kaluga, but the Red Army finally secured it on 30 December. The Russians were back in Mozhaysk by 18 January 1942. By this date they had advanced 200 miles to the north of Moscow, and only a little less to its south. Von Kluge fell back to Vyazma in the centre and Rzhev in the north – some 125 miles from Moscow. Here a complex series of hedgehog all-round defensive positions halted the Russians, and amidst freezing conditions their advance in turn petered out. Moscow had been saved – but at horrendous cost to both armies. Since June the Red Army had lost well over 4,000,000 casualties, the Germans probably more than 1,000,000. War on such a scale was unique.

Narvik

Date: 10 and 13 April; and 24 April – 9 June 1940.

Location: Northern Norway; Narvik stands on the Vestforjorden.

Object: In the naval engagement, the Royal Navy set out to destroy the German warships in the fiord; in the land battle, the Allies challenged German control of the port and area, but ultimately had to be evacuated.

Opposing sides: (a) General Nikolaus von Falkenhorst commanding the Wehrmacht; (b) Admiral Lord Cork and Orrery commanding the Allied Narvik Expedition, with General H. Massey directing operations from London.

Forces engaged: Infantry and mountain troops forming part of the German invasion force. Total: approx. 20,000 by early June; (b) 5,000 Norwegian troops joined by some 20,000 British, French and Poles. Total: approx. 26,000 (Narvik sector) by late May.

Casualties: (a) approx. 1,300 Germans; (b) approx. 5,000 Allies.

Result: The completion of the German conquest of Norway.

Suggested Reading: J. L. Moulton. *The Norwegian Campaign of 1940* (London, 1966); Lord Strabolgi. *Narvik and After* (London, *c.* 1942); B. Pitt (ed.). *The Purnell History of the Second World War* vol. 1, No. 6 (London, 1966).

Germany's desire to secure Swedish iron-ore supplies caused Hitler to invade both Denmark and Norway on 9 April 1940. Little resistance was encountered in Denmark, but the Norwegians fought back, and the German capture of Oslo and six sea-ports was costly. At Narvik (terminus of the Lapland Railway to Sweden), ten German destroyers landed 2,000 troops in a successful surprise attack as part of the overall invasion.

The Royal Navy (which had already taken a toll of Norwegian-bound German shipping) sent Captain Warburton-Lee and six destroyers in a raid up the Vestforjorden to surprise the German naval forces off Narvik. In a spirited engagement on the 10th, the British sank two German destroyers and damaged more before withdrawing, for a loss of two vessels. Three days later the battleship HMS *Warspite* and nine destroyers returned to the scene of action and eliminated the eight remaining German destroyers.

As the Norwegians fought on amidst the hills and mountains, British, French and Free Polish forces were being sent to their assistance. Despite marked German air superiority, a number of successful landings were made from 15 to 18 April, at Aandalesnes, Namsos and Harstad (close by Narvik). This last force comprised the 24th Guards Brigade, French and Polish troops and (later) the British 6th Division, under Major-General Mackesy, with Admiral Lord Cork and Orrery in overall command. Once again German air attacks were heavy, and disagreements between the admiral and the general as to how to exploit the landing – the former wanting a bold attack on Narvik, the latter a more cautious consolidation – caused valuable days to slip by, while valiant Norwegian troops fought on

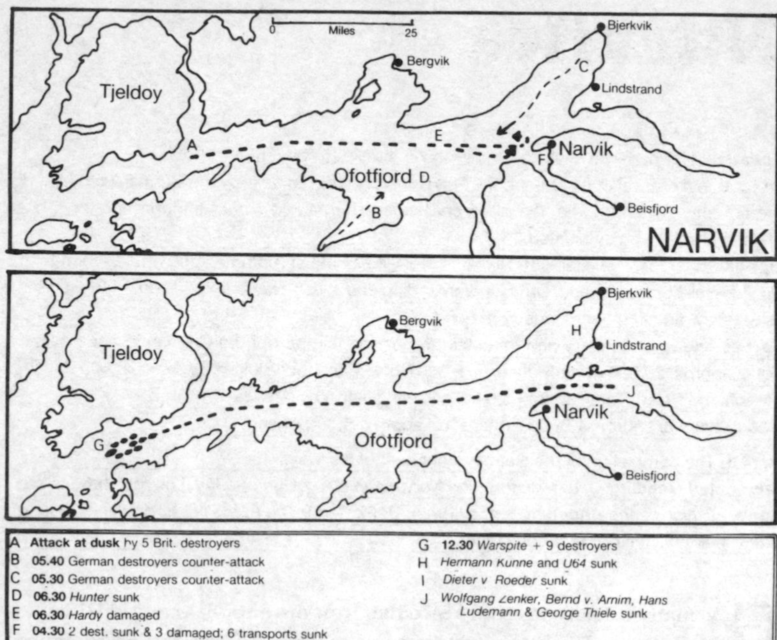

in the mountains under General Fleischer. Some 6,000 Germans were besieged in Narvik itself.

Further south the Germans had reacted vigorously to the threats to Trondheim constituted by Major-General Bernard Paget's two brigades at Aandalesnes and Lieutenant-General Carton de Wiat's force operating from Namsos. In due course both bridgeheads had to be re-embarked in early May – but not before King Haakon of Norway, most of his ministers and much gold bullion had been safely shipped to England from Molde near Aandalesnes.

At last the 20,000 Allies around Narvik began to move. Lieutenant-General Claude Auchinleck had assumed command on land from 12 May. French Foreign Legionaries approached Narvik on 13 May, and the town fell to the Allies on the 28th. However, the arrival of the German 2nd Mountain Division and continual Luftwaffe air attacks checked exploitation inland.

Meanwhile the Battle for France was at a critical stage, and the British and French Governments decided that their troops must pull out of Norway. The embarkation was completed on 8 June. Next day, Norway capitulated. The Allied intervention had been 'too little, too late'.

Okinawa

Date: 1 April – 22 June 1945.

Location: Okinawa is the southernmost island of the Japanese Archipelago.

Object: The start of the conquest of the Japanese homeland was an important step towards achieving an Allied final victory in the Far East.

Opposing sides: (a) Admiral Chester Nimitz and General MacArthur, Allied Supreme Commander; (b) General Mitsuru Ushijima commanding the Japanese defence.

Forces engaged: (a) General Simon Buckner Jnr.'s US Tenth Army, three marine divisions and three infantry divisions. Total: approx. 150,000 men; (b) General Ushijima's Japanese 32nd Army and associated forces. Total: 120,000 men.

Casualties: (a) approx. 40,000 men; (b) 100,000 killed and 10,000 taken prisoner.

Result: The capture of Okinawa was dearly bought, but was psychologically important as it involved the occupation of Japanese native soil. The loses incurred convinced Truman of the need to use the atomic bombs later in the year.

Suggested reading: S. E. Morison. *US Naval Operations in World War Two* (Boston, 1962); C. Nichols and H. Shaw. *Okinawa, Victory in the Pacific* (New York, 1955); J. A. Isely and P. A. Crowl. *The US Marines and Amphibious War* (Princeton, 1956); B. Pitt (ed.). *The Purnell History of the Second World War* vol. 6, No. 12 (London, 1968).

As the perimeter of the Japanese 'Co-Prosperity Sphere' began to crumble the American planners in the Pacific had to address the problem of conquering Japan itself. The redoubtable reputation of the Japanese soldier was not comforting: the war might be won at sea (apart from the continuing *Kamikaze* threat), and the air war dominated, but the prospect of conquering Imperial Japan yard by yard against fanatical opposition was hardly attractive.

Operation 'Iceberg' was to be the first stage in the conquest of the Japanese homeland – a process that was expected to extend well into 1946 if not beyond. The Japanese strategy was to hold the Naha-Shuri-Yonabaru Line across the southern fifth of the island to the last, while massive *Kamikaze* attacks destroyed the US 5th Fleet off-shore. Admiral Nimitz deployed Admiral Turner's amphibious assault force, the key component of which was the experienced General Buckner's US Tenth Army. The preliminary phase envisaged heavy air attacks to neutralize Japanese air bases on Formosa and other islands together with softening-up raids against Okinawa itself. On 26 March the Kerama and Keise Islands off south-west Okinawa were occupied – and all was almost ready for the main landing on the beaches around Hagushi on the west coast of the island, ten miles north of the main Japanese defence line.

As the fleets assembled the Japanese *Kamikaze* offensive opened. So effective, however, were the counter-measures that had been devised (mainly carefully coordinated and 'boxed' anti-aircraft fire), that of 196 suicide sorties only 27 penetrated the wall of fire to reach a target. This was encouraging given the damage that had been sustained in the previous year.

On 1 April the invasion began. The US III Amphibious Corps landed north of Hagushi, the US XXIV Corps to its south, and by nightfall 50,000 men were ashore in a bridgehead eight miles by four. Two days later and a corridor had been forced to the east coast, isolating Okinawa's main positions. For the next three weeks the main attention of the III Amphibious Corps was taken up in clearing the rest of the 794 square-mile island lying north of the Japanese prepared lines, a process completed for fairly heavy loss by 20 April. But the main battle had still to be won.

Meanwhile US XXIV Corps had been fighting a desperate battle to close with the main Japanese positions. By 8 April Japanese resistance had become ferocious, and the US 7th (left) and 96th (right) Divisions made only very slow progress: every yard had to be contended for. When the 27th Division was brought into the action on the west coast approaches on the 19th, a major battle opened that lasted for twelve days, but only secured the Americans two miles of ground. The battered 27th and 96th American divisions had to be rested, and so the III Amphibious Corps was reassigned the right wing, and the 77th Division was brought up to aid the XXIV Corps on the left.

Early May saw a major Japanese counter-offensive, as Ushijima attacked strongly against Tenth Army's eastern flank. This proved an error, for by leaving their strong positions the Japanese exposed themselves to the superior American artillery and air attacks in the open, and more than 6,200 were killed for an American loss of 714 casualties during the two days (4 and 5 May) of the attack. Despite drenching monsoon rains, Buckner resumed the offensive on the 11th, bringing in the rested 96th to relieve the tired 7th Division on the extreme left. A battle of meat-grinder attrition followed, as the Americans penetrated the Japanese positions bunker by bunker, but on 23 May a major success was achieved when the 6th Marine Division successfully turned the Japanese left flank capturing Naha. Six days later, the 6th Marine Division stormed Shuri Castle in the centre, while XXIV Corps managed to achieve a break-through on the east. The Japanese position was clearly crumbling.

The Japanese soldier is never more formidable than when facing defeat, and so the Americans decided to launch another body-blow by using their total maritime and amphibious supremacy to launch another major landing. So on 4 June the US 6th Marine Division made a shore-to-shore assault on the Oroku Peninsula south of Naha to penetrate still deeper behind the collapsing Japanese front. It took ten more days of fearful fighting to clear the tenacious enemy from the peninsula, but eventually the 8th Regiment was able to join in the main southward advance towards the southernmost tip of Okinawa. A major blow was the death, on 18 June, of General Buckner – and he was replaced by Marine General Roy Geiger for the last stages of the battle. On the 21st American marines reached the

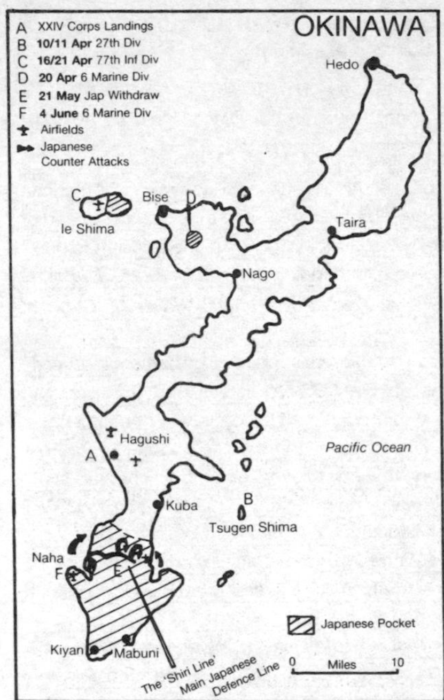

south of the island – but it still remained to wipe out pockets of fanatical resistance inland, a process that was declared complete on 2 July.

The Japanese 32nd Army had been wiped out, but at horrendous cost to the Americans, who lost 8,513 killed and 31,807 wounded. Japanese civilian casualties had also been heavy.

All this time the battle at sea had been continuing. The Japanese air force was making a supreme effort, but some 1,900 *Kamikaze* sorties throughout the whole period managed to sink only 36 US ships and damage in varying degree almost 370 more. The USN lost 4,900 sailors killed and as many more wounded, but by the end of the battle an estimated 7,800 Japanese aircraft had been destroyed for an American loss of 763 aircraft. In addition to their loss of all initiative at sea, the Japanese had now effectively lost the power to intervene in the air.

The Allies braced themselves for the next assault – due to be launched against Kyushu Island in November. General 'Vinegar Joe' Stilwell arrived from south-east Asia to take over US Tenth Army, and plans were afoot for the transfer of the US First Army from north-western Europe – to form an Army Group under General Douglas MacArthur's overall command. But developments in the New Mexico desert were destined to forestall the need to undertake the next stage of the conquest of Japan – and six weeks after the ending of the battle of Okinawa the Japanese Emperor Hirohito would announce the unconditional surrender of his country.

Pearl Harbor

Date: 7 December 1941.

Location: The island of Oahu in the Hawaiian Group, central Pacific Ocean.

Object: The Japanese Imperial Fleet and Naval Air Arm planned to destroy the American Pacific Fleet in its base by means of a surprise pre-emptive strike, and thus gain command of the seas and a high measure of strategic primacy throughout the Asian and Pacific regions.

Opposing sides: (a) Vice-Admiral Chuichi Nagumo commanding the First Air Fleet; (b) Admiral Husband E. Kimmel commanding the US Pacific Fleet and General Walter C. Short in command of the American garrison.

Forces engaged: (a) Six Japanese fleet and two light carriers supported by battleships, heavy cruisers and supporting flotilla. Total: 360 aircraft; (b) Eight US battleships, twelve cruisers and flotilla. Total: 250 Marine Corps and 231 Army Air Force aircraft (all operating from airfields).

Casualties: (a) Five midget submarines and 29 aircraft – approx. 110 Japanese; (b) Four battleships sunk or capsized, three light cruisers, three destroyers and other light craft sunk; remaining battleships and many other vessels badly damaged; 65 USAAF and 196 USMC aircraft destroyed – approx. 3,226 Americans killed and 1,272 wounded.

Result: The entry of the USA into the Second World War; the effective neutralization of the American Pacific Fleet except for its three carriers, which were at sea, earned Japan a year of naval supremacy, making possible the conquest of South-East Asia.

Suggested reading: S. E. Morison. *History of United States Naval Operations in World War Two* vol. 1 (Boston, 1962); H. P. Willmott. *Pearl Harbor* (London, 1980); H. P. Willmott. *Empires in the Balance* (Annapolis, 1984); B. Pitt (ed.). *The Purnell History of the Second World War* vol. 2, No. 12 (London, 1967).

Tension between the USA and Japan had been rising for a considerable period, but the continuation of negotiations at governmental level led many to hope that peace might be preserved. However, the government of General Tojo ordered the Japanese Imperial Navy under Admiral Isoruku Yamamoto to prepare a strategic plan for both the elimination of the American Pacific Fleet and the conquest of South-East Asia.

Vice-Admiral Nagumo sailed from Japan in great secrecy on 26 November 1941, and by 6 December was within air-strike range of Pearl Harbor. Although it was common knowledge that war was imminent, and some indications of a possible surprise attack had been received, the Americans were still observing peacetime routine. There were no patrols operating although an unidentified submarine had been depth-charged in the harbour, and the radar operators were stood down after the dawn-watch. All was at typical Sunday-morning routine on 'Battleship Row'.

The Japanese launched their first strike of 183 aircraft from a point 275 miles north of Pearl Harbor. Shortly before 0800 hours, they attacked the harbour and a neighbouring airfield, followed by a second wave of 170 aircraft forty minutes later. The havoc they wrought was immense. Bombs and torpedoes accounted for large numbers of undispersed American aircraft and, above all, for the battleships *Arizona* (which blew up), *West Virginia* and *California* (both of which sank at their moorings), and

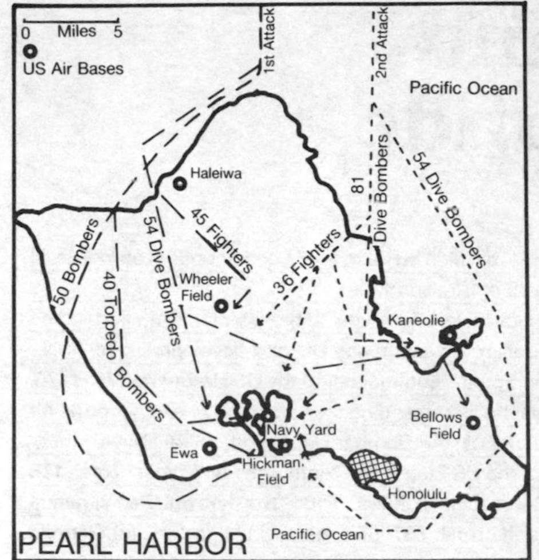

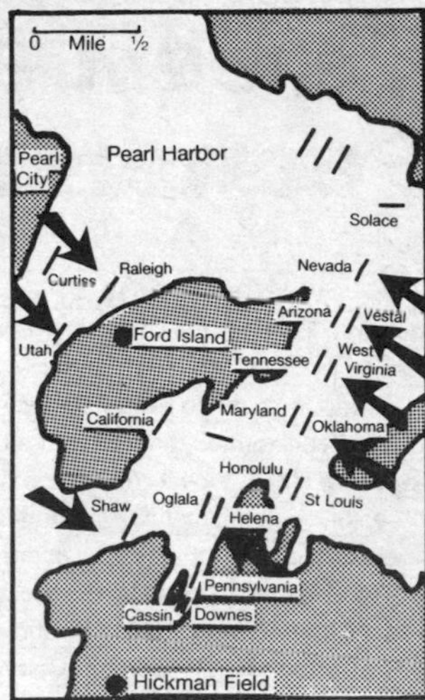

Oklahoma (which capsized). Much damage was also inflicted on the remaining four capital ships and other naval vessels and installations.

Although the attack had been well-planned and boldly executed, it failed to complete its mission. The three US fleet carriers were absent from Pearl Harbor on an exercise, and Nagumo decided against launching a third strike to seek them out. The Japanese also failed to destroy the oil tanks – the loss of which would have fully crippled what was left of the US Pacific Fleet. The blow was infamous in that it was launched in time of peace without warning, and it permitted Japan to commence its period of conquest. Moreover, as Yamamoto warned his superiors, that success was likely to be limited to one year's duration.

Ploesti and Peenemunde

Date: 1 and 17/18 August 1943.

Location: Ploesti is the centre of a group of oilfields in Roumania; Peenemunde is an industrial town on the Baltic coast of Germany, east of Stralsund.

Object: In the case to Ploesti to destroy oil installations vital to the German war effort; in the case of Peenemunde, to destroy the German V-weapon test site and development centre.

Opposing sides: Ploesti (a) General Carl Spaatz, commander of the US North-West Africa Air Force; (b) Reichsmarschall Hermann Goering, commanding the *Luftwaffe*. Peenemunde (a) Air Chief Marshal Sir Arthur Harris, commander of RAF Bomber Command; (b) As above.

Forces engaged: Ploesti (a) Bombers of the US Eighth and Ninth Army Air Forces. Total: 178 B-24s (Liberators); (b) German and Roumanian fighters. Total: Not known. Peenemunde (a) Squadrons of RAF Bomber Command. Total: 597 Stirlings and Lancasters; (b) German fighters and Flak commands. Total: Not known.

Casualties: Ploesti (a) 54 B-24s and 532 aircrew shot down; (b) Not known, but considerable. Peenemunde (a) 40 RAF bombers destroyed; (b) Not known, but considerable on the ground.

Result: At Ploesti heavy – but repairable – damage was inflicted on the oil refineries, causing a drop in output. At Peenemunde, heavy damage was inflicted which delayed the production of the V-2 rocket.

Suggested reading: Anon. *The Effects of Strategic Bombing on the German War Economy* (Washington, 1954); N. Frankland. *The Bombing Offensive Against Germany* (London, 1965); A. Harris. *The Bomber Offensive* (London, 1947); Hans Rumpf. *The Bombing of Germany* (Bonn, 1963); B. Pitt (ed.). *The Purnell History of the Second World War* vol. 6, No. 2 (London, 1968).

The development of the Allied bomber offensive of Germany was a gradual affair. Before the entry of the United States into the war, the RAF raids were divided between naval, military and industrial targets, mainly attacked by night. The USAAF preferred more accurate daylight bombing. The first RAF 1,000-bomber raid was against Cologne on 30 May 1942, and from August the US Eighth Army Air Force entered the fray. The all-out raids against German centres of industry and population would only develop fully in 1944, but the previous year saw many major raids.

Two that typify the different air philosophies of the Allies are Ploesti and Peenemunde. In the first instance the Liberator bomber with its 2,850-mile range made it possible to strike the Roumanian oil fields from North Africa. The 178 aircraft, each carrying 4,000lb of bombs, reached the targets in two waves, having become unintentionally separated. One force flew over Bucharest, alerting the defences. The first daylight attack was pressed home at low level through heavy flak, but was only partly successful; the main force bombed through the dense pall of smoke covering the Ploesti area, causing extensive fires. A heavy toll was exacted by the defence, and oil output was only temporarily affected. Deadly damage

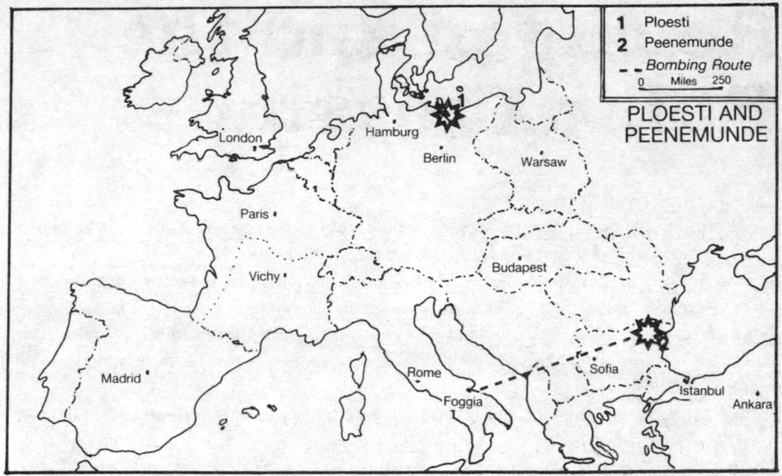

would be inflicted in 1944, but the August attack in 1943 was the first air-raid to penetrate over 1,000 miles into Axis Europe.

'Bomber' Harris's name is usually associated with carpet night-bombing of centres of dense industry and population such as Hamburg or Dresden. On occasion, however, RAF Bomber Command also undertook pin-point raids on highly significant targets. One such was the attack on Peenemunde. Intelligence had revealed that German scientists were fast developing a range of 'Victory' weapons, the V-1 pilotless flying-bomb and the V-2 faster than sound rockets at a secret base near Peenemunde. A large night-raid was mounted on 17/18 August 1943, and in moonlight – aided by radar target-spotting – significant damage was inflicted.

Remagen and the Rhine Crossings

Date: 7–31 March 1945.

Location: At Remagen, midway between Bonn and Koblenz, and later near Boppard, Duisburg, and between Bonn and Mainz for the major crossings.

Object: To force a crossing or series of crossings over the Rhine to expose the Ruhr and German industrial heartland to Allied conquest, ending the war.

Opposing sides: (a) General Dwight D. Eisenhower, SACEUR; (b) Field Marshal Gerd von Rundstedt (soon replaced by Field Marshal Albrecht Kesselring) commanding the German forces in the West.

Forces engaged: (a) Elements of US 21st, 12th and 6th Army Groups; (b) Elements of German Army Groups H, B and G.

Casualties: (a) Overall, 6,570 American and 15,628 British and Canadians; (b) Overall, 90,000 German casualties and 259,000 taken prisoners-of-war.

Result: The crossing of the last great psychological barrier defending Germany from the west, and the near-destruction of the remaining German land forces who were incapable of holding up the Allied final advance.

Suggested reading: K.Hechler. *The Bridge at Remagen* (Edinburgh, 1957); C. P.Stacey. *The Victory Campaign* (Ottawa, 1960); F.de Guingand. *Operation Victory* (London, 1960); B.Pitt (ed.). *The Purnell History of the Second World War* vol. 6, No. 6 (London, 1968).

Following the hard battle in the Ardennes, the bitter winter-weather of 1945 slowed Allied progress towards the Rhine. A ghastly battle was fought in the Reichswald from 8 February to 9 March amidst freezing flood-water which proved the German soldier was still capable of resolute defence of German soil. Gradually the Allies inched-up to the west bank of the Rhine, eliminating pockets of German resistance as they did so. This barrier had a symbolic significance which Dr. Goebbels' propaganda was not slow to exploit, and the Allies were apprehensive.

However, by a fluke of military history, the Ludendorff Railway Bridge at Remagen fell intact into American hands. Advancing from Stadt Meckenheim nine miles to the west of Remagen, Lieutenant Carl Timmerman, of Company A, 27th US Armoured Infantry Battalion, part of General Hodge's US First Army, came upon the undemolished bridge at 1045 hours on 7 March. Directed by Lieutenant Colonel Engeman, his force penetrated the town, and as they approached the bridge at 1440 hours the German defenders attempted to blow it. However, for reasons still undiscovered, the main charges failed to ignite, and when the dust settled the bridge had still not fallen into the Rhine. Sergeant Drabik was first across, closely followed by Timmerman, and while engineers wrestled to defuze the main charges, the Americans created a tiny bridgehead east of the Rhine.

With commendable flexibility, US First Army changed its misson to exploit this unforeseen success (which earned 13 Distinguished Service

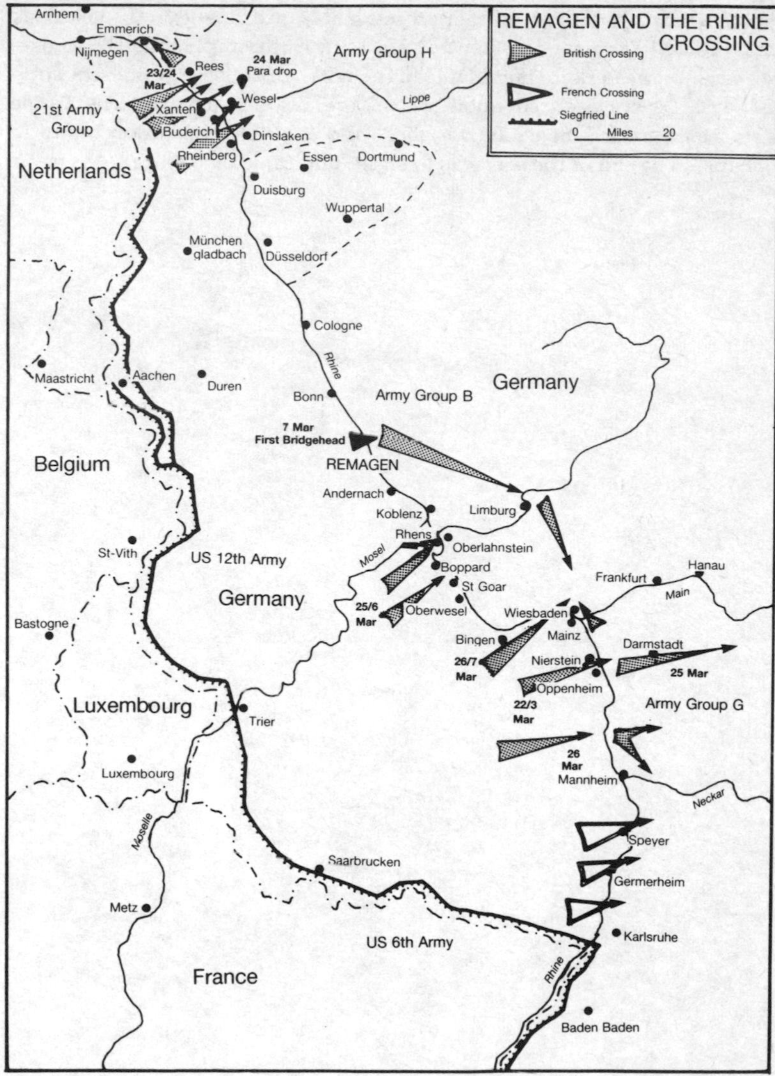

Crosses and a Presidential Citation), and eventually five divisions entered the bridgehead. They were slow to break-out, but the psychological boost was immense for the Allies and devastating for the Germans. Goebbels called it 'a raving scandal', and Hitler sent down a court-martial team which condemned five officers to death (of whom four were shot, but subsequently exonerated). On the 17th the bridge collapsed, but it had served its purpose, and perhaps gained seven days.

Heartened by news of the 'miracle' of Remagen, the main Allied crossings a few weeks later got off to a flying start. On 24 March Patton's

US Third Army secured another crossing at Boppard, and in the last week of March, Montgomery master-minded a hugh crossing, hidden by smoke-screens, between Bonn and Mainz to the north of Duisburg. Subsequently General Devers secured another passage near Strasburg. The Rhine defences were irremediably breached, and cohesive opposition began to collapse. The end of the war was in sight, and came on 9 May.

Repulse and Prince of Wales

Date: 10 December 1941.

Location: Off Kuantan on the east coast of the Malayan Peninsula.

Object: The British capital ships were returning southwards after vainly trying to intercept Japanese invasion convoys heading for Malaya when the Japanese discovered their position and launched heavy air attacks upon them.

Opposing sides: (a) The Japanese air force commander in southern Indo-China; (b) Admiral Sir Tom Phillips commanding the RN Force Z.

Forces engaged: (a) Torpedo-bombers and other elements of the Japanese Imperial Air Force, approx. 70 in all; (b) HMSS *Repulse* and *Prince of Wales* with four escorting destroyers.

Casualties: (a) Not known, but slight; (b) Both capital ships were sunk. Some 2,080 survivors were picked up, but 840 were drowned.

Result: The destruction of the British naval force put the seal on Japanese supremacy at sea in the Far East, and illustrated the vulnerability to air attack of capital ships operating without air cover.

Suggested reading: S. W. Roskill. *The Navy at War* (London, 1960); H. P. Willmott. *Empires in the Balance* (Annapolis, 1984); B. Pitt (ed.). *The Purnell History of the Second World War* vol. 2, No. 13 (London, 1967).

As the situation in the Far East worsened, and the likelihood of war war with Japan increased, in late October 1941 the British War Cabinet decided to send a strong naval deterrent force to Singapore. The new battleship, *Prince of Wales*, and the fast First World War battlecruiser *Repulse*, were selected for the task, and by the plan were to be accompanied by the new aircraft-carrier *Indomitable*. Unfortunately this vessel was under repair after an accident during her working-up trials, but it was still decided to send off the two capital ships with four destroyers in the hope that their presence in the Far East might dissuade the Japanese Government from taking extreme action, or at least provide a telling naval presence in the Indian Ocean.

The squadron, commanded by Admiral Sir Tom Phillips, reached Singapore on 2 December – barely five days before the outbreak of war. Phillips flew to Manila to discuss strategy with the American Admiral Hart on the 5th, but plans were overwhelmed by news of Pearl Harbor. On 8 December Phillips decided to sail north to intercept Japanese invasion convoys, but insisted that surprise and air cover would be vital. As Force Z sailed north on the 9th, it received a message that air-cover over Singora would not be feasible. That evening the ships were spotted by a Japanese aircraft (in fact their position had already been reported by an enemy submarine that afternoon), and Phillips regretfully abandoned his mission and turned south. At midnight, a message indicating a Japanese invasion force heading for Kuantan caused the Admiral to swing west, hoping that Singapore would send air cover without having to be signalled to that effect, breaking radio silence.

On investigation this information proved false, and Force Z again headed away, but at 1119 hours on 10 December nine Japanese bombers attacked. One bomb hit *Repulse*, but not seriously. Then at 1144 hours a second wave of seventeen torpedo-bombers appeared, and two torpedoes struck *Prince of Wales*, seriously damaging her port engine room. She began to list, as at noon a third raid came in. *Repulse* managed to avoid nineteen torpedoes, but Captain Tennant, worried for the flagship, decided to summon air assistance from Singapore, and signalled accordingly. But another large raid swept in, and *Prince of Wales* received four more torpedo hits, and *Repulse* five. Both ships were sinking, and the destroyers closed to take off survivors. Fighters from Singapore arrived at 1320 hours – too late. Force Z had been destroyed, and its commander drowned.

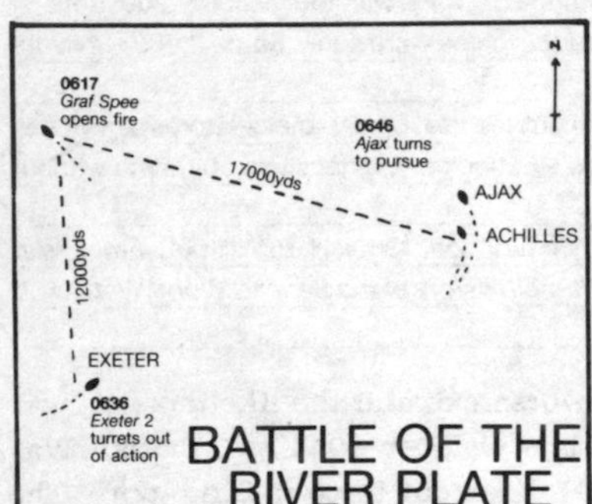

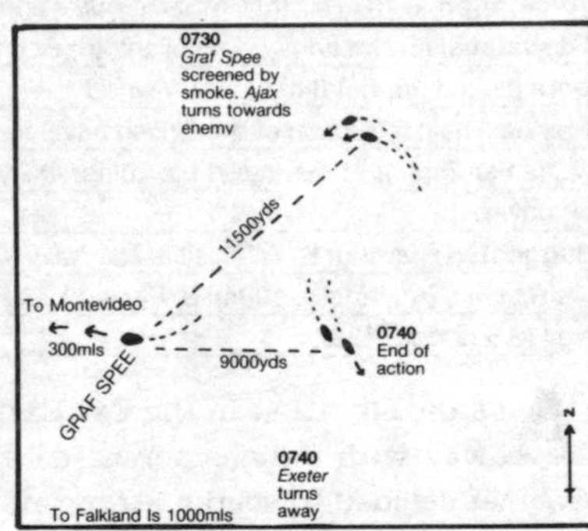

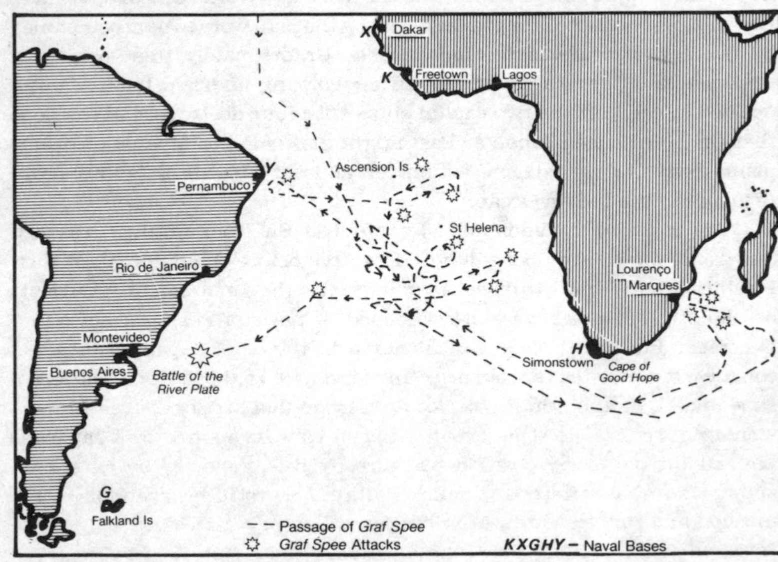

River Plate

Date: 13 December 1939

Location: Off the River Plate estuary, Montevideo, Uruguay, South America.

Object: The Royal Navy was seeking to destroy the German raider, the pocket-battleship *Graf Spee*.

Opposing sides: (a) Commodore Henry Harwood commanding the British squadron; (b) Captain Hans Langsdorff commanding the *Graf Spee*.

Forces in action: (a) HMSS *Exeter* (six 8in guns), *Ajax* and *Achilles* (eight 6in guns each); (b) *Graf Spee* (six 11in and eight 5.9in guns).

Casualties: (a) approx. 150; (b) approx. 50, and 800 interned.

Result: *Graf Spee* scuttled herself on Hitler's orders.

Suggested Reading: D. Pope. *Battle of the River Plate* (London, 1956); E. Millington-Drake. *The Drama of the Graf Spee and the Battle of the River Plate* (London, 1964); B. Pitt (ed.). *The Purnell History of the Second World War* vol. 1, Nos. 4 & 5 (London, 1966).

From the outset of the war, the 10,000-ton German pocket-battleship *Graf Spee* had been cruising the South Atlantic, supported by the supply ship *Altmark*, attacking Allied merchant shipping. By December she had accounted for eleven vessels, and a massive ocean-wide hunt for the raider was being mounted by the Royal Navy with French assistance.

Early on 13 December Force G, comprising Commodore Harwood's three cruisers, sighted *Graf Spee* east of the River Plate estuary, and in spite of a marked inferiority in fire-power, immediately engaged. Instead of keeping his distance and destroying his attackers at long range, Captain Langsdorff decided to close with them. Harwood, flying his flag in *Ajax*, implemented a preconceived plan designed to divide his powerful opponent's attention and prevent Langsdorff from bringing all his big guns against each ship in turn. The heavy cruiser, *Exeter*, attacked one flank, the two light cruisers the other. *Graf Spee* turned her main armament against *Exeter* and inflicted grave damage, silencing her turrets, damaging the bridge, and setting the ship on fire. *Ajax* and *Achilles* darted in to distract the enemy, using smokescreens to confuse the German gunlayers. Their 6in guns scored a number of hits, but in return fire *Graf Spee* put half of *Ajax*'s main guns out of action and inflicted serious damage on *Achilles*. The action had now been engaged for more than a hour. *Exeter* was forced to withdraw from the battle, and headed south towards the Falklands to seek repairs.

Just when it seemed the Germans were winning the engagement, Captain Langsdorff, whose ship had sustained some damage, decided to break off the action. Fearing British torpedo attacks, he sailed west into the River Plate estuary to carry out repairs in neutral waters off Montevideo. Harwood's remaining ships waited off the river mouth, signalling for reinforcements. Fortunately the British heavy cruiser, *Cumberland*, was close enough to be able to respond.

A period of hectic diplomatic activity ensued. Under international law a warship was entitled to 72 hours' sanctuary in a neutral port – and German envoys vainly tried to win an extension from Uruguay and Argentina. British representatives watched every move closely, hoping that enough time would elapse to bring *Cumberland* off the River Plate. At the same time the impression was given that other major British units were closing in. These measures fooled Langsdorff, and on orders from Hitler he took all but a skeleton crew off *Graf Spee*, sailed into mid-estuary, and scuttled his ship on 17 December. Two days later he shot himself. The German crew was interned.

London hailed the end of *Graf Spee* as a naval victory. Harwood was knighted and promoted to Rear-Admiral. As a postscript, the hunt switched to find the *Altmark* with 300 British merchant seamen captives on board – the crews of *Graf Spee*'s prizes. On the night of 16/17 February 1940 she was found in Josing Fiord in Norwegian waters, and the British destroyer *Cossack* rescued the seamen by a bold action that was a technical violation of neutral waters.

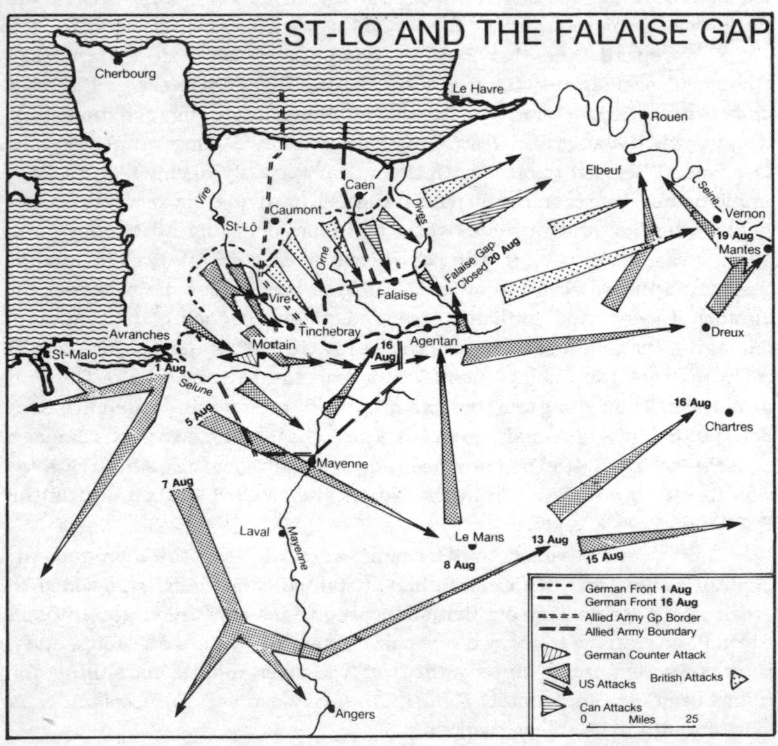

St-Lô and Falaise

Date: 24 July – 22 August 1944.

Location: Twenty miles south-west of Bayeux on the River Vire.

Object: The US First Army was attempting to break out from the Normandy bridgehead to the west and south, and then to trap the German Seventh Army.

Opposing sides: (a) Field Marshal Sir Bernard Montgomery commanding 21st Army Group, including Lieutenant General Omar Bradley commanding the US First Army and Lieutenant General George Patton commanding the US Third Army; (b) Field Marshal Günther von Kluge commanding Army Group B (General Hausser's Seventh Army and Panzer Group West).

Forces engaged: (a) Four US armoured and eleven infantry divisions. Total: approx. 250,000 men; (b) Two Panzer and eleven 'composite' divisions. Total: 150,000 men (both operations).

Casualties: (a) estimated 25,000 troops; (b) estimated 100,000 troops.

Result: The success of Operation 'Cobra' marked the final defeat of German attempts to contain the Normandy bridgehead, and led to the German disaster at Falaise.

Suggested reading: C. Wilmot. *The Struggle for Europe* (London, 1952); L.F. Ellis. *Victory in the West* vol. 1 (London, 1962); M. Blumenson. *The U.S. Army in World War II – Breakout and Pursuit* (Washington, 1961); O. Bradley. *A Soldier's Story* (New York, 1951); B. Pitt (ed.). *The Purnell History of the Second World War* vol. 5, No. 9 (London, 1968).

As the British Second Army battled around Caen, pinning down large numbers of German formations, particularly armour, Montgomery and Bradley planned Operation 'Cobra' – the break-out from the Normandy beachhead (still contained by the Germans six weeks after D-Day).

On 25 July Allied bombers dropped a carpet of 4,200 tons of bombs in an hour and a half on an area measuring 2,500 yards broad by 6,000 yards deep, stunning the Germans and also causing more than 550 American casualties in front-line units. The US VII Corps then attacked west of St-Lô and made progress for the loss of 1,000 casualties. Next day the US 3rd Armored and 1st Infantry Divisions pressed ahead in two mobile columns, while over by Caen British Second Army began to advance south towards the German Seventh Army's rear. The easternmost American column defied heavy German counter-attacks, while to the west the second column forced its way into Coutances on the 28th and two days later reached Avranches.

Massively outnumbered in tanks, the German cohesion was slipping when Patton's US Third Army swept forward into Brittany, exploiting the success. On 10 August, VIII Corps reached Nantes on the Loire estuary, while Brest, Lorient and St-Nazaire were bypassed, being strongly garrisoned by the Germans following their 'port denial' strategy. Soon three corps of Patton's army were sweeping on south and east to envelop the rear of Hausser's army. In desperation, on 6 August Hitler ordered five Panzer divisions to reinforce Seventh Army to mount a drive towards the coast, but the resulting battle of Mortain (6–10 August) saw Kluge's attacks decimated by Allied air strikes, and ultimately halted.

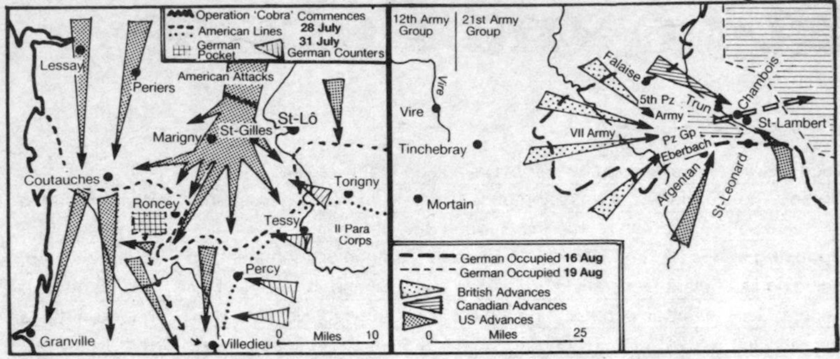

Meanwhile on 8 August Patton, despite serious petrol shortages, had swung his tanks northwards through Le Mans towards Argentan threatening to trap Kluge's entire Army Group in the Mortain-Falaise pocket as British Second Army pressed southwards. US V Corps took Argentan on 14 August, while General Henry Crerar's Canadian First Army fought south towards Falaise. Defying Hitler's orders, Kluge began to withdraw his three nearly trapped armies out of the pocket, and was promptly replaced by Field Marshal Walther Model on the 18th. But withdrawal was the only course open to the Germans, who managed to keep a 10-mile gap open for five vital days, through which their manpower streamed, abandoning almost all their tanks, guns and vehicles in the process to Allied air attack. The ring at last closed on 19 August, and three days later all Germans had surrendered. They lost 10,000 killed and 50,000 captives. The road to the Seine and Paris now lay invitingly open to the Allies.

Salerno

Date: 9–18 September 1943.

Location: Between Paestum and Maiori south of Naples on the west coast of Italy.

Object: The Allies wished to exploit their success in Sicily by landing in strength on the Italian mainland to seize the great port and city of Naples in association with a landing in Calabria, and in the process complete the destabilization of the Mussolini regime.

Opposing sides: (a) General Dwight D. Eisenhower, Allied Supreme Commander, and General Sir Harold Alexander commanding the Allied 15th Army Group; (b) Field Marshal Albert Kesselring commanding German forces in southern Italy.

Forces engaged: (a) Lieutenant General Mark W. Clark commanding the US Fifth Army, comprising the British X and American VI Corps. Total: approx. 85,000 men; (b) General Heinrich von Vietinghoff commanding the German Tenth Army including four Panzer and two Panzer-Grenadier divisions. Total: approx. 50,000.

Casualties: (a) 15,000 Allies killed and wounded; (b) 8,000 German casualties.

Result: The eventual capture of Naples on 1 October, but only after the narrow defeat of the rapid and effective German riposte following Mussolini's fall and Italy's subsequent surrender.

Suggested reading: G. A. Shepperd. *The Italian Campaign, 1943–1945* (London, 1968); A. Kesselring. *Memoirs* (London, 1954); M. W. Clark. *Calculated Risk* (London, 1950); H. Pond. *Salerno* (London, 1961); R. Lamb. *Montgomery in Europe. 1943–45 – Success or Failure?* (London, 1983); B. Pitt (ed.). *The Purnell History of the Second World War* vol. 4, No. 7 (London, 1967).

With the rapid collapse of Axis resistance in Sicily, the Allies decided to make the most of intelligence of the collapse of Mussolini's Fascist government in Rome on 25 July by launching a double attack against the Italian mainland. The British Eighth Army was to mount Operation 'Baytown' over the Straits of Messina into Calabria, while the US Fifth Army was convoyed to make an amphibious attack against Salerno, near the important objective of Naples, codenamed Operation 'Avalanche'.

On 3 September Montgomery made a successful attack on Calabria, and soon the associated Operation 'Slapstick' captured Taranto. But when Mark Clark's sea-borne invasion force began to land on 9 September – its troops elated by the released news that Italy had surrendered (in fact on the 3rd) – they found unexpectedly bitter fighting awaiting them. The Germans under Kesselring had reacted with great swiftness and efficiency to Italy's leaving the war. Five German divisions rapidly sealed-off the invasion bridgehead, and a truly desperate battle began. On 11 September a strong German attempt to split the beachhead in two by an armoured onslaught through Battipaglia reached to within two miles of the coast, and only well-directed battleship fire and heavy air attacks (2,000 sorties alone on 15 September) blunted their attack. German air and glider-bomb attacks inflicted severe damage on three Allied capital ships, but the worst was over by the 15th. General Alexander had meantime sent in the US 82nd Airborne and the British 7th Armoured Divisions to reinforce the bridgehead. The Allied build-up slowly progressed, and by the 16th

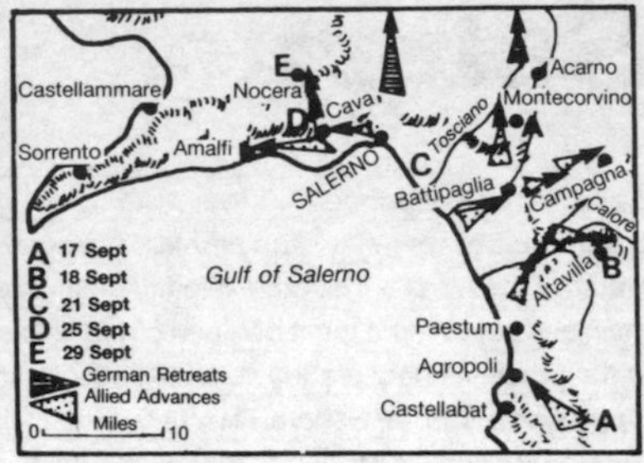

Kesselring had begun to pull back his hard-fighting Panzers aware that Montgomery was advancing from the south. The bridgehead was finally consolidated on the 18th, Montgomery and Clark having established contact from the 16th.

Naples was occupied on 1 October, but the Germans had some reason for claiming a strategic victory in that they had held up the superior Allied armies and air forces, with their complete mastery of the sea, despite the Italian surrender. Nevertheless, the Allied conquest of Italy could now be developed northward towards Rome and the Sangro.

Sedan

Date: 13–15 May 1940.

Location: On the River Meuse, in the Ardennes region.

Object: Army Group A was seeking a major crossing over the Meuse at the outset of the main German onslaught against France.

Opposing sides: (a) General Gerd von Rundstedt commanding Army Group A; (b) General Gaston Billotte commanding the French First Army Group.

Forces engaged: (a) 45 divisions including seven armoured. Total (whole sector): approx. 500,000 Germans; (b) 22 divisions including two light mechanized. Total (whole sector): approx 300,000 French.

Casualties: (a) 60,000 killed and wounded (to 4 June, all sectors); (b) included more than one million prisoners (to 4 June, all sectors).

Result: The creation of a 50-mile gap through the Allied lines north of the Maginot Line led to the rapid German advance to the Channel and the cutting off of the French Seventh Army and the British Expeditionary Force. Effectively, this blow decided the outcome of the campaign.

Suggested reading: A. Horne. *To Lose a Battle* (London, 1969); A. Goutard. *The Battle of France, 1940* (London, 1958); B. Pitt (ed.). *The Purnell History of the Second World War* vol. 1, No. 8 (London, 1966).

As, on 10 May 1940, the BEF and French Seventh and First Armies swung into Belgium (to meet what they believed to be the main German attack), Army Group A, spearheaded by General von Kleist's Panzer Group, began to press forward through the wooded hills of the Ardennes (regarded by General Gamelin, the French Commander-in-Chief, as wholly unsuitable for armoured formations) to close with the River Meuse. Ahead of them were General Corap's French Ninth Army (some nine divisions) and the X Corps (3 divisions) of General Huntziger's French Second Army – both containing large contingents of reservists, and neither expecting to be seriously attacked. According to the Manstein Plan, however, the 70-mile sector between Namur and Sedan was in fact designated the key target for Operation 'Sichelschnitt' ('Sickle-cut') – the great German *Blitzkreig* attack in the west. No less than seven of the ten available Panzer divisions were assigned to General von Rundstedt for the attack, although the German staff did not envisage any more than the securing of bridgeheads over the Meuse. In the event they were to be amazingly surprised by the unforeseen opportunity that awaited them.

The German armour was organized into three corps. In the north – moving on Namur and Dinant – were General Hoth's corps of two Panzers, including Rommel's 7th. In the centre – heading for Monthermé – moved General Reinhardt's two Panzers. To the south came the greater part of Kleist's command, General Guderian's corps comprising the 1st, 2nd and 10th Panzer divisions, driving for the Meuse between Donchery and the river bank to the south of Sedan. The light Belgian and French motorized formations that had been advanced east of the Meuse to delay any German advance found themselves bundled back unceremoniously as the Germans made far better time through the Ardennes than anybody had deemed possible. Obstructions and demolitions placed in the Germans' path were rapidly tackled by well-trained engineer battalions, and the sweep of the advance barely faltered. Overhead the Luftwaffe reduced Allied air intervention to a minimum. In any case most of Gamelin's attention was concentrated away to the north, where von Bock's Army Group B was acting as the 'matador's red cloak' – drawing the best Allied forces deep into Belgium.

On the afternoon of 12 May, 1st Panzer Division entered the streets of a virtually undefended Sedan, while behind it the rest of Guderian's XIX Panzer Corps crossed the River Semos. By evening most of his formations were near the eastern banks of the Meuse. Away to the north, meanwhile, Rommel's 7th Panzer Division had found an undemolished and undefended weir near Dinant, and, using this to cross the Meuse, by nightfall his motor-cycle battalion had formed a weak bridgehead on the west bank. The truly critical battle was to be fought next day, however, around Sedan.

Early on the 13th Guderian had issued his orders. The 2nd Panzer was to attempt a crossing at Donchery – but there was some doubt whether it would arrive at the start-line in time. The 10th was to force a passage south of Sedan. But the main enterprise, just north of Sedan, was entrusted to the reinforced 1st Panzer Division under General Kirchner.

The Meuse at Sedan is a wide and deep river; with its bridges blown-up, and its banks overlooked by considerable hills to the west, it should have proved a formidable obstacle to cross. But although French artillery caused considerable casualties as the Germans moved down to the river, the expenditure of shells was strictly rationed, and in any case the French high command did not expect a major crossing attempt for some five days as they believed the Germans would need that long to bring up their heavy artillery. In this calculation, however, they were hopelessly wrong. The Germans would use Dornier bombers and above all Stuka dive-bombers, protected by Messerschmitt fighters, to make up for their deficiency in large guns.

Before midday the air bombardment opened, and for more than four hours the French soldiers cowered in their trenches as Stukas shrieked down to bomb and machine-gun in an unceasing series of attacks. The damage the dive-bombers wrought was far more psychological than physical – but the reservists had never been warned to anticipate anything like this. At 1600 hours the Germans began to cross the 60-yards-wide river. First came assault engineers and then infantry in rubber boats. As soon as they were over the Meuse they attacked the first line of French pillboxes – finding many of them manned by stunned and demoralized Frenchmen. Behind the assault wave, the first German tanks were moved over the river on ferries, while German pontoon troops worked frantically to construct bridges. By late afternoon a large bridgehead had been created on 1st Panzer's front, and the overlooking Marfée Heights occupied.

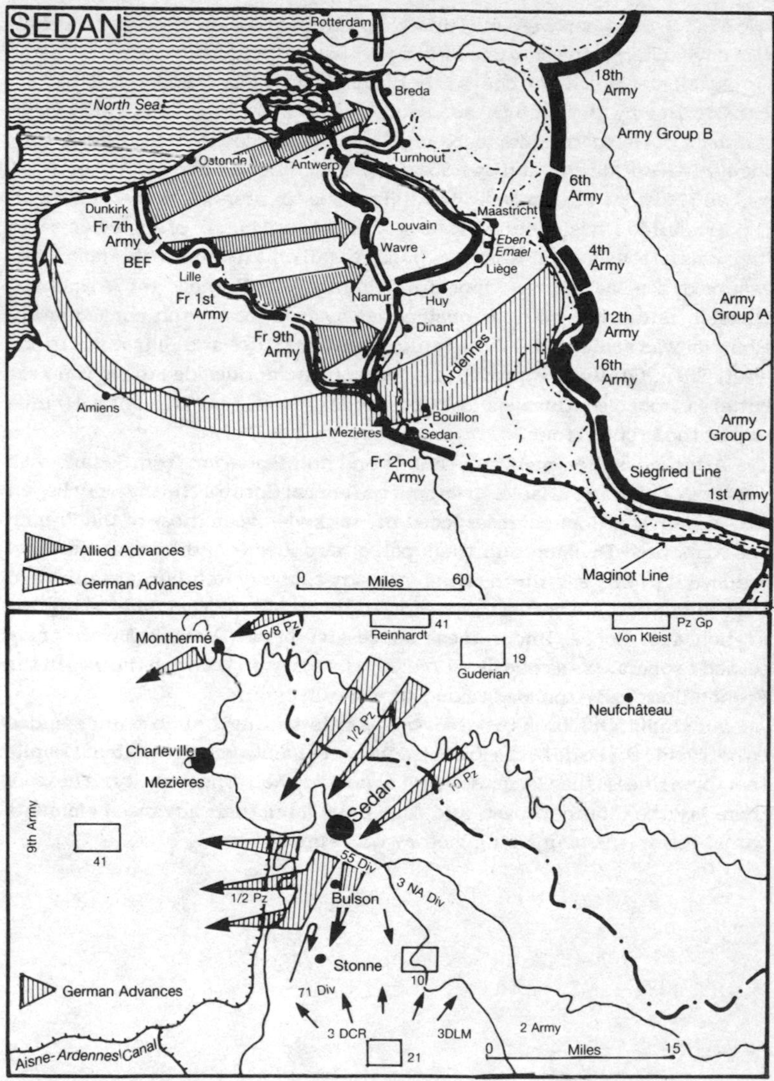

General Lafontaine's French 55th Division dissolved into a horde of fugitives. To the south, 10th Panzer had also made a successful crossing but at some loss, and by nightfall Guderian had a bridgehead three miles wide by between four and six miles deep – into which the mass of his armour began to cross ready to break-out. To the north, Reinhardt's corps had less success at Monthermé due to lack of air support, while away to the right Rommel's bridgehead remained very tenuous. Thus only on Guderian's sector had a high level of success been achieved on the 13th. But two French divisions were in ruins, the 55th and 71st, and an ominous gap was developing between their Ninth and Second Armies.

Much depended on the French ability to mount effective counter-attacks. But by the time these began on the morning of the 14th, large numbers of German tanks were over the Meuse. The French tanks found themselves outfought, and by mid-afternoon Guderian had most of both 1st and 2nd Panzer Divisions ready to strike. The counter-stroke by the French 3rd Armoured Division failed to attack the exposed flank of Guderian's two divisions as they swung west and north to fall on French Ninth Army – but assumed the defensive. Opposite Dinant, the French 1st Armoured Division found its progress obstructed by refugees – and consequently Rommel was able to get all his tanks over the Meuse and four miles to the west. Then, fatally as it proved, General Huntziger decided to regroup his battered troops southwards towards the Maginot Line. This left a 10-mile gap in the French front.

Attacked by Rommel from Dinant and now Guderian from Sedan, with ceaseless Luftwaffe attacks in support, General Corap's Ninth Army began to disintegrate. Rommel interposed his tanks between those of the French 1st Armoured Division and their petrol supplies – and by nightfall had reduced it to only seventeen tanks. Already that day Reinhardt's tanks had surged out of the Monthermé pocket, to reach Montcornet, shattering the French 41st Corps. Under these successive blows, French Ninth Army ceased to operate as a cohesive force, and by early on the 16th the gap in the French lines had expanded to one 45 miles in extent.

As Guderian's tanks roared westwards through almost undefended countryside the scale of the French débâcle began to be appreciated. Despite their weariness, the Germans were aware of their opportunity. Ahead of them lay the Channel coast, and four days later their advanced elements would reach it. A staggering victory was almost won.

Sidi Barrani

Date: 9–11 December 1940.

Location: On the Mediterranean coast of Egypt, 80 miles west of Mersa Matruh and 60 miles east of the Libyan frontier.

Object: Western Desert Force was attempting to drive the Italians out of Egypt by means of a surprise offensive.

Opposing sides: (a) Lieutenant-General Richard O'Connor, Western Desert Force; (b) Marshal Rodolfo Graziani commanding the Italian Forces in Libya.

Forces engaged: (a) 7th Armoured and 4th Indian Divisions. Total: 31,000 men; (b) Four and a half Italian divisions. Total: approx. 50,000 men.

Casualties: (a) 624 troops; (b) 40,000, including 38,000 prisoners.

Result: The complete rout of the Italians, leading to a rapid exploitation and the conquest of Cyrenaica as far as El Agheila.

Suggested reading: A Moorehead. *African Trilogy* (London, 1956); C. Barnett. *The Desert Generals* (London, 1960); J. Connell. *Wavell* vol. 1 (London, 1964); R. Lewin. *The Chief* (London, 1980); B. Pitt (ed.). *The Purnell History of the Second World War* vol. 1, No. 15 (London, 1966).

Italy entered the war on 11 June, but it was only on 13 September that Marshal Graziani, on Mussolini's prompting, invaded Egypt. The British frontier covering force fell back before him until the Italian impetus died out at Sidi Barrani five days later. O'Connor's Western Desert Force based itself at Mersa Matruh and began to prepare for a counter-offensive. Meantime the Italians remained entirely quiescent.

General Sir Archibald Wavell, CinC, Middle East, had barely 50,000 fighting troops to garrison nine countries, and besides the 200,000 Italians in Libya there were 250,000 more in Abyssinia to the south. Anticipating Australian and New Zealand reinforcements, Wavell strongly encouraged Lieutenant-General Sir Henry Maitland Wilson, GOC, Egypt, to take the offensive in Egypt at the earliest possible moment. The arrival of a large convoy from Britain in October built up tank and aircraft levels.

The Italians were occupying two groups of camps, around Mektila and Sofafi, separated by a 50-mile gap, with headquarters at Sidi Barrani. General O'Connor determined to exploit this separation. On 19 November mobile forces moved inconspicuously into the gap, and after rehearsing 4th Indian Division for a standard frontal attack, on the 26th the plan was changed to an artillery bombardment of the east-facing Italian defences while the infantry and tanks attacked the camps from the rear.

Great secrecy was maintained, and on 7 December the main forces moved forward to their start-lines between Nibeiwa and Sofafi while Selby Force prepared to attack Sidi Barrani up the coast road. Operation 'Compass' began at dawn on the 9th. The bombardment began without prior registration, and the Italians were taken completely by surprise. By midday Nibeiwa Camp had been taken with 2,000 prisoners and 55 tanks

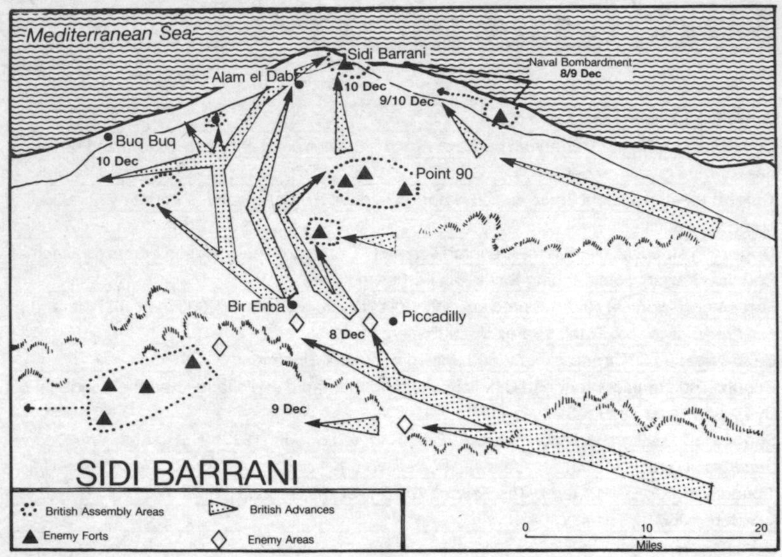

destroyed or captured for just 56 casualties. Two further fortified camps, the Tummars west and east, had shared the same fate by late afternoon whilst 7th Armoured Division sealed off the inland Sofafi positions. The only check was on the coastal sector, where Colonel Selby failed to capture Mektila, and the Italians there managed to escape briefly.

Western Desert Force was scenting victory. O'Connor used his armoured division to overrun the Sofafi positions, and then swung them north towards Buq Buq on the coast road west of Sidi Barrani. This envelopment destroyed what little fight remained in the Italians, and on the 11th Sidi Barrani was reoccupied. To date the Italians had lost 38,000 prisoners-of-war, 73 tanks and 237 guns. Overhead, the supposedly superior Aeronautica had been driven from the skies by the few squadrons of Hurricanes available. O'Connor swept west for the frontier wire and towards Sollum and Bardia, only now learning that a crisis in far-away Eritrea would cost him the use of 4th Indian Division. The 6th Australian Division – new to the theatre – would join him before Bardia which was invested on the 16th. A major success was in the making.

Singapore

Date: 8–15 February 1942.

Location: An island at the southern extremity of the Malayan Peninsula.

Object: As part of their campaign to establish the 'South-East Asia Co-Prosperity Sphere', the Japanese were determined to complete their rapid conquest of Malaya by occupying Singapore and its important naval base, freeing their hands for the attack on Burma and the threat to India.

Opposing sides: (a) General Tomoyuki Yamashita commanding the Japanese Imperial 25th Army; (b) Lieutenant-General Arthur Percival commanding the British garrison, including III Indian Corps.

Forces engaged: (a) The Japanese 5th and 18th Divisions and Takumi Force, with strong air force support. Total: approx. 40,000 troops; (b) The 9th and 11th Indian Divisions, the British 18th Division and Australian troops with limited air support. Total: approx. 107,000 troops (about 80,000 combatants).

Casualties: (a) (whole campaign) approx. 9,800 men; (b) (whole campaign) 8,000 killed and 130,000 made prisoners-of war.

Result: The humiliating loss by Great Britain of 'the Gibraltar of Asia' and a great military triumph for the Imperial Japanese Army.

Suggested reading: S. L. Falk. *Seventy Days to Singapore – the Malayan Campaign, 1941–2* (London, 1975); M. Tsuji. *Singapore – the Japanese Version* (London, 1972); H. P. Willmott. *Empires in the Balance* (Annapolis, 1984); E. R. Holmes and A. Kemp. *The Bitter End: Singapore, 1942* (London, 1982); B. Pitt (ed.). *The Purnell History of the Second World War,* vol. 2, No. 13 (London 1967).

Singapore was reputed to be the strongest island fortress in South-East Asia. Its defences mounted 29 coastal guns, but these were sited to guard the seaward approaches – nobody in the 1930s anticipating an attack from the Malayan Peninsula over the Straits of Johore as was in fact to take place in February 1942.

On 8 December 1941, the day after their attack on Pearl Harbor, Japanese forces – eventually some 100,000 strong – landed at Singora and Patani in neutral Thailand and at Kota Bahru and two other points in Malaya. After moving south through mountainous border country, their main attack was concentrated on the state of Kedah in north-west Malaya, and thence southwards down the west coast plain. The troops of III Indian Corps attempted numerous holding actions, but were beaten back from one position to the next, and by late December the Japanese were in Ipoh, 200 miles from Singapore. Enjoying complete air and naval superiority, there was no stopping the Japanese, who were far more adept at jungle warfare than the defenders, and were able to mount a series of amphibious landings along the coast behind each successive British defence line. On 31 January 1942 General Percival withdrew his last weary troops over the causeway into Singapore Island.

The defences extended over 30 miles, and although efforts were made to traverse the large guns to fire inland, and Percival could also deploy 156

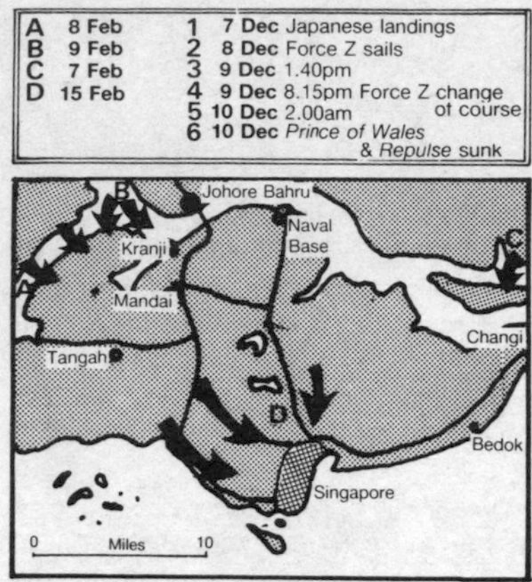

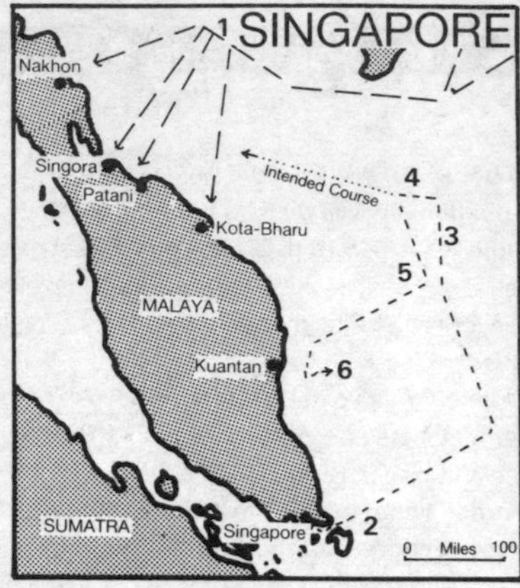

field and mountain guns and a further 144 anti-aircraft guns, they were over-dispersed. Singapore was crowded with a million refugees and many of the troops were of 'tail' rather than 'teeth' formations.

The Japanese had fewer guns and fewer men under command after their long and rapid advance, but their morale was high. On 7 February they launched a feint attack on the island of Pulau Ubin at the north-eastern end of the Johore Straits, but made their main onslaught over the next two days to the west of the partially-destroyed causeway. After establishing bridgeheads, they repaired the causeway, and sent light tanks and 25,000 men over into Singapore Island. Percival tried to evacuate specialist personnel on the 13th as Yamashita's troops occupied the already air-damaged city water reservoirs. Fierce fighting continued until the 15th when Percival surrendered as water-supplies ran low. Churchill called this débâcle 'the greatest disaster in the history of the British Empire'.

Stalingrad

Date: 24 August 1942 – 2 February 1943.

Location: In southern Russia on the River Volga; today the city is called Volgagrad.

Object: Despite the hesitations of his senior advisers, Hitler insisted that Stalingrad must be taken in order to close the Volga to Russian shipping and to guard the left flank of the Caucasian offensive.

Opposing sides: (a) General Andrei Yeremenko commanding the Stalingrad Front; (b) Field Marshal Maximilian von Weichs commanding Army Group B.

Forces engaged: (a) General Vasilii Chuikov, commanding the 62nd Red Army, Total: 300,000 men; (b) General Freidrich Paulus, commanding the German Sixth Army and parts of neighbouring formations. Total: 22 divisions, approx. 230,000 men.

Casualties: (a) approx. 200,000 men; (b) 140,000 killed and 90,000 prisoners-of-war.

Result: The total destruction of Sixth Army – and the failure of the German drive on the Caucasus and the Volga. Stalingrad is regarded as the turning-point of the war on the Eastern Front.

Suggested reading: V. I. Chuikov. *The Beginning of the Road* (London, 1963); J. Erikson. *The Road to Stalingrad* (London, 1982); E. von Manstein. *Lost Victories* (London, 1958); R. Seth. *Stalingrad, Point of No-Return* (London, 1959); W. Goerlitz. *Paulus and Stalingrad* (London, 1963); B. Pitt (ed.). *The Purnell History of the Second World War* vol. 3, Nos. 9 and 15 (London, 1967).

In 1942 Hitler insisted that the main German effort should be made on the southern flank of the Russian front, involving Army Groups A and B. The former was to aim at capturing the oil-rich Caucasian region linking the Black and Caspian seas, while the latter (which included Paulus's Sixth Army) was to head for the strategically important city of Stalingrad. For propaganda as well as strategic reasons Stalin was determined that the Germans should not gain the city.

The German campaign began slowly, and Field Marshal von Bock was replaced by Field Marshal von Weichs on 13 July after a setback at Voronezh on the River Don. Further south, however, Hoth's Fourth Panzer Army made rapid progress eastwards between the Don and the Donetz rivers, and with its aid Kleist's First Panzer Army crossed the former and spearheaded a 300-mile advance deep into the Caucasus. Although there were still some dissenting voices, General Paulus's Sixth Army was directed towards Stalingrad on the Volga to the north of the great break-through. By 24 August the leading elements of his Sixth Army reached the Volga north of the large city which lay sprawled for almost 20 miles along the west bank of the river.

The German attack began with a 3-day aerial *Blitz*, causing much damage and many casualties. The Russian authorities ordered the evacuation of the old and all women and children, but the great factories remained in production and would remain so throughout the long battle. For the defence of the city and area the Russian High Command created the 'Stalingrad Front' – comprising the 57th, 62nd and 64th Red Armies –

under General Yeremenko. His three-man Military Council included Nikita Kruschev as senior political commissar. The task was to prevent the fall of Stalingrad and the denial of the west bank of the Volga to the enemy. Access to the city could only be by boat.

The Germans began a series of assaults on the western and northern suburbs, and block by block and house by house inched and blasted their way into the city. They faced a totally determined defence by the Russians who fought for every yard, feeding reinforcements over the river by night and evacuating their wounded by the same route. A notable German success was the capture on 14 September of the important feature, Mamaiev Hill, from which they could dominate the river with their artillery fire. The Russians responded by bringing a Guards Division over the Volga under heavy fire, and by the end of the 15th they had regained the hill and the neighbouring sector of river bank.

Ferocious street fighting continued over the succeeding weeks, the Germans gaining only half a mile, but regaining Mamiev Hill and taking the extensive Tractor Plant. One Russian division holding the area of the Red October Factory was attacked on 100 separate occasions over one month – the worst day seeing 23 tank attacks. The Russians were reduced to holding four small bridgeheads – but there they indomitably stood. Their city was reduced to rubble, but still limited tank production continued in the remaining factories.

Meantime, the Russian High Command had been preparing their counter-blow. On 19 November, well to the north-west of the city, Rokossovsky's 65th Army broke through the Axis lines at Kremenskaya. Next day, Yeremenko crossed the Volga six miles south of Stalingrad. Two concentric attacks began to develop, the Russian aim being to surround the German Sixth Army. The northern pincer made excellent progress, crossing the River Don near Kalach after just two days, which permitted General Vatutin to press through to defeat three under-equipped satellite armies in turn – the Third Roumanian, Eighth Italian and Second Hungarian – and then beat-off a counter-attack by Panzer Corps H. South of the city, Yeremenko smashed the Fourth Roumanian Army taking 65,000 prisoners. Finally, 23 November saw the two Russian prongs join up at Kalach. Paulus was trapped in a pocket 30 miles wide by 25 deep.

At this stage Sixth Army could have fought its way out, but Hitler ordered Paulus to hold his ground and await relief in 'Fortress Stalingrad'. Reichsminister Goering promised the Führer that his Luftwaffe would be able to fly in 500 tons of stores a day. Neither Weichs nor Paulus believed this, .and by the 24th Sixth Army had 130 tanks and 57,000 men poised to break out. But Hitler countermanded this intention. Instead, he ordered von Manstein to take over the new Army Group Don (comprising the beleagured Sixth, the Fourth Panzer Army and two Roumanian armies) and to relieve Stalingrad. Operation '*Winterblitz*' began on 12 December, striving to reach Paulus from the south, and by the 19th was within 30

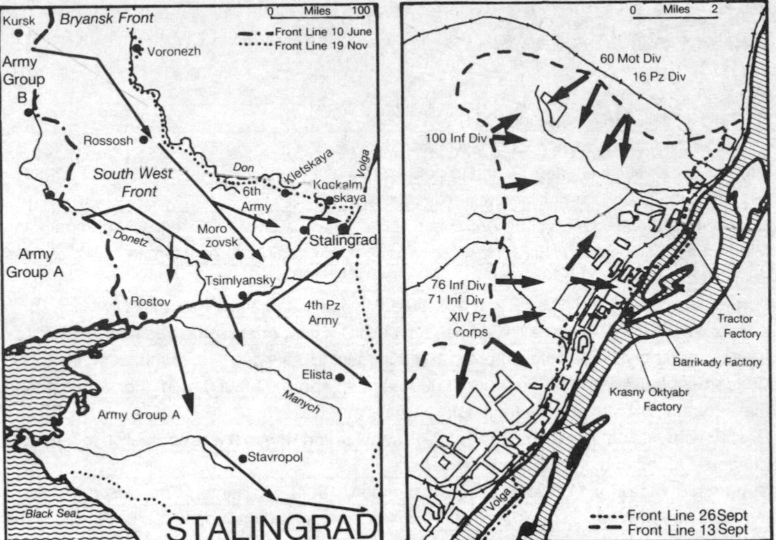

miles of the city. Manstein then ordered Paulus to break out – and Hitler agreed – but also insisted that Sixth Army should continue to hold its perimeter. Paulus, short of fuel (Goering's promises had proved valueless) and unwilling to earn Hitler's censure, hesitated. Then new Russian attacks towards Rostov forced Manstein (who had lost 300 tanks and 16,000 men in his relief attempt) to look to his flank, and the belt of Soviet-held ground around Stalingrad widened. Anti-aircraft guns were massed to block the air lanes, and many German transport aircraft (eventually 536 in all) were shot down.

At this stage Hitler took over personal command of 'Fortress Stalingrad' from his bunker in Poland, and was persuaded to allow Army Group A to withdraw from the Caucasus, which it succeeded in doing. But for Sixth Army there was no hope. Summoned to surrender on 8 January, Paulus refused – and at once major Russian attacks were launched against his frozen, under-supplied men holding a shrinking perimeter. The average airlift of supplies was now down to 42 tons a day, but the loss of Pitomik airfield – followed by that of Gumrak a few days later – cut the last tenuous links with the outside world. A few supplies continued to be parachuted in, but the end was now in sight.

On the 28th Russian troops reached the Volga, cutting the defenders in two. Paulus proposed surrender to save his wounded, but Hitler refused permission. His answer was to promote Paulus to Field Marshal – because in all German history there had been no instance of one having surrendered. But on 31 January Paulus did surrender – and fighting ended two days later. The Russians – besides 90,000 men – took 60,000 vehicles, 1,500 tanks and 6,000 guns. The tide in Russia had turned.

Tobruk

Dates: 10 April – 26 November 1941.

Location: Mediterranean coast of Cyrenaica, Libya.

Object: The British were determined to hold Tobruk against all German and Italian attempts to recapture the important port and water-filtration plant.

Opposing sides: (a) General Sir Archibald Wavell (later Sir Claude Auchinleck) commanding Middle East Land Forces; (b) Marshal Gariboldi commanding all Axis forces under General Erwin Rommel.

Forces engaged: (a) (initially) 2nd Armoured Division and 9th Australian Division. Total: approx. 23,000 men; (b) (initially) German 5th Light Division, Ariete Armoured Division and four Italian infantry divisions. Total: approx. 100,000 men. (Both sides later much reinforced).

Casualties: (final battle) (a) approx. 18,000 men; (b) approx. 38,000 men. (For whole period the numbers probably require trebling).

Result: Tobruk's defences withstood all Axis attacks, and Rommel was compelled to retreat to El Agheila at the end of Operation 'Crusader'.

Suggested reading: M. Carver. *Tobruk* (London, 1964); C. Barnet. *The Desert Generals* (London, 1960); W. Jackson. *The North African Campaigns* (London, 1974); B. Pitt (ed.). *The Purnell History of the Second World War*, vol. 1. No. 16 and vol. 2, Nos. 7 and 11 (London, 1966).

The name of Tobruk became a symbol of the Second World War, being the focal point of much fighting in the North African Campaigns of 1941-2. General O'Connor had first taken the port from the Italians on 22 January 1941, but the exploitation of his victorious campaign was halted after Beda Fomm owing to the need to send substantial forces to Greece and later Crete. On 12 February, Rommel landed in Tripoli, followed by the first German units to be sent to North Africa. His mission was to secure Tripoli from attack, but typically he determined on a liberal interpretation of his instructions to wage a very active defence. On 24 March elements of 5th Light Division (later to be redesignated 21st Panzer) occupied El Agheila, and after successful operations against the weakened British XIII Corps, on 7 April captured Generals O'Connor, Neame and Parry in a lucky stroke. Rommel immediately sent General von Prittwitz on a dash over the desert; his target – Tobruk.

Wavell was able to reinforce the port in the nick of time, much aided by Admiral Cunningham's Mediterranean Fleet, which was to play a vital role in sustaining the defence of Tobruk over the following months. The defences were rapidly improved by Major-General Leslie Morshead at the head of four Australian infantry brigades and part of British 3rd Armoured Brigade, together with four regiments of 25pdr artillery. On the Egyptian frontier to the east, Brigadier Gott built up a small force with which to attempt to hold Bardia and maintain contact by land with Tobruk.

All parties were fully aware of the place's importance – not least Winston Churchill in London – and an epic struggle was about to begin. It began badly for XIII Corps with the loss of Benghazi and Bardia to Rommel

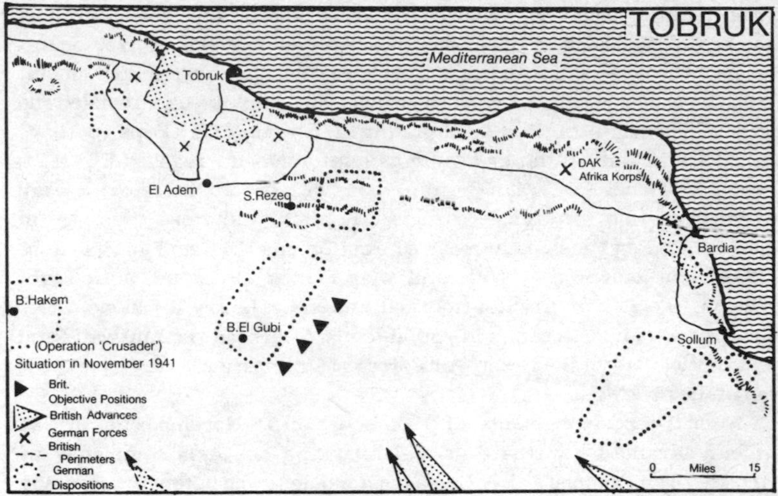

on 4 and 9 April respectively. Next day the Australian 9th Division fell back into the Tobruk perimeter, the Germans hard behind them, and within three days Morshead was tightly besieged. Von Prittwitz was killed in a skirmish, and Rommel took over command of a series of improvised assaults which the defence withstood. Time and again the German tanks and dive-bombers attacked the defences, but the minefields and prepared positions denied them success. Frustrated of his objective, Rommel had no recourse but to begin a regular siege – bringing up Italian infantry divisions to hold the ring. But there was no denying that – Tobruk apart – his rapid first offensive had nullified most of O'Connor's hard-won gains of the previous winter. But as Tobruk was the only sizeable port between Alexandria and Tripoli, its denial to the Axis was a matter of the first importance. Without taking it, Rommel would not be able to invade Egypt for fear of his communications being attacked from Tobruk. The fact that the port was never wholly closed to Allied seaward access was an important factor in what was to follow.

On 30 April Rommel launched a well-prepared attack from the air and on the ground, making some progress, but the Australian defences held, and the German salient was contained. The battle raged until 4 May when the Germans pulled back a short distance. Churchill meanwhile was insisting that Wavell should launch a counter-offensive to relieve Tobruk. Wavell deemed it his duty to comply, and the results were the failure of Operation 'Brevity' in mid-May and Operation 'Battleaxe' (15–16 June). By this time Rommel had received 15th Panzer Division from Europe, and he was able to deny XIII Corps the area of the Egyptian-Libyan frontier. As a result Churchill soon decided to replace Wavell with General Sir Claude Auchinleck on 21 June. Meanwhile, the siege of Tobruk continued unabated, the defenders becoming veritable 'desert rats', holed-up in caves for shelter from the incessant bombing.

Auchinleck began to withdraw the weary Australians from Tobruk by sea, replacing them by the Polish Carpathian Brigade of Lieutenant-General Kopanski and then the 70th British Division under Major-General R. Scobie during September. At the same time, Auckinleck entrusted the new British Eighth Army, comprising XIII and XXX Corps (perhaps 118,000 men and 724 tanks strong as reinforcements reached Egypt) to Lieutenant-General Sir Alan Cunningham, with orders to prepare a large battle, Operation 'Crusader', to defeat Rommel and raise the siege of Tobruk. Rommel also had received reinforcements for Panzergruppe Afrika, now comprising 15th and 21st Panzer Divisions, 90th Light Division, the Italian Ariete armoured and six infantry divisions, some 150,000 men and 558 tanks in round totals. Overhead the Luftwaffe and Aeronautica fought the Desert Air Force for air superiority. A major battle was in the making.

After two postponements, at 0600 hours on 18 November the British armour advanced towards Gabr Saleh, taking the Axis completely by surprise as all Rommel's attention at that moment was taken up preparing a new onslaught against Tobruk timed for the 20th. A confused battle ensued – Eighth Army making progress on some sectors but being held on others. The main British intention – to reach Sidi Rezegh in strength and then to make contact with the Tobruk garrison – was thwarted when Rommel launched a counter-stroke on 20 November, seeking to divide the two British corps. The main tank battle of Sidi Rezegh raged on with fluctations of fortune, but despite Cunningham's early optimism it became clear by the evening of the 22nd that the Germans were winning: 7th Armoured Brigade had no tank 'runners' at all – and Eighth Army had lost 207 tanks. Next day Auchinleck flew up and decided to fight on. Rommel was determined to win the battle. Unaware that Auchinleck was virtually running the fight, on 24 November the German commander started off on a rash thrust over the Egyptian frontier, attacking several Allied headquarters on the way. 'The Matruh Stakes' were on, and some confusion ensued. But Auchinleck knew that the ridges around Sidi Rezegh were the key to the battlefield, and refused to fall back. So it was that on the 25th Rommel realized that his enemy was not conforming to his move, and furthermore his petrol supplies were fast running out. The lull gave XXX Corps and 4th and 22nd Armoured Brigades time to regroup, and for Auchinleck to replace the over-tired Cunningham by Lieutenant-General Sir Neil Ritchie in overall command of Eighth Army.

As Rommel turned back towards Libya, the 1st New Zealand Division at last captured Sidi Rezegh from the German 90th Light Division. And on the 26th, as the Tobruk garrison sortied out in strength to take the El Duda escarpment, Eighth Army at last made contact with Scobie's defenders. The siege of Tobruk had been raised. After more fighting around Sidi Rezegh, Rommel acknowledged defeat, and by 8 December he was in full retreat.

Warsaw

Date: 1–27 September 1939.

Location: The critical battles took place around Warsaw and Lodz.

Object: The Germans (in association with the USSR) were intent on conquering Poland.

Opposing sides: (a) General Walter von Brauschitsch commanding the *Wehrmacht*; (b) Marshal Edward Smigly-Rydz commanding the Polish Army.

Forces engaged: (a) Fourteen Panzer divisions and 44 infantry divisions in five armies. Total: approx. 1,250,000 Germans; (b) 30 infantry and cavalry divisions, one motorized brigade in six armies. Total: 800,000 Poles.

Casualties: (a) approx. 43,000; (b) approx. 266,000 killed and wounded and 690,000 taken prisoners-of-war.

Result: The conquest of Poland and its subsequent partition between Germany and the USSR. The attack caused Britain and France to declare war on Germany (3 September).

Suggested reading: N. Bethall. *The War Hitler Won* (London, 1972); J. Gardinsky. *Poland in the Second World War* (London, 1985); B. Pitt (ed.). *The Purnell History of the Second World War* vol. 1, No. 3 (London, 1966).

Without declaring war and prefaced by a heavy air bombardment, the Germans invaded Poland on 1 September 1939. Their armoured spearheads rapidly broke through the Polish defences, and made good progress eastwards over the Polish plains. General von Bock's Third and Fourth Armies attacked from each side of the Danzig Corridor in the north, while General von Rundstedt's Eighth, Tenth and Fourteenth Armies swept into Galicia and Upper Silesia from the west and south. The intention was to develop this double-penetration into a double-envelopment by the two army groups to the east of Warsaw.

From the outset the mostly out-dated Polish air force – 900 aircraft strong – was outclassed by the 1,400 modern aircraft of the Luftwaffe and by 3 September (the day Britain and France declared war in support of their distant Polish ally) had been virtually swept from the skies, many having been destroyed on their airfields. Ruthless German air attacks on centres of population spread terror, and repeated attacks on Polish General Headquarters (whose locations were pinpointed by spies) destroyed communications. Meanwhile away in the Baltic the small Polish Navy was eliminated.

On land, the German progress seemed irresistible. From East Prussia, General Kuechler's German Third Army bore down remorselessly on the Army of Modlin and Narew Group, heading for Brest-Litovsk. In the south, von List's German Fourteenth Army swept past Cracow, while on its left von Reichenau's German Tenth Army – including the mass of their armour – headed for the River Vistula and Warsaw. A second, inner pincer-movement by Kluge's German Fourth and von Blaskowitz's German Eighth Armies was soon in progress, intent on trapping Polish forces on the Vistula and San river lines, while the outer envelopment beyond the River Bug was continued by the Third and Fourteenth Armies.

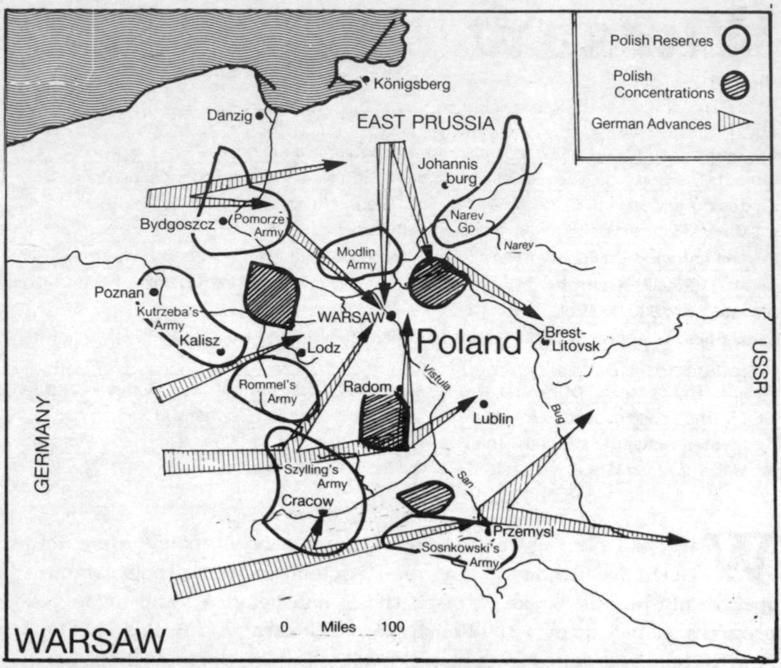

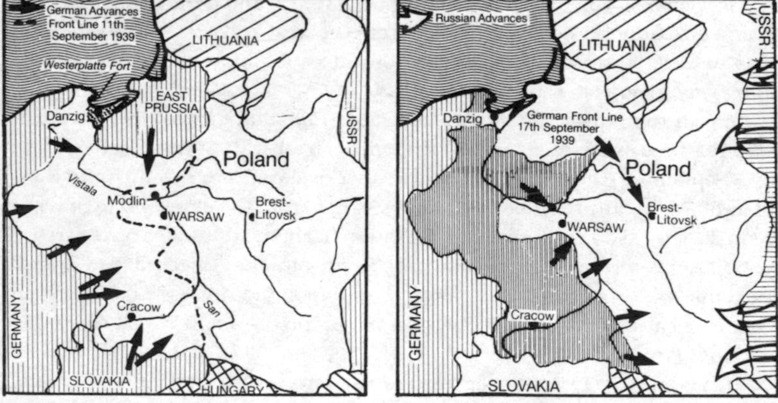

Outnumbered and outclassed, the Poles fought back with great gallantry, but soon they were being isolated into groups. However, Reichenau's attempt to enter Warsaw on the 8th – after covering 145 miles in a single week – was repulsed by Polish counter-attacks, in some cases horsed cavalry sacrificing themselves in charges against tanks. Resistance soon centred around Warsaw and the fortress of Modlin, and, further to the west, around Kutno and Lodz. By the 17th Warsaw was surrounded, and the city was suffering heavy artillery and air bombardment. That same day also saw the failure of a break-out attempt from the Lodz pocket (the Polish troops there being forced to capitulate). The 17th also saw the start of the secretly agreed Russian invasion of eastern Poland, strong columns moving north and south of the Pripet marshes. Facing the outbreak of typhoid fever, starving Warsaw surrendered on the 27th, and all resistance ended at Kock on 5 October.

The speed of the conquest astounded the world. The close co-ordination of highly mobile all-arm Panzer divisions with air attacks by Stuka dive-bombers and other aircraft had shown the offensive power of *Blitzkrieg* warfare; and the futility of armies adopting a cordon defence against such a concentrated and fast-moving series of onslaughts had been convincingly demonstrated. Britain and France had proved incapable of influencing the campaign in practical terms, Poland being beyond bomber range and the Allies being unprepared for an early offensive towards the Rhine – as had been feared by the German General Staff. However, Hitler's intuition that a rapid victory was obtainable had been proved correct, the intervention of Russia being the *coup de grâce* for the unfortunate Poles.

Chronology of Battles

Date	Battle	Location	Antagonists	Nature of Battle
1939				
1-27 Sept	Warsaw	E Europe	Ger versus Pol	land/air
13 Dec	River Plate	S America	Brit v. Ger	naval
1940				
10 & 13 April &	Narvik	N Europe	Brit v. Ger	land/naval
24 April-9 June			Brit/Fr/Nor/Pol v. Ger	land/naval
10-11 May	Eben Emael	W Europe	Ger v. Bel	land/para
13-15 May	Sedan	W Europe	Ger v. Fr	land
21 May	Arras	W Europe	Brit v. Ger	land
26 May-4 June	Dunkirk	W Europe	Ger v. Brit/Fr	land/naval/air
10 July-12 Oct	Battle of Britain	W Europe	Brit v. Ger	air
17 Aug-12 Nov(44)	Atlantic	Atlantic	Brit v. Ger	naval
7 Sept-17 Mar(45)	The *Blitz*	W Europe	Brit v. Ger	air
9-11 Dec	Sidi Barrani	N Africa	Brit v. Ital	land
1941				
3-5 Feb	Beda Fomm	N Africa	Brit/Aust v. Ital	land
April-June(43)	Malta	Mediterranean	Brit/Malt v. Ger/Ital	air
10 April-26 Nov	Tobruk	N Africa	Brit/Aust v. Ger/Ital	land
18-27 May	*Bismarck*	Atlantic	Brit v. Ger	naval
20 May-1 June	Crete	Mediterranean	Brit/Aust/NZ/ Greek v. Ger	land/para
22 June-21 Aug	'Barbarossa'	E Europe/Russia	Ger v. Rus	land
8 Sept-25 Jan(44)	Leningrad	Russia	Ger/Finn v. Rus	land
9-23 Sept	Kiev	Russia	Ger v. Rus	land/air
8 Oct-30 April(42)	Moscow	Russia	Ger v. Rus	land/air
29 Oct-3 July(42)	Crimea & Sevastopol	Russia	Ger v. Rus	land/naval
7 Dec	Pearl Harbor	Pacific	Jap v. Amer	air
10 Dec	*Repulse* & *Prince of Wales*	SE Asia	Jap v. Brit	air/naval
1942				
2 Jan-6 May	Bataan & Corregidor	SE Asia	Jap v. Amer	land

Date	Battle	Location	Antagonists	Nature of Battle
8-15 Feb	Singapore	SE Asia	Jap v. Brit/Ind/ Aust	land
26 May-21 June	Gazala	N Africa	Ger/Ital v. Brit/SA	land
4-6 June	Midway	Pacific	Jap v. Amer	naval
1-27 July & 23 Oct-4 Nov	Alamein (1st & 2nd)	N Africa	Brit v. Ger	land
7 Aug-7 Feb(43)	Guadalcanal	Pacific	Jap v. Amer	land/naval
24 Aug-2 Feb(43)	Stalingrad	Russia	Rus v. Ger/Roum/ Hung/Ital	land
1943				
14-22 Feb & 20-26 Mar	Kasserine & Mareth Line	N Africa	Brit/Amer/Fr/NZ/ v. Ger/Ital	land
5-16 July	Kursk	Russia	Rus v. Ger	land
9 July-17 Aug	Mount Etna (Invasion of Sicily)	Mediterranean	Brit/Amer/Can v. Ger/Ital	land
1 Aug	Ploesti	E Europe	Amer v. Ger	air
17-18 Aug	Peenemunde	N Europe	Brit v. Ger	air
9-18 Sept	Salerno	Mediterranean	Brit/Amer v. Ger	naval/land
1944				
17 Jan-22 May	Cassino	Mediterranean	Brit/Amer/Pol/ Fr/Ind/NZ v. Ger	land/air
22 Jan-22 May	Anzio	Mediterranean	Brit/Amer v. Ger	naval/land
8 Mar-22 June	Kohima-Imphal	SE Asia	Brit/Ind v. Jap	land/air
6 June	D-Day	NW Europe	Brit/Amer v. Ger	naval/land
7 June-25 July	Caen	NW Europe	Brit v. Ger	land/air
24 July-22 Aug	St-Lô & Falaise	NW Europe	Amer/Brit/Can v. Ger	land/air
17-25 Sept	Arnhem	NW Europe	Brit v. Ger	air/land
2 Oct-31 Dec	Leyte Gulf	SE Asia	Amer v. Jap	naval/land
4 Oct-1 Dec	Aachen	NW Europe	Amer v. Ger	land
19-22 Nov	Belfort	NW Europe	Fr/Amer/ v. Ger	land
16 Dec-1 Feb(45)	Ardennes	NW Europe	Brit/Amer v. Ger	land
1945				
14 Jan-31 Mar	Mandalay-Meiktila	SE Asia	Brit/Ind/Chin v. Jap/Ind	land
7-31 Mar	Remagen & Rhine Crossings	NW Europe	Amer/Brit v. Ger	land/air
1 April-22 June	Okinawa	Pacific	Amer v. Jap	naval/land
16 April-2 May	Berlin	NW Europe	Rus v. Ger	land
6 and 9 Aug	Hiroshima & Nagasaki	NE Asia	Amer v. Jap	air
9-17 Aug	Manchuria	N Asia	Rus v. Jap	land

Index